Building Machine Learning Systems with Python

Master the art of machine learning with Python and build effective machine learning systems with this intensive hands-on guide

Willi Richert

Luis Pedro Coelho

[PACKT] open source ✣
PUBLISHING   community experience distilled

BIRMINGHAM - MUMBAI

Building Machine Learning Systems with Python

First published: July 2013

Production Reference: 1200713

Published by Packt Publishing Ltd.
Livery Place
35 Livery Street
Birmingham B3 2PB, UK.

ISBN 978-1-78216-140-0

www.packtpub.com

Cover Image by Asher Wishkerman (a.wishkerman@mpic.de)

Credits

Authors
Willi Richert
Luis Pedro Coelho

Reviewers
Matthieu Brucher
Mike Driscoll
Maurice HT Ling

Acquisition Editor
Kartikey Pandey

Lead Technical Editor
Mayur Hule

Technical Editors
Sharvari H. Baet
Ruchita Bhansali
Athira Laji
Zafeer Rais

Copy Editors
Insiya Morbiwala
Aditya Nair
Alfida Paiva
Laxmi Subramanian

Project Coordinator
Anurag Banerjee

Proofreader
Paul Hindle

Indexer
Tejal R. Soni

Graphics
Abhinash Sahu

Production Coordinator
Aditi Gajjar

Cover Work
Aditi Gajjar

About the Authors

Willi Richert has a PhD in Machine Learning and Robotics, and he currently works for Microsoft in the Core Relevance Team of Bing, where he is involved in a variety of machine learning areas such as active learning and statistical machine translation.

This book would not have been possible without the support of my wife Natalie and my sons Linus and Moritz. I am also especially grateful for the many fruitful discussions with my current and previous managers, Andreas Bode, Clemens Marschner, Hongyan Zhou, and Eric Crestan, as well as my colleagues and friends, Tomasz Marciniak, Cristian Eigel, Oliver Niehoerster, and Philipp Adelt. The interesting ideas are most likely from them; the bugs belong to me.

Luis Pedro Coelho is a Computational Biologist: someone who uses computers as a tool to understand biological systems. Within this large field, Luis works in Bioimage Informatics, which is the application of machine learning techniques to the analysis of images of biological specimens. His main focus is on the processing of large scale image data. With robotic microscopes, it is possible to acquire hundreds of thousands of images in a day, and visual inspection of all the images becomes impossible.

Luis has a PhD from Carnegie Mellon University, which is one of the leading universities in the world in the area of machine learning. He is also the author of several scientific publications.

Luis started developing open source software in 1998 as a way to apply to real code what he was learning in his computer science courses at the Technical University of Lisbon. In 2004, he started developing in Python and has contributed to several open source libraries in this language. He is the lead developer on mahotas, the popular computer vision package for Python, and is the contributor of several machine learning codes.

I thank my wife Rita for all her love and support, and I thank my daughter Anna for being the best thing ever.

About the Reviewers

Matthieu Brucher holds an Engineering degree from the Ecole Superieure d'Electricite (Information, Signals, Measures), France, and has a PhD in Unsupervised Manifold Learning from the Universite de Strasbourg, France. He currently holds an HPC Software Developer position in an oil company and works on next generation reservoir simulation.

Mike Driscoll has been programming in Python since Spring 2006. He enjoys writing about Python on his blog at http://www.blog.pythonlibrary.org/. Mike also occasionally writes for the Python Software Foundation, i-Programmer, and Developer Zone. He enjoys photography and reading a good book. Mike has also been a technical reviewer for the following Packt Publishing books: *Python 3 Object Oriented Programming*, *Python 2.6 Graphics Cookbook*, and *Python Web Development Beginner's Guide*.

> I would like to thank my wife, Evangeline, for always supporting me. I would also like to thank my friends and family for all that they do to help me. And I would like to thank Jesus Christ for saving me.

Maurice HT Ling completed his PhD. in Bioinformatics and BSc (Hons) in Molecular and Cell Biology at the University of Melbourne. He is currently a research fellow at Nanyang Technological University, Singapore, and an honorary fellow at the University of Melbourne, Australia. He co-edits the Python papers and has co-founded the Python User Group (Singapore), where he has served as vice president since 2010. His research interests lie in life — biological life, artificial life, and artificial intelligence — using computer science and statistics as tools to understand life and its numerous aspects. You can find his website at: http://maurice.vodien.com

www.PacktPub.com

Support files, eBooks, discount offers and more

You might want to visit www.PacktPub.com for support files and downloads related to your book.

Did you know that Packt offers eBook versions of every book published, with PDF and ePub files available? You can upgrade to the eBook version at www.PacktPub.com and as a print book customer, you are entitled to a discount on the eBook copy. Get in touch with us at service@packtpub.com for more details.

At www.PacktPub.com, you can also read a collection of free technical articles, sign up for a range of free newsletters and receive exclusive discounts and offers on Packt books and eBooks.

http://PacktLib.PacktPub.com

Do you need instant solutions to your IT questions? PacktLib is Packt's online digital book library. Here, you can access, read and search across Packt's entire library of books.

Why Subscribe?

- Fully searchable across every book published by Packt
- Copy and paste, print and bookmark content
- On demand and accessible via web browser

Free Access for Packt account holders

If you have an account with Packt at www.PacktPub.com, you can use this to access PacktLib today and view nine entirely free books. Simply use your login credentials for immediate access.

Table of Contents

Preface

You could argue that it is a fortunate coincidence that you are holding this book in your hands (or your e-book reader). After all, there are millions of books printed every year, which are read by millions of readers; and then there is this book read by you. You could also argue that a couple of machine learning algorithms played their role in leading you to this book (or this book to you). And we, the authors, are happy that you want to understand more about the how and why.

Most of this book will cover the how. How should the data be processed so that machine learning algorithms can make the most out of it? How should you choose the right algorithm for a problem at hand?

Occasionally, we will also cover the why. Why is it important to measure correctly? Why does one algorithm outperform another one in a given scenario?

We know that there is much more to learn to be an expert in the field. After all, we only covered some of the "hows" and just a tiny fraction of the "whys". But at the end, we hope that this mixture will help you to get up and running as quickly as possible.

What this book covers

Chapter 1, Getting Started with Python Machine Learning, introduces the basic idea of machine learning with a very simple example. Despite its simplicity, it will challenge us with the risk of overfitting.

Chapter 2, Learning How to Classify with Real-world Examples, explains the use of real data to learn about classification, whereby we train a computer to be able to distinguish between different classes of flowers.

Chapter 3, Clustering – Finding Related Posts, explains how powerful the bag-of-words approach is when we apply it to finding similar posts without really understanding them.

Chapter 4, Topic Modeling, takes us beyond assigning each post to a single cluster and shows us how assigning them to several topics as real text can deal with multiple topics.

Chapter 5, Classification – Detecting Poor Answers, explains how to use logistic regression to find whether a user's answer to a question is good or bad. Behind the scenes, we will learn how to use the bias-variance trade-off to debug machine learning models.

Chapter 6, Classification II – Sentiment Analysis, introduces how Naive Bayes works, and how to use it to classify tweets in order to see whether they are positive or negative.

Chapter 7, Regression – Recommendations, discusses a classical topic in handling data, but it is still relevant today. We will use it to build recommendation systems, a system that can take user input about the likes and dislikes to recommend new products.

Chapter 8, Regression – Recommendations Improved, improves our recommendations by using multiple methods at once. We will also see how to build recommendations just from shopping data without the need of rating data (which users do not always provide).

Chapter 9, Classification III – Music Genre Classification, illustrates how if someone has scrambled our huge music collection, then our only hope to create an order is to let a machine learner classify our songs. It will turn out that it is sometimes better to trust someone else's expertise than creating features ourselves.

Chapter 10, Computer Vision – Pattern Recognition, explains how to apply classifications in the specific context of handling images, a field known as pattern recognition.

Chapter 11, Dimensionality Reduction, teaches us what other methods exist that can help us in downsizing data so that it is chewable by our machine learning algorithms.

Chapter 12, Big(ger) Data, explains how data sizes keep getting bigger, and how this often becomes a problem for the analysis. In this chapter, we explore some approaches to deal with larger data by taking advantage of multiple core or computing clusters. We also have an introduction to using cloud computing (using Amazon's Web Services as our cloud provider).

Appendix, Where to Learn More about Machine Learning, covers a list of wonderful resources available for machine learning.

What you need for this book

This book assumes you know Python and how to install a library using `easy_install` or `pip`. We do not rely on any advanced mathematics such as calculus or matrix algebra.

To summarize it, we are using the following versions throughout this book, but you should be fine with any more recent one:

- Python: 2.7
- NumPy: 1.6.2
- SciPy: 0.11
- Scikit-learn: 0.13

Who this book is for

This book is for Python programmers who want to learn how to perform machine learning using open source libraries. We will walk through the basic modes of machine learning based on realistic examples.

This book is also for machine learners who want to start using Python to build their systems. Python is a flexible language for rapid prototyping, while the underlying algorithms are all written in optimized C or C++. Therefore, the resulting code is fast and robust enough to be usable in production as well.

Conventions

In this book, you will find a number of styles of text that distinguish between different kinds of information. Here are some examples of these styles, and an explanation of their meaning.

Code words in text are shown as follows: "We can include other contexts through the use of the `include` directive".

A block of code is set as follows:

```
def nn_movie(movie_likeness, reviews, uid, mid):
    likes = movie_likeness[mid].argsort()
  # reverse the sorting so that most alike are in
   # beginning
    likes = likes[::-1]
  # returns the rating for the most similar movie available
    for ell in likes:
        if reviews[u,ell] > 0:
            return reviews[u,ell]
```

When we wish to draw your attention to a particular part of a code block, the relevant lines or items are set in bold:

```
def nn_movie(movie_likeness, reviews, uid, mid):
    likes = movie_likeness[mid].argsort()
  # reverse the sorting so that most alike are in
   # beginning
    likes = likes[::-1]
  # returns the rating for the most similar movie available
    for ell in likes:
        if reviews[u,ell] > 0:
            return reviews[u,ell]
```

New terms and **important words** are shown in bold. Words that you see on the screen, in menus or dialog boxes for example, appear in the text like this: "clicking on the **Next** button moves you to the next screen".

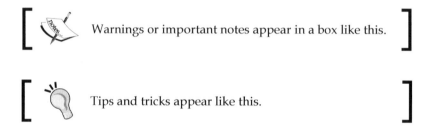

Warnings or important notes appear in a box like this.

Tips and tricks appear like this.

Reader feedback

Feedback from our readers is always welcome. Let us know what you think about this book—what you liked or may have disliked. Reader feedback is important for us to develop titles that you really get the most out of.

To send us general feedback, simply send an e-mail to feedback@packtpub.com, and mention the book title via the subject of your message. If there is a topic that you have expertise in and you are interested in either writing or contributing to a book, see our author guide on www.packtpub.com/authors.

Customer support

Now that you are the proud owner of a Packt book, we have a number of things to help you to get the most from your purchase.

Downloading the example code

You can download the example code files for all Packt books you have purchased from your account at http://www.packtpub.com. If you purchased this book elsewhere, you can visit http://www.packtpub.com/support and register to have the files e-mailed directly to you.

Errata

Although we have taken every care to ensure the accuracy of our content, mistakes do happen. If you find a mistake in one of our books — maybe a mistake in the text or the code — we would be grateful if you would report this to us. By doing so, you can save other readers from frustration and help us improve subsequent versions of this book. If you find any errata, please report them by visiting http://www.packtpub.com/submit-errata, selecting your book, clicking on the **errata submission form** link, and entering the details of your errata. Once your errata are verified, your submission will be accepted and the errata will be uploaded on our website, or added to any list of existing errata, under the Errata section of that title. Any existing errata can be viewed by selecting your title from http://www.packtpub.com/support.

Piracy

Piracy of copyright material on the Internet is an ongoing problem across all media. At Packt, we take the protection of our copyright and licenses very seriously. If you come across any illegal copies of our works, in any form, on the Internet, please provide us with the location address or website name immediately so that we can pursue a remedy.

Please contact us at copyright@packtpub.com with a link to the suspected pirated material.

We appreciate your help in protecting our authors, and our ability to bring you valuable content.

Questions

You can contact us at questions@packtpub.com if you are having a problem with any aspect of the book, and we will do our best to address it.

1
Getting Started with Python Machine Learning

Machine learning (ML) teaches machines how to carry out tasks by themselves. It is that simple. The complexity comes with the details, and that is most likely the reason you are reading this book.

Maybe you have too much data and too little insight, and you hoped that using machine learning algorithms will help you solve this challenge. So you started to dig into random algorithms. But after some time you were puzzled: which of the myriad of algorithms should you actually choose?

Or maybe you are broadly interested in machine learning and have been reading a few blogs and articles about it for some time. Everything seemed to be magic and cool, so you started your exploration and fed some toy data into a decision tree or a support vector machine. But after you successfully applied it to some other data, you wondered, was the whole setting right? Did you get the optimal results? And how do you know there are no better algorithms? Or whether your data was "the right one"?

Welcome to the club! We, the authors, were at those stages once upon a time, looking for information that tells the real story behind the theoretical textbooks on machine learning. It turned out that much of that information was "black art", not usually taught in standard textbooks. So, in a sense, we wrote this book to our younger selves; a book that not only gives a quick introduction to machine learning, but also teaches you lessons that we have learned along the way. We hope that it will also give you, the reader, a smoother entry into one of the most exciting fields in Computer Science.

Machine learning and Python – the dream team

The goal of machine learning is to teach machines (software) to carry out tasks by providing them with a couple of examples (how to do or not do a task). Let us assume that each morning when you turn on your computer, you perform the same task of moving e-mails around so that only those e-mails belonging to a particular topic end up in the same folder. After some time, you feel bored and think of automating this chore. One way would be to start analyzing your brain and writing down all the rules your brain processes while you are shuffling your e-mails. However, this will be quite cumbersome and always imperfect. While you will miss some rules, you will over-specify others. A better and more future-proof way would be to automate this process by choosing a set of e-mail meta information and body/folder name pairs and let an algorithm come up with the best rule set. The pairs would be your training data, and the resulting rule set (also called model) could then be applied to future e-mails that we have not yet seen. This is machine learning in its simplest form.

Of course, machine learning (often also referred to as data mining or predictive analysis) is not a brand new field in itself. Quite the contrary, its success over recent years can be attributed to the pragmatic way of using rock-solid techniques and insights from other successful fields; for example, statistics. There, the purpose is for us humans to get insights into the data by learning more about the underlying patterns and relationships. As you read more and more about successful applications of machine learning (you have checked out kaggle.com already, haven't you?), you will see that applied statistics is a common field among machine learning experts.

As you will see later, the process of coming up with a decent ML approach is never a waterfall-like process. Instead, you will see yourself going back and forth in your analysis, trying out different versions of your input data on diverse sets of ML algorithms. It is this explorative nature that lends itself perfectly to Python. Being an interpreted high-level programming language, it may seem that Python was designed specifically for the process of trying out different things. What is more, it does this very fast. Sure enough, it is slower than C or similar statically-typed programming languages; nevertheless, with a myriad of easy-to-use libraries that are often written in C, you don't have to sacrifice speed for agility.

What the book will teach you (and what it will not)

This book will give you a broad overview of the types of learning algorithms that are currently used in the diverse fields of machine learning and what to watch out for when applying them. From our own experience, however, we know that doing the "cool" stuff—using and tweaking machine learning algorithms such as **support vector machines (SVM)**, **nearest neighbor search (NNS)**, or ensembles thereof—will only consume a tiny fraction of the overall time of a good machine learning expert. Looking at the following typical workflow, we see that most of our time will be spent in rather mundane tasks:

1. Reading the data and cleaning it.
2. Exploring and understanding the input data.
3. Analyzing how best to present the data to the learning algorithm.
4. Choosing the right model and learning algorithm.
5. Measuring the performance correctly.

When talking about exploring and understanding the input data, we will need a bit of statistics and basic math. But while doing this, you will see that those topics, which seemed so dry in your math class, can actually be really exciting when you use them to look at interesting data.

The journey begins when you read in the data. When you have to face issues such as invalid or missing values, you will see that this is more an art than a precise science. And a very rewarding one, as doing this part right will open your data to more machine learning algorithms, and thus increase the likelihood of success.

With the data being ready in your program's data structures, you will want to get a real feeling of what kind of animal you are working with. Do you have enough data to answer your questions? If not, you might want to think about additional ways to get more of it. Do you maybe even have too much data? Then you probably want to think about how best to extract a sample of it.

Often you will not feed the data directly into your machine learning algorithm. Instead, you will find that you can refine parts of the data before training. Many times, the machine learning algorithm will reward you with increased performance. You will even find that a simple algorithm with refined data generally outperforms a very sophisticated algorithm with raw data. This part of the machine learning workflow is called **feature engineering**, and it is generally a very exciting and rewarding challenge. Creative and intelligent that you are, you will immediately see the results.

Choosing the right learning algorithm is not simply a shootout of the three or four that are in your toolbox (there will be more algorithms in your toolbox that you will see). It is more of a thoughtful process of weighing different performance and functional requirements. Do you need fast results and are willing to sacrifice quality? Or would you rather spend more time to get the best possible result? Do you have a clear idea of the future data or should you be a bit more conservative on that side?

Finally, measuring the performance is the part where most mistakes are waiting for the aspiring ML learner. There are easy ones, such as testing your approach with the same data on which you have trained. But there are more difficult ones; for example, when you have imbalanced training data. Again, data is the part that determines whether your undertaking will fail or succeed.

We see that only the fourth point is dealing with the fancy algorithms. Nevertheless, we hope that this book will convince you that the other four tasks are not simply chores, but can be equally important if not more exciting. Our hope is that by the end of the book you will have truly fallen in love with data instead of learned algorithms.

To that end, we will not overwhelm you with the theoretical aspects of the diverse ML algorithms, as there are already excellent books in that area (you will find pointers in *Appendix, Where to Learn More about Machine Learning*). Instead, we will try to provide an intuition of the underlying approaches in the individual chapters—just enough for you to get the idea and be able to undertake your first steps. Hence, this book is by no means "the definitive guide" to machine learning. It is more a kind of starter kit. We hope that it ignites your curiosity enough to keep you eager in trying to learn more and more about this interesting field.

In the rest of this chapter, we will set up and get to know the basic Python libraries, NumPy and SciPy, and then train our first machine learning using scikit-learn. During this endeavor, we will introduce basic ML concepts that will later be used throughout the book. The rest of the chapters will then go into more detail through the five steps described earlier, highlighting different aspects of machine learning in Python using diverse application scenarios.

What to do when you are stuck

We try to convey every idea necessary to reproduce the steps throughout this book. Nevertheless, there will be situations when you might get stuck. The reasons might range from simple typos over odd combinations of package versions to problems in understanding.

In such a situation, there are many different ways to get help. Most likely, your problem will already have been raised and solved in the following excellent Q&A sites:

- `http://metaoptimize.com/qa` – This Q&A site is laser-focused on machine learning topics. For almost every question, it contains above-average answers from machine learning experts. Even if you don't have any questions, it is a good habit to check it out every now and then and read through some of the questions and answers.

- `http://stats.stackexchange.com` – This Q&A site, named Cross Validated, is similar to MetaOptimized, but focuses more on statistics problems.

- `http://stackoverflow.com` – This Q&A site is similar to the previous ones, but with a broader focus on general programming topics. It contains, for example, more questions on some of the packages that we will use in this book (SciPy and Matplotlib).

- `#machinelearning` on Freenode – This IRC channel is focused on machine learning topics. It is a small but very active and helpful community of machine learning experts.

- `http://www.TwoToReal.com` – This is an instant Q&A site written by us, the authors, to support you in topics that don't fit in any of the above buckets. If you post your question, we will get an instant message; if any of us are online, we will be drawn into a chat with you.

As stated at the beginning, this book tries to help you get started quickly on your machine learning journey. We therefore highly encourage you to build up your own list of machine learning-related blogs and check them out regularly. This is the best way to get to know what works and what does not.

The only blog we want to highlight right here is `http://blog.kaggle.com`, the blog of the Kaggle company, which is carrying out machine learning competitions (more links are provided in *Appendix, Where to Learn More about Machine Learning*). Typically, they encourage the winners of the competitions to write down how they approached the competition, what strategies did not work, and how they arrived at the winning strategy. If you don't read anything else, fine; but this is a must.

Getting started

Assuming that you have already installed Python (everything at least as recent as 2.7 should be fine), we need to install NumPy and SciPy for numerical operations as well as Matplotlib for visualization.

Introduction to NumPy, SciPy, and Matplotlib

Before we can talk about concrete machine learning algorithms, we have to talk about how best to store the data we will chew through. This is important as the most advanced learning algorithm will not be of any help to us if they will never finish. This may be simply because accessing the data is too slow. Or maybe its representation forces the operating system to swap all day. Add to this that Python is an interpreted language (a highly optimized one, though) that is slow for many numerically heavy algorithms compared to C or Fortran. So we might ask why on earth so many scientists and companies are betting their fortune on Python even in the highly computation-intensive areas?

The answer is that in Python, it is very easy to offload number-crunching tasks to the lower layer in the form of a C or Fortran extension. That is exactly what NumPy and SciPy do (http://scipy.org/install.html). In this tandem, NumPy provides the support of highly optimized multidimensional arrays, which are the basic data structure of most state-of-the-art algorithms. SciPy uses those arrays to provide a set of fast numerical recipes. Finally, Matplotlib (http://matplotlib.org/) is probably the most convenient and feature-rich library to plot high-quality graphs using Python.

Installing Python

Luckily, for all the major operating systems, namely Windows, Mac, and Linux, there are targeted installers for NumPy, SciPy, and Matplotlib. If you are unsure about the installation process, you might want to install Enthought Python Distribution (https://www.enthought.com/products/epd_free.php) or Python(x,y) (http://code.google.com/p/pythonxy/wiki/Downloads), which come with all the earlier mentioned packages included.

Chewing data efficiently with NumPy and intelligently with SciPy

Let us quickly walk through some basic NumPy examples and then take a look at what SciPy provides on top of it. On the way, we will get our feet wet with plotting using the marvelous Matplotlib package.

You will find more interesting examples of what NumPy can offer at http://www.scipy.org/Tentative_NumPy_Tutorial.

You will also find the book *NumPy Beginner's Guide - Second Edition, Ivan Idris, Packt Publishing* very valuable. Additional tutorial style guides are at `http://scipy-lectures.github.com`; you may also visit the official SciPy tutorial at `http://docs.scipy.org/doc/scipy/reference/tutorial`.

In this book, we will use NumPy Version 1.6.2 and SciPy Version 0.11.0.

Learning NumPy

So let us import NumPy and play a bit with it. For that, we need to start the Python interactive shell.

```
>>> import numpy
>>> numpy.version.full_version
1.6.2
```

As we do not want to pollute our namespace, we certainly should not do the following:

```
>>> from numpy import *
```

The `numpy.array` array will potentially shadow the array package that is included in standard Python. Instead, we will use the following convenient shortcut:

```
>>> import numpy as np
>>> a = np.array([0,1,2,3,4,5])
>>> a
array([0, 1, 2, 3, 4, 5])
>>> a.ndim
1
>>> a.shape
(6,)
```

We just created an array in a similar way to how we would create a list in Python. However, NumPy arrays have additional information about the shape. In this case, it is a one-dimensional array of five elements. No surprises so far.

We can now transform this array in to a 2D matrix.

```
>>> b = a.reshape((3,2))
>>> b
array([[0, 1],
       [2, 3],
       [4, 5]])
>>> b.ndim
2
>>> b.shape
(3, 2)
```

The funny thing starts when we realize just how much the NumPy package is optimized. For example, it avoids copies wherever possible.

```
>>> b[1][0]=77
>>> b
array([[ 0,  1],
       [77,  3],
       [ 4,  5]])
>>> a
array([ 0,  1, 77,  3,  4,  5])
```

In this case, we have modified the value 2 to 77 in b, and we can immediately see the same change reflected in a as well. Keep that in mind whenever you need a true copy.

```
>>> c = a.reshape((3,2)).copy()
>>> c
array([[ 0,  1],
       [77,  3],
       [ 4,  5]])
>>> c[0][0] = -99
>>> a
array([ 0,  1, 77,  3,  4,  5])
>>> c
array([[-99,  1],
       [ 77,  3],
       [  4,  5]])
```

Here, c and a are totally independent copies.

Another big advantage of NumPy arrays is that the operations are propagated to the individual elements.

```
>>> a*2
array([ 2,  4,  6,  8, 10])
>>> a**2
array([ 1,  4,  9, 16, 25])
Contrast that to ordinary Python lists:
>>> [1,2,3,4,5]*2
[1, 2, 3, 4, 5, 1, 2, 3, 4, 5]
>>> [1,2,3,4,5]**2
Traceback (most recent call last):
  File "<stdin>", line 1, in <module>
TypeError: unsupported operand type(s) for ** or pow(): 'list' and
'int'
```

Of course, by using NumPy arrays we sacrifice the agility Python lists offer. Simple operations like adding or removing are a bit complex for NumPy arrays. Luckily, we have both at our disposal, and we will use the right one for the task at hand.

Indexing

Part of the power of NumPy comes from the versatile ways in which its arrays can be accessed.

In addition to normal list indexing, it allows us to use arrays themselves as indices.

```
>>> a[np.array([2,3,4])]
array([77,  3,  4])
```

In addition to the fact that conditions are now propagated to the individual elements, we gain a very convenient way to access our data.

```
>>> a>4
array([False, False,  True, False, False,  True], dtype=bool)
>>> a[a>4]
array([77,  5])
```

This can also be used to trim outliers.

```
>>> a[a>4] = 4
>>> a
array([0, 1, 4, 3, 4, 4])
```

As this is a frequent use case, there is a special clip function for it, clipping the values at both ends of an interval with one function call as follows:

```
>>> a.clip(0,4)
array([0, 1, 4, 3, 4, 4])
```

Handling non-existing values

The power of NumPy's indexing capabilities comes in handy when preprocessing data that we have just read in from a text file. It will most likely contain invalid values, which we will mark as not being a real number using numpy.NAN as follows:

```
c = np.array([1, 2, np.NAN, 3, 4]) # let's pretend we have read this
from a text file
>>> c
array([ 1.,   2.,   nan,   3.,   4.])
>>> np.isnan(c)
array([False, False,  True, False, False], dtype=bool)
```

```
>>> c[~np.isnan(c)]
array([ 1.,   2.,   3.,   4.])
>>> np.mean(c[~np.isnan(c)])
2.5
```

Comparing runtime behaviors

Let us compare the runtime behavior of NumPy with normal Python lists. In the following code, we will calculate the sum of all squared numbers of 1 to 1000 and see how much time the calculation will take. We do it 10000 times and report the total time so that our measurement is accurate enough.

```
import timeit
normal_py_sec = timeit.timeit('sum(x*x for x in xrange(1000))',
                              number=10000)
naive_np_sec = timeit.timeit('sum(na*na)',
                                setup="import numpy as np; na=np.
arange(1000)",
                                number=10000)
good_np_sec = timeit.timeit('na.dot(na)',
                                setup="import numpy as np; na=np.
arange(1000)",
                                number=10000)

print("Normal Python: %f sec"%normal_py_sec)
print("Naive NumPy: %f sec"%naive_np_sec)
print("Good NumPy: %f sec"%good_np_sec)

Normal Python: 1.157467 sec
Naive NumPy: 4.061293 sec
Good NumPy: 0.033419 sec
```

We make two interesting observations. First, just using NumPy as data storage (Naive NumPy) takes 3.5 times longer, which is surprising since we believe it must be much faster as it is written as a C extension. One reason for this is that the access of individual elements from Python itself is rather costly. Only when we are able to apply algorithms inside the optimized extension code do we get speed improvements, and tremendous ones at that: using the dot() function of NumPy, we are more than 25 times faster. In summary, in every algorithm we are about to implement, we should always look at how we can move loops over individual elements from Python to some of the highly optimized NumPy or SciPy extension functions.

However, the speed comes at a price. Using NumPy arrays, we no longer have the incredible flexibility of Python lists, which can hold basically anything. NumPy arrays always have only one datatype.

```
>>> a = np.array([1,2,3])
>>> a.dtype
dtype('int64')
```

If we try to use elements of different types, NumPy will do its best to coerce them to the most reasonable common datatype:

```
>>> np.array([1, "stringy"])
array(['1', 'stringy'], dtype='|S8')
>>> np.array([1, "stringy", set([1,2,3])])
array([1, stringy, set([1, 2, 3])], dtype=object)
```

Learning SciPy

On top of the efficient data structures of NumPy, SciPy offers a magnitude of algorithms working on those arrays. Whatever numerical-heavy algorithm you take from current books on numerical recipes, you will most likely find support for them in SciPy in one way or another. Whether it is matrix manipulation, linear algebra, optimization, clustering, spatial operations, or even Fast Fourier transformation, the toolbox is readily filled. Therefore, it is a good habit to always inspect the `scipy` module before you start implementing a numerical algorithm.

For convenience, the complete namespace of NumPy is also accessible via SciPy. So, from now on, we will use NumPy's machinery via the SciPy namespace. You can check this easily by comparing the function references of any base function; for example:

```
>>> import scipy, numpy
>>> scipy.version.full_version
0.11.0
>>> scipy.dot is numpy.dot
True
```

The diverse algorithms are grouped into the following toolboxes:

SciPy package	Functionality
cluster	Hierarchical clustering (cluster.hierarchy)
	Vector quantization / K-Means (cluster.vq)

SciPy package	Functionality
constants	Physical and mathematical constants
	Conversion methods
fftpack	Discrete Fourier transform algorithms
integrate	Integration routines
interpolate	Interpolation (linear, cubic, and so on)
io	Data input and output
linalg	Linear algebra routines using the optimized BLAS and LAPACK libraries
maxentropy	Functions for fitting maximum entropy models
ndimage	n-dimensional image package
odr	Orthogonal distance regression
optimize	Optimization (finding minima and roots)
signal	Signal processing
sparse	Sparse matrices
spatial	Spatial data structures and algorithms
special	Special mathematical functions such as Bessel or Jacobian
stats	Statistics toolkit

The toolboxes most interesting to our endeavor are `scipy.stats`, `scipy. interpolate`, `scipy.cluster`, and `scipy.signal`. For the sake of brevity, we will briefly explore some features of the `stats` package and leave the others to be explained when they show up in the chapters.

Our first (tiny) machine learning application

Let us get our hands dirty and have a look at our hypothetical web startup, MLAAS, which sells the service of providing machine learning algorithms via HTTP. With the increasing success of our company, the demand for better infrastructure also increases to serve all incoming web requests successfully. We don't want to allocate too many resources as that would be too costly. On the other hand, we will lose money if we have not reserved enough resources for serving all incoming requests. The question now is, when will we hit the limit of our current infrastructure, which we estimated being 100,000 requests per hour. We would like to know in advance when we have to request additional servers in the cloud to serve all the incoming requests successfully without paying for unused ones.

Reading in the data

We have collected the web stats for the last month and aggregated them in `ch01/data/web_traffic.tsv` (tsv because it contains tab separated values). They are stored as the number of hits per hour. Each line contains consecutive hours and the number of web hits in that hour.

The first few lines look like the following:

Using SciPy's `genfromtxt()`, we can easily read in the data.

```
import scipy as sp
data = sp.genfromtxt("web_traffic.tsv", delimiter="\t")
```

We have to specify tab as the delimiter so that the columns are correctly determined.

A quick check shows that we have correctly read in the data.

```
>>> print(data[:10])
[[  1.00000000e+00   2.27200000e+03]
 [  2.00000000e+00              nan]
 [  3.00000000e+00   1.38600000e+03]
 [  4.00000000e+00   1.36500000e+03]
 [  5.00000000e+00   1.48800000e+03]
 [  6.00000000e+00   1.33700000e+03]
 [  7.00000000e+00   1.88300000e+03]
 [  8.00000000e+00   2.28300000e+03]
 [  9.00000000e+00   1.33500000e+03]
 [  1.00000000e+01   1.02500000e+03]]
>>> print(data.shape)
(743, 2)
```

We have 743 data points with two dimensions.

Preprocessing and cleaning the data

It is more convenient for SciPy to separate the dimensions into two vectors, each of size 743. The first vector, x, will contain the hours and the other, y, will contain the web hits in that particular hour. This splitting is done using the special index notation of SciPy, using which we can choose the columns individually.

```
x = data[:,0]
y = data[:,1]
```

> There is much more to the way data can be selected from a SciPy array. Check out `http://www.scipy.org/Tentative_NumPy_Tutorial` for more details on indexing, slicing, and iterating.

One caveat is that we still have some values in y that contain invalid values, `nan`. The question is, what can we do with them? Let us check how many hours contain invalid data.

```
>>> sp.sum(sp.isnan(y))
8
```

We are missing only 8 out of 743 entries, so we can afford to remove them. Remember that we can index a SciPy array with another array. `sp.isnan(y)` returns an array of Booleans indicating whether an entry is not a number. Using ~, we logically negate that array so that we choose only those elements from x and y where y does contain valid numbers.

```
x = x[~sp.isnan(y)]
y = y[~sp.isnan(y)]
```

To get a first impression of our data, let us plot the data in a scatter plot using Matplotlib. Matplotlib contains the `pyplot` package, which tries to mimic Matlab's interface—a very convenient and easy-to-use one (you will find more tutorials on plotting at `http://matplotlib.org/users/pyplot_tutorial.html`).

```
import matplotlib.pyplot as plt
plt.scatter(x,y)
plt.title("Web traffic over the last month")
plt.xlabel("Time")
plt.ylabel("Hits/hour")
plt.xticks([w*7*24 for w in range(10)],
    ['week %i'%w for w in range(10)])
plt.autoscale(tight=True)
plt.grid()
plt.show()
```

In the resulting chart, we can see that while in the first weeks the traffic stayed more or less the same, the last week shows a steep increase:

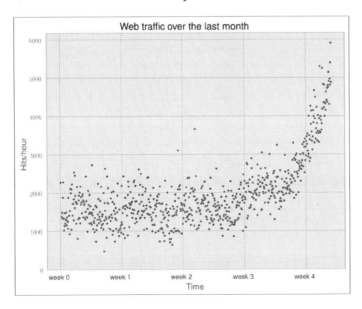

Choosing the right model and learning algorithm

Now that we have a first impression of the data, we return to the initial question: how long will our server handle the incoming web traffic? To answer this we have to:

- Find the real model behind the noisy data points
- Use the model to extrapolate into the future to find the point in time where our infrastructure has to be extended

Before building our first model

When we talk about models, you can think of them as simplified theoretical approximations of the complex reality. As such there is always some inferiority involved, also called the approximation error. This error will guide us in choosing the right model among the myriad of choices we have. This error will be calculated as the squared distance of the model's prediction to the real data. That is, for a learned model function, f, the error is calculated as follows:

```
def error(f, x, y):
    return sp.sum((f(x)-y)**2)
```

The vectors x and y contain the web stats data that we have extracted before. It is the beauty of SciPy's vectorized functions that we exploit here with f(x). The trained model is assumed to take a vector and return the results again as a vector of the same size so that we can use it to calculate the difference to y.

Starting with a simple straight line

Let us assume for a second that the underlying model is a straight line. The challenge then is how to best put that line into the chart so that it results in the smallest approximation error. SciPy's polyfit() function does exactly that. Given data x and y and the desired order of the polynomial (straight line has order 1), it finds the model function that minimizes the error function defined earlier.

```
fp1, residuals, rank, sv, rcond = sp.polyfit(x, y, 1, full=True)
```

The polyfit() function returns the parameters of the fitted model function, fp1; and by setting full to True, we also get additional background information on the fitting process. Of it, only residuals are of interest, which is exactly the error of the approximation.

```
>>> print("Model parameters: %s" % fp1)
Model parameters: [   2.59619213   989.02487106]
```

```
>>> print(res)
[   3.17389767e+08]
```

This means that the best straight line fit is the following function:

```
f(x) = 2.59619213 * x + 989.02487106.
```

We then use `poly1d()` to create a model function from the model parameters.

```
>>> f1 = sp.poly1d(fp1)
>>> print(error(f1, x, y))
317389767.34
```

We have used `full=True` to retrieve more details on the fitting process. Normally, we would not need it, in which case only the model parameters would be returned.

> In fact, what we do here is simple curve fitting. You can find out more about it on Wikipedia by going to http://en.wikipedia.org/wiki/Curve_fitting.

We can now use `f1()` to plot our first trained model. In addition to the earlier plotting instructions, we simply add the following:

```
fx = sp.linspace(0,x[-1], 1000) # generate X-values for plotting
plt.plot(fx, f1(fx), linewidth=4)
plt.legend(["d=%i" % f1.order], loc="upper left")
```

The following graph shows our first trained model:

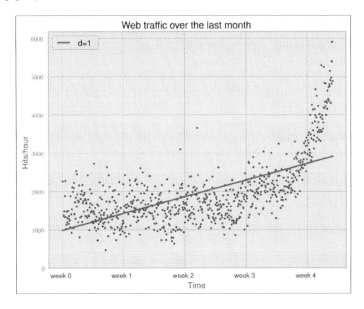

It seems like the first four weeks are not that far off, although we clearly see that there is something wrong with our initial assumption that the underlying model is a straight line. Plus, how good or bad actually is the error of 317,389,767.34?

The absolute value of the error is seldom of use in isolation. However, when comparing two competing models, we can use their errors to judge which one of them is better. Although our first model clearly is not the one we would use, it serves a very important purpose in the workflow: we will use it as our baseline until we find a better one. Whatever model we will come up with in the future, we will compare it against the current baseline.

Towards some advanced stuff

Let us now fit a more complex model, a polynomial of degree 2, to see whether it better "understands" our data:

```
>>> f2p = sp.polyfit(x, y, 2)
>>> print(f2p)
array([  1.05322215e-02,  -5.26545650e+00,   1.97476082e+03])
>>> f2 = sp.poly1d(f2p)
>>> print(error(f2, x, y))
179983507.878
```

The following chart shows the model we trained before (straight line of one degree) with our newly trained, more complex model with two degrees (dashed):

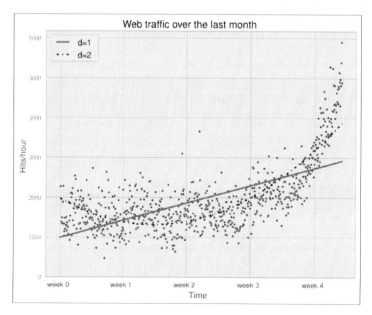

The error is 179,983,507.878, which is almost half the error of the straight-line model. This is good; however, it comes with a price. We now have a more complex function, meaning that we have one more parameter to tune inside `polyfit()`. The fitted polynomial is as follows:

```
f(x) = 0.0105322215 * x**2  - 5.26545650 * x + 1974.76082
```

So, if more complexity gives better results, why not increase the complexity even more? Let's try it for degree 3, 10, and 100.

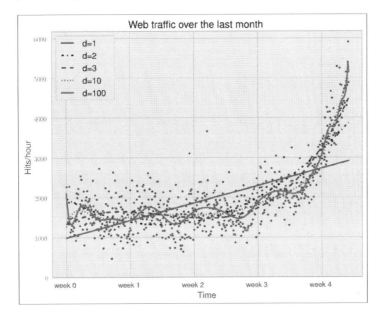

The more complex the data gets, the curves capture it and make it fit better. The errors seem to tell the same story.

```
Error d=1:   317,389,767.339778
Error d=2:   179,983,507.878179
Error d=3:   139,350,144.031725
Error d=10:  121,942,326.363461
Error d=100: 109,318,004.475556
```

However, taking a closer look at the fitted curves, we start to wonder whether they also capture the true process that generated this data. Framed differently, do our models correctly represent the underlying mass behavior of customers visiting our website? Looking at the polynomial of degree 10 and 100, we see wildly oscillating behavior. It seems that the models are fitted too much to the data. So much that it is now capturing not only the underlying process but also the noise. This is called **overfitting**.

At this point, we have the following choices:

- Selecting one of the fitted polynomial models.
- Switching to another more complex model class; splines?
- Thinking differently about the data and starting again.

Of the five fitted models, the first-order model clearly is too simple, and the models of order 10 and 100 are clearly overfitting. Only the second- and third-order models seem to somehow match the data. However, if we extrapolate them at both borders, we see them going berserk.

Switching to a more complex class also seems to be the wrong way to go about it. What arguments would back which class? At this point, we realize that we probably have not completely understood our data.

Stepping back to go forward – another look at our data

So, we step back and take another look at the data. It seems that there is an inflection point between weeks 3 and 4. So let us separate the data and train two lines using week 3.5 as a separation point. We train the first line with the data up to week 3, and the second line with the remaining data.

```
inflection = 3.5*7*24 # calculate the inflection point in hours
xa = x[:inflection] # data before the inflection point
ya = y[:inflection]
xb = x[inflection:] # data after
yb = y[inflection:]

fa = sp.poly1d(sp.polyfit(xa, ya, 1))
fb = sp.poly1d(sp.polyfit(xb, yb, 1))

fa_error = error(fa, xa, ya)
fb_error = error(fb, xb, yb)
print("Error inflection=%f" % (fa + fb_error))
Error inflection=156,639,407.701523
```

Plotting the two models for the two data ranges gives the following chart:

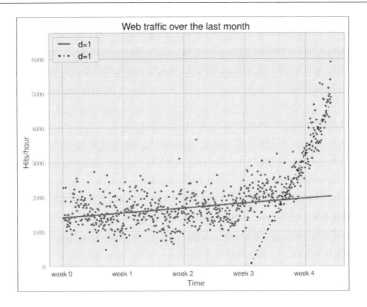

Clearly, the combination of these two lines seems to be a much better fit to the data than anything we have modeled before. But still, the combined error is higher than the higher-order polynomials. Can we trust the error at the end?

Asked differently, why do we trust the straight line fitted only at the last week of our data more than any of the more complex models? It is because we assume that it will capture future data better. If we plot the models into the future, we see how right we are (**d=1** is again our initially straight line).

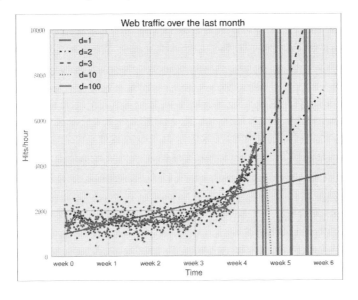

The models of degree 10 and 100 don't seem to expect a bright future for our startup. They tried so hard to model the given data correctly that they are clearly useless to extrapolate further. This is called overfitting. On the other hand, the lower-degree models do not seem to be capable of capturing the data properly. This is called underfitting.

So let us play fair to the models of degree 2 and above and try out how they behave if we fit them *only* to the data of the last week. After all, we believe that the last week says more about the future than the data before. The result can be seen in the following psychedelic chart, which shows even more clearly how bad the problem of overfitting is:

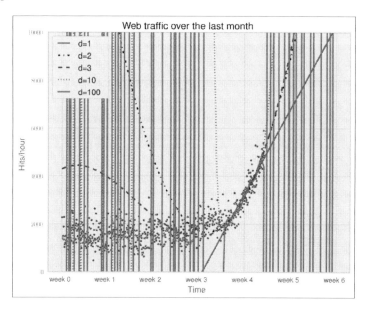

Still, judging from the errors of the models when trained only on the data from week 3.5 and after, we should still choose the most complex one.

```
Error d=1:    22143941.107618
Error d=2:    19768846.989176
Error d=3:    19766452.361027
Error d=10:   18949339.348539
Error d=100:  16915159.603877
```

Training and testing

If only we had some data from the future that we could use to measure our models against, we should be able to judge our model choice only on the resulting approximation error.

Although we cannot look into the future, we can and should simulate a similar effect by holding out a part of our data. Let us remove, for instance, a certain percentage of the data and train on the remaining one. Then we use the hold-out data to calculate the error. As the model has been trained not knowing the hold-out data, we should get a more realistic picture of how the model will behave in the future.

The test errors for the models trained only on the time after the inflection point now show a completely different picture.

```
Error d=1:     7,917,335.831122
Error d=2:     6,993,880.348870
Error d=3:     7,137,471.177363
Error d=10:    8,805,551.189738
Error d=100:  10,877,646.621984
```

The result can be seen in the following chart:

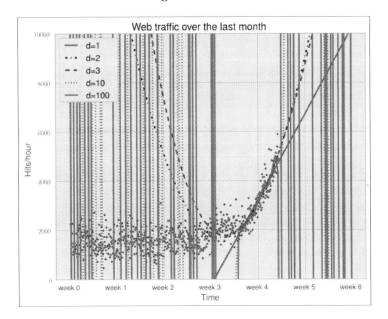

It seems we finally have a clear winner. The model with degree 2 has the lowest test error, which is the error when measured using data that the model did not see during training. And this is what lets us trust that we won't get bad surprises when future data arrives.

Answering our initial question

Finally, we have arrived at a model that we think represents the underlying process best; it is now a simple task of finding out when our infrastructure will reach 100,000 requests per hour. We have to calculate when our model function reaches the value 100,000.

Having a polynomial of degree 2, we could simply compute the inverse of the function and calculate its value at 100,000. Of course, we would like to have an approach that is applicable to any model function easily.

This can be done by subtracting 100,000 from the polynomial, which results in another polynomial, and finding the root of it. SciPy's `optimize` module has the `fsolve` function to achieve this when providing an initial starting position. Let `fbt2` be the winning polynomial of degree 2:

```
>>> print(fbt2)
         2
0.08844 x - 97.31 x + 2.853e+04
>>> print(fbt2-100000)
         2
0.08844 x - 97.31 x - 7.147e+04

>>> from scipy.optimize import fsolve
>>> reached_max = fsolve(fbt2-100000, 800)/(7*24)
>>> print("100,000 hits/hour expected at week %f" % reached_max[0])
100,000 hits/hour expected at week 9.827613
```

Our model tells us that given the current user behavior and traction of our startup, it will take another month until we have reached our threshold capacity.

Of course, there is a certain uncertainty involved with our prediction. To get the real picture, you can draw in more sophisticated statistics to find out about the variance that we have to expect when looking farther and further into the future.

And then there are the user and underlying user behavior dynamics that we cannot model accurately. However, at this point we are fine with the current predictions. After all, we can prepare all the time-consuming actions now. If we then monitor our web traffic closely, we will see in time when we have to allocate new resources.

Summary

Congratulations! You just learned two important things. Of these, the most important one is that as a typical machine learning operator, you will spend most of your time understanding and refining the data—exactly what we just did in our first tiny machine learning example. And we hope that the example helped you to start switching your mental focus from algorithms to data. Later, you learned how important it is to have the correct experiment setup, and that it is vital to not mix up training and testing.

Admittedly, the use of polynomial fitting is not the coolest thing in the machine learning world. We have chosen it so as not to distract you with the coolness of some shiny algorithm, which encompasses the two most important points we just summarized above.

So, let's move to the next chapter, in which we will dive deep into SciKits-learn, the marvelous machine learning toolkit, give an overview of different types of learning, and show you the beauty of feature engineering.

2

Learning How to Classify with Real-world Examples

Can a machine distinguish between flower species based on images? From a machine learning perspective, we approach this problem by having the machine learn how to perform this task based on examples of each species so that it can classify images where the species are not marked. This process is called **classification** (or **supervised learning**), and is a classic problem that goes back a few decades.

We will explore small datasets using a few simple algorithms that we can implement manually. The goal is to be able to understand the basic principles of classification. This will be a solid foundation to understanding later chapters as we introduce more complex methods that will, by necessity, rely on code written by others.

The Iris dataset

The Iris dataset is a classic dataset from the 1930s; it is one of the first modern examples of statistical classification.

The setting is that of Iris flowers, of which there are multiple species that can be identified by their morphology. Today, the species would be defined by their genomic signatures, but in the 1930s, DNA had not even been identified as the carrier of genetic information.

The following four attributes of each plant were measured:

- Sepal length
- Sepal width
- Petal length
- Petal width

In general, we will call any measurement from our data as **features**.

Additionally, for each plant, the species was recorded. The question now is: if we saw a new flower out in the field, could we make a good prediction about its species from its measurements?

This is the **supervised learning** or **classification** problem; given labeled examples, we can design a rule that will eventually be applied to other examples. This is the same setting that is used for spam classification; given the examples of spam and ham (non-spam e-mail) that the user gave the system, can we determine whether a new, incoming message is spam or not?

For the moment, the Iris dataset serves our purposes well. It is small (150 examples, 4 features each) and can easily be visualized and manipulated.

The first step is visualization

Because this dataset is so small, we can easily plot all of the points and all two-dimensional projections on a page. We will thus build intuitions that can then be extended to datasets with many more dimensions and datapoints. Each subplot in the following screenshot shows all the points projected into two of the dimensions. The outlying group (triangles) are the Iris Setosa plants, while Iris Versicolor plants are in the center (circle) and Iris Virginica are indicated with "x" marks. We can see that there are two large groups: one is of Iris Setosa and another is a mixture of Iris Versicolor and Iris Virginica.

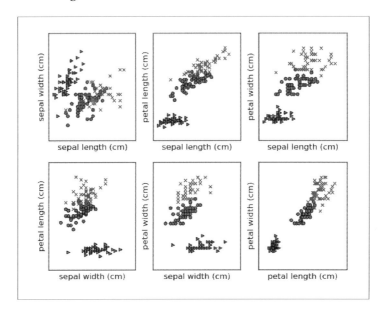

We are using Matplotlib; it is the most well-known plotting package for Python. We present the code to generate the top-left plot. The code for the other plots is similar to the following code:

```
from matplotlib import pyplot as plt
from sklearn.datasets import load_iris
import numpy as np

# We load the data with load_iris from sklearn
data = load_iris()
features = data['data']
feature_names = data['feature_names']
target = data['target']

for t,marker,c in zip(xrange(3),">ox","rgb"):
    # We plot each class on its own to get different colored markers
    plt.scatter(features[target == t,0],
                features[target == t,1],
                marker=marker,
                c=c)
```

Building our first classification model

If the goal is to separate the three types of flower, we can immediately make a few suggestions. For example, the petal length seems to be able to separate Iris Setosa from the other two flower species on its own. We can write a little bit of code to discover where the cutoff is as follows:

```
plength = features[:, 2]
# use numpy operations to get setosa features
is_setosa = (labels == 'setosa')
# This is the important step:
max_setosa =plength[is_setosa].max()
min_non_setosa = plength[~is_setosa].min()
print('Maximum of setosa: {0}.'.format(max_setosa))
print('Minimum of others: {0}.'.format(min_non_setosa))
```

This prints **1.9** and **3.0**. Therefore, we can build a simple model: *if the petal length is smaller than two, this is an Iris Setosa flower; otherwise, it is either Iris Virginica or Iris Versicolor.*

```
if features[:,2] < 2: print 'Iris Setosa'
else: print 'Iris Virginica or Iris Versicolour'
```

This is our first model, and it works very well in that it separates the Iris Setosa flowers from the other two species without making any mistakes.

What we had here was a simple structure; a simple threshold on one of the dimensions. Then we searched for the best dimension threshold. We performed this visually and with some calculation; machine learning happens when we write code to perform this for us.

The example where we distinguished Iris Setosa from the other two species was very easy. However, we cannot immediately see what the best threshold is for distinguishing Iris Virginica from Iris Versicolor. We can even see that we will never achieve perfect separation. We can, however, try to do it the best possible way. For this, we will perform a little computation.

We first select only the non-Setosa features and labels:

```
features = features[~is_setosa]
labels = labels[~is_setosa]
virginica = (labels == 'virginica')
```

Here we are heavily using NumPy operations on the arrays. `is_setosa` is a Boolean array, and we use it to select a subset of the other two arrays, `features` and `labels`. Finally, we build a new Boolean array, `virginica`, using an equality comparison on labels.

Now, we run a loop over all possible features and thresholds to see which one results in better accuracy. *Accuracy* is simply the fraction of examples that the model classifies correctly:

```
best_acc = -1.0
for fi in xrange(features.shape[1]):
  # We are going to generate all possible threshold for this feature
  thresh = features[:,fi].copy()
  thresh.sort()
  # Now test all thresholds:
  for t in thresh:
    pred = (features[:,fi] > t)
    acc = (pred == virginica).mean()
    if acc > best_acc:
      best_acc = acc
      best_fi = fi
      best_t = t
```

The last few lines select the best model. First we compare the predictions, `pred`, with the actual labels, `virginica`. The little trick of computing the mean of the comparisons gives us the fraction of correct results, the accuracy. At the end of the `for` loop, all possible thresholds for all possible features have been tested, and the `best_fi` and `best_t` variables hold our model. To apply it to a new example, we perform the following:

```
if example[best_fi] > t: print 'virginica'
else: print 'versicolor'
```

What does this model look like? If we run it on the whole data, the best model that we get is split on the petal length. We can visualize the decision boundary. In the following screenshot, we see two regions: one is white and the other is shaded in grey. Anything that falls in the white region will be called Iris Virginica and anything that falls on the shaded side will be classified as Iris Versicolor:

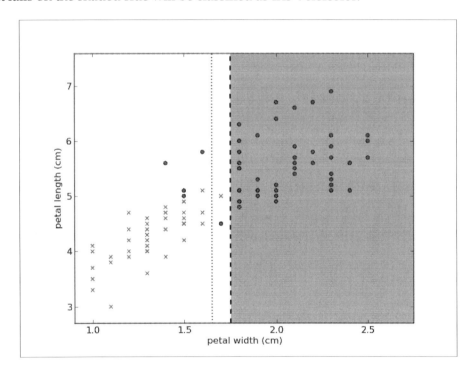

In a threshold model, the decision boundary will always be a line that is parallel to one of the axes. The plot in the preceding screenshot shows the decision boundary and the two regions where the points are classified as either white or grey. It also shows (as a dashed line) an alternative threshold that will achieve exactly the same accuracy. Our method chose the first threshold, but that was an arbitrary choice.

Evaluation – holding out data and cross-validation

The model discussed in the preceding section is a simple model; it achieves 94 percent accuracy on its training data. However, this evaluation may be overly optimistic. We used the data to define what the threshold would be, and then we used the same data to evaluate the model. Of course, the model will perform better than anything else we have tried on this dataset. The logic is circular.

What we really want to do is estimate the ability of the model to generalize to new instances. We should measure its performance in instances that the algorithm has not seen at training. Therefore, we are going to do a more rigorous evaluation and use held-out data. For this, we are going to break up the data into two blocks: on one block, we'll train the model, and on the other — the one we held out of training — we'll test it. The output is as follows:

```
Training error was 96.0%.
Testing error was 90.0% (N = 50).
```

The result of the testing data is lower than that of the training error. This may surprise an inexperienced machine learner, but it is expected and typical. To see why, look back at the plot that showed the decision boundary. See if some of the examples close to the boundary were not there or if one of the ones in between the two lines was missing. It is easy to imagine that the boundary would then move a little bit to the right or to the left so as to put them on the "wrong" side of the border.

 The error on the training data is called a **training error** and is always an overly optimistic estimate of how well your algorithm is doing. We should always measure and report the **testing error**; the error on a collection of examples that were not used for training.

These concepts will become more and more important as the models become more complex. In this example, the difference between the two errors is not very large. When using a complex model, it is possible to get 100 percent accuracy in training and do no better than random guessing on testing!

One possible problem with what we did previously, which was to hold off data from training, is that we only used part of the data (in this case, we used half of it) for training. On the other hand, if we use too little data for testing, the error estimation is performed on a very small number of examples. Ideally, we would like to use all of the data for training and all of the data for testing as well.

We can achieve something quite similar by **cross-validation**. One extreme (but sometimes useful) form of cross-validation is leave-one-out. We will take an example out of the training data, learn a model without this example, and then see if the model classifies this example correctly:

```
error = 0.0
for ei in range(len(features)):
    # select all but the one at position 'ei':
        training = np.ones(len(features), bool)
        training[ei] = False
        testing = ~training
        model = learn_model(features[training], virginica[training])
        predictions = apply_model(features[testing],
                                    virginica[testing], model)
    error += np.sum(predictions != virginica[testing])
```

At the end of this loop, we will have tested a series of models on all the examples. However, there is no circularity problem because each example was tested on a model that was built without taking the model into account. Therefore, the overall estimate is a reliable estimate of how well the models would generalize.

The major problem with leave-one-out cross-validation is that we are now being forced to perform 100 times more work. In fact, we must learn a whole new model for each and every example, and this will grow as our dataset grows.

We can get most of the benefits of leave-one-out at a fraction of the cost by using x-fold cross-validation; here, "x" stands for a small number, say, five. In order to perform five-fold cross-validation, we break up the data in five groups, that is, five folds.

Then we learn five models, leaving one fold out of each. The resulting code will be similar to the code given earlier in this section, but here we leave 20 percent of the data out instead of just one element. We test each of these models on the left out fold and average the results:

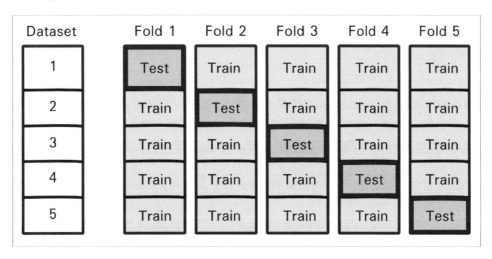

The preceding figure illustrates this process for five blocks; the dataset is split into five pieces. Then for each fold, you hold out one of the blocks for testing and train on the other four. You can use any number of folds you wish. Five or ten fold is typical; it corresponds to training with 80 or 90 percent of your data and should already be close to what you would get from using all the data. In an extreme case, if you have as many folds as datapoints, you can simply perform leave-one-out cross-validation.

When generating the folds, you need to be careful to keep them balanced. For example, if all of the examples in one fold come from the same class, the results will not be representative. We will not go into the details of how to do this because the machine learning packages will handle it for you.

We have now generated several models instead of just one. So, what *final model* do we return and use for the new data? The simplest solution is now to use a single overall model on all your training data. The cross-validation loop gives you an estimate of how well this model should generalize.

 A cross-validation schedule allows you to use all your data to estimate if your methods are doing well. At the end of the cross-validation loop, you can use all your data to train a final model.

Although it was not properly recognized when machine learning was starting out, nowadays it is seen as a very bad sign to even discuss the training error of a classification system. This is because the results can be very misleading. We always want to measure and compare either the error on a held-out dataset or the error estimated using a cross-validation schedule.

Building more complex classifiers

In the previous section, we used a very simple model: a threshold on one of the dimensions. Throughout this book, you will see many other types of models, and we're not even going to cover everything that is out there.

What makes up a classification model? We can break it up into three parts:

- **The structure of the model**: In this, we use a threshold on a single feature.
- **The search procedure**: In this, we try every possible combination of feature and threshold.
- **The loss function**: Using the loss function, we decide which of the possibilities is less bad (because we can rarely talk about the perfect solution). We can use the training error or just define this point the other way around and say that we want the best accuracy. Traditionally, people want the loss function to be minimum.

We can play around with these parts to get different results. For example, we can attempt to build a threshold that achieves minimal training error, but we will only test three values for each feature: the mean value of the features, the mean plus one standard deviation, and the mean minus one standard deviation. This could make sense if testing each value was very costly in terms of computer time (or if we had millions and millions of datapoints). Then the exhaustive search we used would be infeasible, and we would have to perform an approximation like this.

Alternatively, we might have different loss functions. It might be that one type of error is much more costly than another. In a medical setting, false negatives and false positives are not equivalent. A **false negative** (when the result of a test comes back negative, but that is false) might lead to the patient not receiving treatment for a serious disease. A **false positive** (when the test comes back positive even though the patient does not actually have that disease) might lead to additional tests for confirmation purposes or unnecessary treatment (which can still have costs, including side effects from the treatment). Therefore, depending on the exact setting, different trade-offs can make sense. At one extreme, if the disease is fatal and treatment is cheap with very few negative side effects, you want to minimize the false negatives as much as you can. With spam filtering, we may face the same problem; incorrectly deleting a non-spam e-mail can be very dangerous for the user, while letting a spam e-mail through is just a minor annoyance.

What the **cost function** should be is always dependent on the exact problem you are working on. When we present a general-purpose algorithm, we often focus on minimizing the number of mistakes (achieving the highest accuracy). However, if some mistakes are more costly than others, it might be better to accept a lower overall accuracy to minimize overall costs.

Finally, we can also have other classification structures. A simple threshold rule is very limiting and will only work in the very simplest cases, such as with the Iris dataset.

A more complex dataset and a more complex classifier

We will now look at a slightly more complex dataset. This will motivate the introduction of a new classification algorithm and a few other ideas.

Learning about the Seeds dataset

We will now look at another agricultural dataset; it is still small, but now too big to comfortably plot exhaustively as we did with Iris. This is a dataset of the measurements of wheat seeds. Seven features are present, as follows:

- Area (A)
- Perimeter (P)
- Compactness ($C = 4\pi A/P^2$)
- Length of kernel
- Width of kernel
- Asymmetry coefficient
- Length of kernel groove

There are three classes that correspond to three wheat varieties: Canadian, Koma, and Rosa. As before, the goal is to be able to classify the species based on these morphological measurements.

Unlike the Iris dataset, which was collected in the 1930s, this is a very recent dataset, and its features were automatically computed from digital images.

This is how image pattern recognition can be implemented: you can take images in digital form, compute a few relevant features from them, and use a generic classification system. In a later chapter, we will work through the computer vision side of this problem and compute features in images. For the moment, we will work with the features that are given to us.

UCI Machine Learning Dataset Repository

The **University of California at Irvine (UCI)** maintains an online repository of machine learning datasets (at the time of writing, they are listing 233 datasets). Both the Iris and Seeds dataset used in this chapter were taken from there.

The repository is available online:
http://archive.ics.uci.edu/ml/

Features and feature engineering

One interesting aspect of these features is that the compactness feature is not actually a new measurement, but a function of the previous two features, area and perimeter. It is often very useful to derive new combined features. This is a general area normally termed **feature engineering**; it is sometimes seen as less glamorous than algorithms, but it may matter more for performance (a simple algorithm on well-chosen features will perform better than a fancy algorithm on not-so-good features).

In this case, the original researchers computed the "compactness", which is a typical feature for shapes (also called "roundness"). This feature will have the same value for two kernels, one of which is twice as big as the other one, but with the same shape. However, it will have different values for kernels that are very round (when the feature is close to one) as compared to kernels that are elongated (when the feature is close to zero).

The goals of a good feature are to simultaneously vary with what matters and be invariant with what does not. For example, compactness does not vary with size but varies with the shape. In practice, it might be hard to achieve both objectives perfectly, but we want to approximate this ideal.

You will need to use background knowledge to intuit which will be good features. Fortunately, for many problem domains, there is already a vast literature of possible features and feature types that you can build upon. For images, all of the previously mentioned features are typical, and computer vision libraries will compute them for you. In text-based problems too, there are standard solutions that you can mix and match (we will also see this in a later chapter). Often though, you can use your knowledge of the specific problem to design a specific feature.

Even before you have data, you must decide which data is worthwhile to collect. Then, you need to hand all your features to the machine to evaluate and compute the best classifier.

A natural question is whether or not we can select good features automatically. This problem is known as **feature selection**. There are many methods that have been proposed for this problem, but in practice, very simple ideas work best. It does not make sense to use feature selection in these small problems, but if you had thousands of features, throwing out most of them might make the rest of the process much faster.

Nearest neighbor classification

With this dataset, even if we just try to separate two classes using the previous method, we do not get very good results. Let me introduce , therefore, a new classifier: the nearest neighbor classifier.

If we consider that each example is represented by its features (in mathematical terms, as a point in N-dimensional space), we can compute the distance between examples. We can choose different ways of computing the distance, for example:

```
def distance(p0, p1):
    'Computes squared euclidean distance'
    return np.sum( (p0-p1)**2)
```

Now when classifying, we adopt a simple rule: given a new example, we look at the dataset for the point that is closest to it (its nearest neighbor) and look at its label:

```
def nn_classify(training_set, training_labels, new_example):
    dists = np.array([distance(t, new_example)
        for t in training_set])
    nearest = dists.argmin()
    return training_labels[nearest]
```

In this case, our model involves saving all of the training data and labels and computing everything at classification time. A better implementation would be to actually index these at learning time to speed up classification, but this implementation is a complex algorithm.

Now, note that this model performs perfectly on its training data! For each point, its closest neighbor is itself, and so its label matches perfectly (unless two examples have exactly the same features but different labels, which can happen). Therefore, it is essential to test using a cross-validation protocol.

Using ten folds for cross-validation for this dataset with this algorithm, we obtain 88 percent accuracy. As we discussed in the earlier section, the cross-validation accuracy is lower than the training accuracy, but this is a more credible estimate of the performance of the model.

We will now examine the decision boundary. For this, we will be forced to simplify and look at only two dimensions (just so that we can plot it on paper).

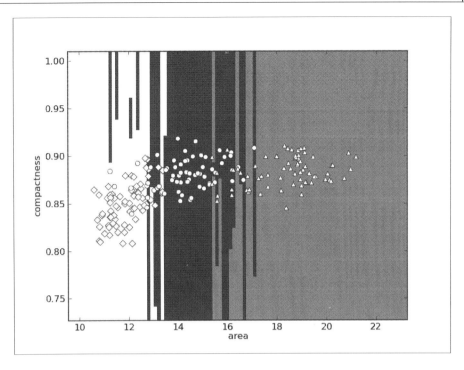

In the preceding screenshot, the Canadian examples are shown as diamonds, Kama seeds as circles, and Rosa seeds as triangles. Their respective areas are shown as white, black, and grey. You might be wondering why the regions are so horizontal, almost weirdly so. The problem is that the x axis (area) ranges from 10 to 22 while the y axis (compactness) ranges from 0.75 to 1.0. This means that a small change in x is actually much larger than a small change in y. So, when we compute the distance according to the preceding function, we are, for the most part, only taking the x axis into account.

If you have a physics background, you might have already noticed that we had been summing up lengths, areas, and dimensionless quantities, mixing up our units (which is something you never want to do in a physical system). We need to normalize all of the features to a common scale. There are many solutions to this problem; a simple one is to normalize to Z-scores. The Z-score of a value is how far away from the mean it is in terms of units of standard deviation. It comes down to this simple pair of operations:

```
# subtract the mean for each feature:
features -= features.mean(axis=0)
# divide each feature by its standard deviation
features /= features.std(axis=0)
```

Independent of what the original values were, after Z-scoring, a value of zero is the mean and positive values are above the mean and negative values are below it.

Now every feature is in the same unit (technically, every feature is now dimensionless; it has no units) and we can mix dimensions more confidently. In fact, if we now run our nearest neighbor classifier, we obtain 94 percent accuracy!

Look at the decision space again in two dimensions; it looks as shown in the following screenshot:

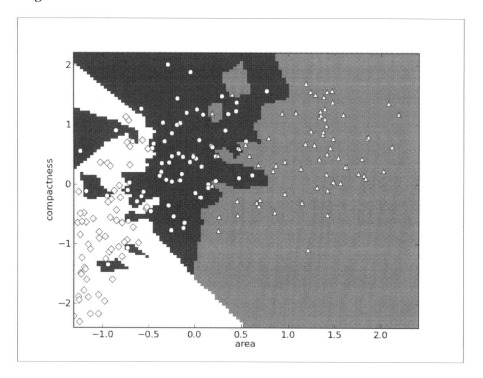

The boundaries are now much more complex and there is interaction between the two dimensions. In the full dataset, everything is happening in a seven-dimensional space that is very hard to visualize, but the same principle applies: where before a few dimensions were dominant, now they are all given the same importance.

The nearest neighbor classifier is simple, but sometimes good enough. We can generalize it to a *k-nearest* neighbor classifier by considering not just the closest point but the *k* closest points. All *k* neighbors vote to select the label. *k* is typically a small number, such as 5, but can be larger, particularly if the dataset is very large.

Binary and multiclass classification

The first classifier we saw, the threshold classifier, was a simple binary classifier (the result is either one class or the other as a point is either above the threshold or it is not). The second classifier we used, the nearest neighbor classifier, was a naturally multiclass classifier (the output can be one of several classes).

It is often simpler to define a simple binary method than one that works on multiclass problems. However, we can reduce the multiclass problem to a series of binary decisions. This is what we did earlier in the Iris dataset in a haphazard way; we observed that it was easy to separate one of the initial classes and focused on the other two, reducing the problem to two binary decisions:

- Is it an Iris Setosa (yes or no)?
- If no, check whether it is an Iris Virginica (yes or no).

Of course, we want to leave this sort of reasoning to the computer. As usual, there are several solutions to this multiclass reduction.

The simplest is to use a series of "one classifier versus the rest of the classifiers". For each possible label ℓ, we build a classifier of the type "is this ℓ or something else?". When applying the rule, exactly one of the classifiers would say "yes" and we would have our solution. Unfortunately, this does not always happen, so we have to decide how to deal with either multiple positive answers or no positive answers.

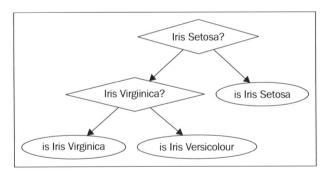

Alternatively, we can build a classification tree. Split the possible labels in two and build a classifier that asks "should this example go to the left or the right bin?" We can perform this splitting recursively until we obtain a single label. The preceding diagram depicts the tree of reasoning for the Iris dataset. Each diamond is a single binary classifier. It is easy to imagine we could make this tree larger and encompass more decisions. This means that any classifier that can be used for binary classification can also be adapted to handle any number of classes in a simple way.

There are many other possible ways of turning a binary method into a multiclass one. There is no single method that is clearly better in all cases. However, which one you use normally does not make much of a difference to the final result.

Most classifiers are binary systems while many real-life problems are naturally multiclass. Several simple protocols reduce a multiclass problem to a series of binary decisions and allow us to apply the binary models to our multiclass problem.

Summary

In a sense, this was a very theoretical chapter, as we introduced generic concepts with simple examples. We went over a few operations with a classic dataset. This, by now, is considered a very small problem. However, it has the advantage that we were able to plot it out and see what we were doing in detail. This is something that will be lost when we move on to problems with many dimensions and many thousands of examples. The intuitions we gained here will all still be valid.

Classification means generalizing from examples to build a model (that is, a rule that can automatically be applied to new, unclassified objects). It is one of the fundamental tools in machine learning, and we will see many more examples of this in forthcoming chapters.

We also learned that the training error is a misleading, over-optimistic estimate of how well the model does. We must, instead, evaluate it on testing data that was not used for training. In order to not waste too many examples in testing, a cross-validation schedule can get us the best of both worlds (at the cost of more computation).

We also had a look at the problem of feature engineering. Features are not something that is predefined for you, but choosing and designing features is an integral part of designing a machine-learning pipeline. In fact, it is often the area where you can get the most improvements in accuracy as better data beats fancier methods. The chapters on computer vision and text-based classification will provide examples for these specific settings.

In this chapter, we wrote all of our own code (except when we used NumPy, of course). This will not be the case for the next few chapters, but we needed to build up intuitions on simple cases to illustrate the basic concepts.

The next chapter looks at how to proceed when your data does not have predefined classes for classification.

3
Clustering – Finding Related Posts

In the previous chapter, we have learned how to find classes or categories of individual data points. With a handful of training data items that were paired with their respective classes, we learned a model that we can now use to classify future data items. We called this supervised learning, as the learning was guided by a teacher; in our case the teacher had the form of correct classifications.

Let us now imagine that we do not possess those labels by which we could learn the classification model. This could be, for example, because they were too expensive to collect. What could we have done in that case?

Well, of course, we would not be able to learn a classification model. Still, we could find some pattern within the data itself. This is what we will do in this chapter, where we consider the challenge of a "question and answer" website. When a user browses our site looking for some particular information, the search engine will most likely point him/her to a specific answer. To improve the user experience, we now want to show all related questions with their answers. If the presented answer is not what he/she was looking for, he/she can easily see the other available answers and hopefully stay on our site.

The naive approach would be to take the post, calculate its similarity to all other posts, and display the top N most similar posts as links on the page. This will quickly become very costly. Instead, we need a method that quickly finds all related posts.

We will achieve this goal in this chapter using clustering. This is a method of arranging items so that similar items are in one cluster and dissimilar items are in distinct ones. The tricky thing that we have to tackle first is how to turn text into something on which we can calculate similarity. With such a measurement for similarity, we will then proceed to investigate how we can leverage that to quickly arrive at a cluster that contains similar posts. Once there, we will only have to check out those documents that also belong to that cluster. To achieve this, we will introduce the marvelous Scikit library, which comes with diverse machine-learning methods that we will also use in the following chapters.

Measuring the relatedness of posts

From the machine learning point of view, raw text is useless. Only if we manage to transform it into meaningful numbers, can we feed it into our machine-learning algorithms such as clustering. The same is true for more mundane operations on text, such as similarity measurement.

How not to do it

One text similarity measure is the Levenshtein distance, which also goes by the name edit distance. Let's say we have two words, "machine" and "mchiene". The similarity between them can be expressed as the minimum set of edits that are necessary to turn one word into the other. In this case, the edit distance would be 2, as we have to add an "a" after "m" and delete the first "e". This algorithm is, however, quite costly, as it is bound by the product of the lengths of the first and second words.

Looking at our posts, we could cheat by treating the whole word as characters and performing the edit distance calculation on the word level. Let's say we have two posts (let's concentrate on the title for the sake of simplicity), "How to format my hard disk" and "Hard disk format problems"; we would have an edit distance of five (removing "how", "to", "format", "my", and then adding "format" and "problems" at the end). Therefore, one could express the difference between two posts as the number of words that have to be added or deleted so that one text morphs into the other. Although we could speed up the overall approach quite a bit, the time complexity stays the same.

Even if it would have been fast enough, there is another problem. The post above the word "format" accounts for an edit distance of two (deleting it first, then adding it). So our distance doesn't seem to be robust enough to take word reordering into account.

How to do it

More robust than edit distance is the so-called **bag-of-word** approach. It uses simple word counts as its basis. For each word in the post, its occurrence is counted and noted in a vector. Not surprisingly, this step is also called vectorization. The vector is typically huge as it contains as many elements as the words that occur in the whole dataset. Take for instance two example posts with the following word counts:

Word	Occurrences in Post 1	Occurrences in Post 2
disk	1	1
format	1	1
how	1	0
hard	1	1
my	1	0
problems	0	1
to	1	0

The columns Post 1 and Post 2 can now be treated as simple vectors. We could simply calculate the Euclidean distance between the vectors of all posts and take the nearest one (too slow, as we have just found out). As such, we can use them later in the form of feature vectors in the following clustering steps:

1. Extract the salient features from each post and store it as a vector per post.

2. Compute clustering on the vectors.

3. Determine the cluster for the post in question.

4. From this cluster, fetch a handful of posts that are different from the post in question. This will increase diversity.

However, there is some more work to be done before we get there, and before we can do that work, we need some data to work on.

Preprocessing – similarity measured as similar number of common words

As we have seen previously, the bag-of-word approach is both fast and robust. However, it is not without challenges. Let's dive directly into them.

Converting raw text into a bag-of-words

We do not have to write a custom code for counting words and representing those counts as a vector. Scikit's `CountVectorizer` does the job very efficiently. It also has a very convenient interface. Scikit's functions and classes are imported via the `sklearn` package as follows:

```
>>> from sklearn.feature_extraction.text import CountVectorizer
>>> vectorizer = CountVectorizer(min_df=1)
```

The parameter `min_df` determines how `CountVectorizer` treats words that are not used frequently (minimum document frequency). If it is set to an integer, all words occurring less than that value will be dropped. If it is a fraction, all words that occur less than that fraction of the overall dataset will be dropped. The parameter `max_df` works in a similar manner. If we print the instance, we see what other parameters Scikit provides together with their default values:

```
>>> print(vectorizer)
CountVectorizer(analyzer=word, binary=False, charset=utf-8,
charset_error=strict, dtype=<type 'long'>, input=content,
lowercase=True, max_df=1.0, max_features=None, max_n=None,
min_df=1, min_n=None, ngram_range=(1, 1), preprocessor=None,
stop_words=None, strip_accents=None, token_pattern=(?u)\b\w\w+\b,
tokenizer=None, vocabulary=None)
```

We see that, as expected, the counting is done at word level (`analyzer=word`) and the words are determined by the regular expression pattern `token_pattern`. It would, for example, tokenize "cross-validated" into "cross" and "validated". Let us ignore the other parameters for now.

```
>>> content = ["How to format my hard disk", " Hard disk format
problems "]
>>> X = vectorizer.fit_transform(content)
>>> vectorizer.get_feature_names()
[u'disk', u'format', u'hard', u'how', u'my', u'problems', u'to']
```

The vectorizer has detected seven words for which we can fetch the counts individually:

```
>>> print(X.toarray().transpose())
array([[1, 1],
       [1, 1],
       [1, 1],
       [1, 0],
       [1, 0],
       [0, 1],
       [1, 0]], dtype=int64)
```

This means that the first sentence contains all the words except for "problems", while the second contains all except "how", "my", and "to". In fact, these are exactly the same columns as seen in the previous table. From X, we can extract a feature vector that we can use to compare the two documents with each other.

First we will start with a naive approach to point out some preprocessing peculiarities we have to account for. So let us pick a random post, for which we will then create the count vector. We will then compare its distance to all the count vectors and fetch the post with the smallest one.

Counting words

Let us play with the toy dataset consisting of the following posts:

Post filename	Post content
01.txt	This is a toy post about machine learning. Actually, it contains not much interesting stuff.
02.txt	Imaging databases can get huge.
03.txt	Most imaging databases safe images permanently.
04.txt	Imaging databases store images.
05.txt	Imaging databases store images. Imaging databases store images. Imaging databases store images.

In this post dataset, we want to find the most similar post for the short post "imaging databases".

Assuming that the posts are located in the folder DIR, we can feed CountVectorizer with it as follows:

```
>>> posts = [open(os.path.join(DIR, f)).read() for f in
os.listdir(DIR)]
>>> from sklearn.feature_extraction.text import CountVectorizer
>>> vectorizer = CountVectorizer(min_df=1)
```

We have to notify the vectorizer about the full dataset so that it knows upfront what words are to be expected, as shown in the following code:

```
>>> X_train = vectorizer.fit_transform(posts)

>>> num_samples, num_features = X_train.shape

>>> print("#samples: %d, #features: %d" % (num_samples,
num_features)) #samples: 5, #features: 25
```

Unsurprisingly, we have five posts with a total of 25 different words. The following words that have been tokenized will be counted:

```
>>> print(vectorizer.get_feature_names())
[u'about', u'actually', u'capabilities', u'contains', u'data',
u'databases', u'images', u'imaging', u'interesting', u'is', u'it',
u'learning', u'machine', u'most', u'much', u'not', u'permanently',
u'post', u'provide', u'safe', u'storage', u'store', u'stuff',
u'this', u'toy']
```

Now we can vectorize our new post as follows:

```
>>> new_post = "imaging databases"
>>> new_post_vec = vectorizer.transform([new_post])
```

Note that the count vectors returned by the `transform` method are sparse. That is, each vector does not store one count value for each word, as most of those counts would be zero (post does not contain the word). Instead, it uses the more memory efficient implementation `coo_matrix` (for "COOrdinate"). Our new post, for instance, actually contains only two elements:

```
>>> print(new_post_vec)
  (0, 7)1
  (0, 5)1
```

Via its member `toarray()`, we can again access full `ndarray` as follows:

```
>>> print(new_post_vec.toarray())
[[0 0 0 0 0 1 0 1 0 0 0 0 0 0 0 0 0 0 0 0 0 0 0 0 0]]
```

We need to use the full array if we want to use it as a vector for similarity calculations. For the similarity measurement (the naive one), we calculate the Euclidean distance between the count vectors of the new post and all the old posts as follows:

```
>>> import scipy as sp
>>> def dist_raw(v1, v2):
>>> delta = v1-v2
>>> return sp.linalg.norm(delta.toarray())
```

The `norm()` function calculates the Euclidean norm (shortest distance). With dist_ raw, we just need to iterate over all the posts and remember the nearest one:

```
>>> import sys
>>> best_doc = None
>>> best_dist = sys.maxint
>>> best_i = None
>>> for i in range(0, num_samples):
```

```
...        post = posts[i]

...        if post==new_post:
...            continue
...        post_vec = X_train.getrow(i)
...        d = dist(post_vec, new_post_vec)
...        print "=== Post %i with dist=%.2f: %s"%(i, d, post)
...        if d<best_dist:
...            best_dist = d
...            best_i = i
>>> print("Best post is %i with dist=%.2f"%(best_i, best_dist))

=== Post 0 with dist=4.00: This is a toy post about machine learning.
Actually, it contains not much interesting stuff.
=== Post 1 with dist=1.73: Imaging databases provide storage
capabilities.
=== Post 2 with dist=2.00: Most imaging databases safe images
permanently.
=== Post 3 with dist=1.41: Imaging databases store data.
=== Post 4 with dist=5.10: Imaging databases store data. Imaging
databases store data. Imaging databases store data.
Best post is 3 with dist=1.41
```

Congratulations! We have our first similarity measurement. Post 0 is most dissimilar from our new post. Quite understandably, it does not have a single word in common with the new post. We can also understand that Post 1 is very similar to the new post, but not to the winner, as it contains one word more than Post 3 that is not contained in the new post.

Looking at posts 3 and 4, however, the picture is not so clear any more. Post 4 is the same as Post 3, duplicated three times. So, it should also be of the same similarity to the new post as Post 3.

Printing the corresponding feature vectors explains the reason:

```
>>> print(X_train.getrow(3).toarray())
[[0 0 0 0 1 1 0 1 0 0 0 0 0 0 0 0 0 0 0 0 1 0 0 0]]
>>> print(X_train.getrow(4).toarray())
[[0 0 0 0 3 3 0 3 0 0 0 0 0 0 0 0 0 0 0 0 3 0 0 0]]
```

Obviously, using only the counts of the raw words is too simple. We will have to normalize them to get vectors of unit length.

Normalizing the word count vectors

We will have to extend `dist_raw` to calculate the vector distance, not on the raw vectors but on the normalized ones instead:

```
>>> def dist_norm(v1, v2):
...     v1_normalized = v1/sp.linalg.norm(v1.toarray())
...     v2_normalized = v2/sp.linalg.norm(v2.toarray())
...     delta = v1_normalized - v2_normalized
...     return sp.linalg.norm(delta.toarray())
```

This leads to the following similarity measurement:

```
=== Post 0 with dist=1.41: This is a toy post about machine learning.
Actually, it contains not much interesting stuff.
=== Post 1 with dist=0.86: Imaging databases provide storage
capabilities.
=== Post 2 with dist=0.92: Most imaging databases safe images
permanently.
=== Post 3 with dist=0.77: Imaging databases store data.
=== Post 4 with dist=0.77: Imaging databases store data. Imaging
databases store data. Imaging databases store data.
Best post is 3 with dist=0.77
```

This looks a bit better now. Post 3 and Post 4 are calculated as being equally similar. One could argue whether that much repetition would be a delight to the reader, but from the point of counting the words in the posts, this seems to be right.

Removing less important words

Let us have another look at Post 2. Of its words that are not in the new post, we have "most", "safe", "images", and "permanently". They are actually quite different in the overall importance to the post. Words such as "most" appear very often in all sorts of different contexts, and words such as this are called stop words. They do not carry as much information, and thus should not be weighed as much as words such as "images", that don't occur often in different contexts. The best option would be to remove all words that are so frequent that they do not help to distinguish between different texts. These words are called stop words.

As this is such a common step in text processing, there is a simple parameter in `CountVectorizer` to achieve this, as follows:

```
>>> vectorizer = CountVectorizer(min_df=1, stop_words='english')
```

If you have a clear picture of what kind of stop words you would want to remove, you can also pass a list of them. Setting `stop_words` to "english" will use a set of 318 English stop words. To find out which ones they are, you can use `get_stop_words()`:

```
>>> sorted(vectorizer.get_stop_words())[0:20]
['a', 'about', 'above', 'across', 'after', 'afterwards', 'again',
'against', 'all', 'almost', 'alone', 'along', 'already', 'also',
'although', 'always', 'am', 'among', 'amongst', 'amoungst']
```

The new word list is seven words lighter:

```
[u'actually', u'capabilities', u'contains', u'data', u'databases',
u'images', u'imaging', u'interesting', u'learning', u'machine',
u'permanently', u'post', u'provide', u'safe', u'storage', u'store',
u'stuff', u'toy']
```

Without stop words, we arrive at the following similarity measurement:

```
=== Post 0 with dist=1.41: This is a toy post about machine learning.
Actually, it contains not much interesting stuff.
=== Post 1 with dist=0.86: Imaging databases provide storage
capabilities.
=== Post 2 with dist=0.86: Most imaging databases safe images
permanently.
=== Post 3 with dist=0.77: Imaging databases store data.
=== Post 4 with dist=0.77: Imaging databases store data. Imaging
databases store data. Imaging databases store data.
Best post is 3 with dist=0.77
```

Post 2 is now on par with Post 1. Overall, it has, however, not changed much as our posts are kept short for demonstration purposes. It will become vital when we look at real-world data.

Stemming

One thing is still missing. We count similar words in different variants as different words. Post 2, for instance, contains "imaging" and "images". It would make sense to count them together. After all, it is the same concept they are referring to.

We need a function that reduces words to their specific word stem. Scikit does not contain a stemmer by default. With the **Natural Language Toolkit (NLTK)**, we can download a free software toolkit, which provides a stemmer that we can easily plug into `CountVectorizer`.

Installing and using NLTK

How to install NLTK on your operating system is described in detail at
`http://nltk.org/install.html`. Basically, you will need to install the two
packages NLTK and PyYAML.

To check whether your installation was successful, open a Python interpreter and
type the following:

```
>>> import nltk
```

 You will find a very nice tutorial for NLTK in the book *Python
Text Processing with NLTK 2.0 Cookbook*. To play a little bit with a
stemmer, you can visit the accompanied web page `http://text-processing.com/demo/stem/`.

NLTK comes with different stemmers. This is necessary, because every language has
a different set of rules for stemming. For English, we can take `SnowballStemmer`.

```
>>> import nltk.stem
>>> s= nltk.stem.SnowballStemmer('english')
>>> s.stem("graphics")
u'graphic'
>>> s.stem("imaging")
u'imag'
>>> s.stem("image")
u'imag'
>>> s.stem("imagination")u'imagin'
>>> s.stem("imagine")
u'imagin'
```

 Note that stemming does not necessarily have to result into valid
English words.

It also works with verbs as follows:

```
>>> s.stem("buys")
u'buy'
>>> s.stem("buying")
u'buy'
>>> s.stem("bought")
u'bought'
```

Extending the vectorizer with NLTK's stemmer

We need to stem the posts before we feed them into CountVectorizer. The class provides several hooks with which we could customize the preprocessing and tokenization stages. The preprocessor and tokenizer can be set in the constructor as parameters. We do not want to place the stemmer into any of them, because we would then have to do the tokenization and normalization by ourselves. Instead, we overwrite the method build_analyzer as follows:

```
>>> import nltk.stem
>>> english_stemmer = nltk.stem.SnowballStemmer('english')
>>> class StemmedCountVectorizer(CountVectorizer):
...     def build_analyzer(self):
...         analyzer = super(StemmedCountVectorizer, self).build_
analyzer()
...         return lambda doc: (english_stemmer.stem(w) for w in
analyzer(doc))
>>> vectorizer = StemmedCountVectorizer(min_df=1, stop_
words='english')
```

This will perform the following steps for each post:

1. Lower casing the raw post in the preprocessing step (done in the parent class).
2. Extracting all individual words in the tokenization step (done in the parent class).
3. Converting each word into its stemmed version.

As a result, we now have one feature less, because "images" and "imaging" collapsed to one. The set of feature names looks like the following:

```
[u'actual', u'capabl', u'contain', u'data', u'databas', u'imag',
u'interest', u'learn', u'machin', u'perman', u'post', u'provid',
u'safe', u'storag', u'store', u'stuff', u'toy']
```

Running our new stemmed vectorizer over our posts, we see that collapsing "imaging" and "images" reveals that Post 2 is actually the most similar post to our new post, as it contains the concept "imag" twice:

```
=== Post 0 with dist=1.41: This is a toy post about machine learning.
Actually, it contains not much interesting stuff.
=== Post 1 with dist=0.86: Imaging databases provide storage
capabilities.
=== Post 2 with dist=0.63: Most imaging databases safe images
permanently.
```

```
=== Post 3 with dist=0.77: Imaging databases store data.
=== Post 4 with dist=0.77: Imaging databases store data. Imaging
databases store data. Imaging databases store data.
Best post is 2 with dist=0.63
```

Stop words on steroids

Now that we have a reasonable way to extract a compact vector from a noisy textual post, let us step back for a while to think about what the feature values actually mean.

The feature values simply count occurrences of terms in a post. We silently assumed that higher values for a term also mean that the term is of greater importance to the given post. But what about, for instance, the word "subject", which naturally occurs in each and every single post? Alright, we could tell CountVectorizer to remove it as well by means of its max_df parameter. We could, for instance, set it to 0.9 so that all words that occur in more than 90 percent of all posts would be always ignored. But what about words that appear in 89 percent of all posts? How low would we be willing to set max_df? The problem is that however we set it, there will always be the problem that some terms are just more discriminative than others.

This can only be solved by counting term frequencies for every post, and in addition, discounting those that appear in many posts. In other words, we want a high value for a given term in a given value if that term occurs often in that particular post and very rarely anywhere else.

This is exactly what **term frequency – inverse document frequency (TF-IDF)** does; TF stands for the counting part, while IDF factors in the discounting. A naive implementation would look like the following:

```
>>> import scipy as sp
>>> def tfidf(term, doc, docset):
...     tf = float(doc.count(term))/sum(doc.count(w) for w in docset)
...     idf = math.log(float(len(docset))/(len([doc for doc in docset
           if term in doc])))
...     return tf * idf
```

For the following document set, docset, consisting of three documents that are already tokenized, we can see how the terms are treated differently, although all appear equally often per document:

```
>>> a, abb, abc = ["a"], ["a", "b", "b"], ["a", "b", "c"]

>>> D = [a, abb, abc]

>>> print(tfidf("a", a, D))
```

```
0.0

>>> print(tfidf("b", abb, D))

0.270310072072

>>> print(tfidf("a", abc, D))

0.0

>>> print(tfidf("b", abc, D))

0.135155036036

>>> print(tfidf("c", abc, D))

0.366204096223
```

We see that a carries no meaning for any document since it is contained everywhere. b is more important for the document abb than for abc as it occurs there twice.

In reality, there are more corner cases to handle than the above example does. Thanks to Scikit, we don't have to think of them, as they are already nicely packaged in TfidfVectorizer, which is inherited from CountVectorizer. Sure enough, we don't want to miss our stemmer:

```
>>> from sklearn.feature_extraction.text import TfidfVectorizer
>>> class StemmedTfidfVectorizer(TfidfVectorizer):
...     def build_analyzer(self):
...         analyzer = super(TfidfVectorizer,
                             self).build_analyzer()
...         return lambda doc: (
                english_stemmer.stem(w) for w in analyzer(doc))
>>> vectorizer = StemmedTfidfVectorizer(min_df=1,
                stop_words='english', charset_error='ignore')
```

The resulting document vectors will not contain counts any more. Instead, they will contain the individual TF-IDF values per term.

Our achievements and goals

Our current text preprocessing phase includes the following steps:

1. Tokenizing the text.
2. Throwing away words that occur way too often to be of any help in detecting relevant posts.

3. Throwing away words that occur so seldom that there is only a small chance that they occur in future posts.

4. Counting the remaining words.

5. Calculating TF-IDF values from the counts, considering the whole text corpus.

Again we can congratulate ourselves. With this process, we are able to convert a bunch of noisy text into a concise representation of feature values.

But, as simple and as powerful as the bag-of-words approach with its extensions is, it has some drawbacks that we should be aware of. They are as follows:

- It does not cover word relations. With the previous vectorization approach, the text "Car hits wall" and "Wall hits car" will both have the same feature vector.

- It does not capture negations correctly. For instance, the text "I will eat ice cream" and "I will not eat ice cream" will look very similar by means of their feature vectors, although they contain quite the opposite meaning. This problem, however, can be easily changed by not only counting individual words, also called unigrams, but also considering bigrams (pairs of words) or trigrams (three words in a row).

- It totally fails with misspelled words. Although it is clear to the readers that "database" and "databas" convey the same meaning, our approach will treat them as totally different words.

For brevity's sake, let us nevertheless stick with the current approach, which we can now use to efficiently build clusters from.

Clustering

Finally, we have our vectors that we believe capture the posts to a sufficient degree. Not surprisingly, there are many ways to group them together. Most clustering algorithms fall into one of the two methods, flat and hierarchical clustering.

Flat clustering divides the posts into a set of clusters without relating the clust[...]
each other. The goal is simply to come up with a partitioning such that all pos[...]
one cluster are most similar to each other while being dissimilar from the post[...]
other clusters. Many flat clustering algorithms require the number of clusters [...]
specified up front.

In hierarchical clustering, the number of clusters does not have to be specified. Instead, the hierarchical clustering creates a hierarchy of clusters. While similar posts are grouped into one cluster, similar clusters are again grouped into one uber-cluster. This is done recursively, until only one cluster is left, which contains everything. In this hierarchy, one can then choose the desired number of clusters. However, this comes at the cost of lower efficiency.

Scikit provides a wide range of clustering approaches in the package `sklearn.cluster`. You can get a quick overview of the advantages and drawbacks of each of them at `http://scikit-learn.org/dev/modules/clustering.html`.

In the following section, we will use the flat clustering method, KMeans, and play a bit with the desired number of clusters.

KMeans

KMeans is the most widely used flat clustering algorithm. After it is initialized with the desired number of clusters, `num_clusters`, it maintains that number of so-called cluster centroids. Initially, it would pick any of the `num_clusters` posts and set the centroids to their feature vector. Then it would go through all other posts and assign them the nearest centroid as their current cluster. Then it will move each centroid into the middle of all the vectors of that particular class. This changes, of course, the cluster assignment. Some posts are now nearer to another cluster. So it will update the assignments for those changed posts. This is done as long as the centroids move a considerable amount. After some iterations, the movements will fall below a threshold and we consider clustering to be converged.

Downloading the example code

You can download the example code files for all Packt books you have purchased from your account at `http://www.packtpub.com`. If you purchased this book elsewhere, you can visit `http://www.packtpub.com/support` and register to have the files e-mailed directly to you.

Let us play this through with a toy example of posts containing only two words. Each point in the following chart represents one document:

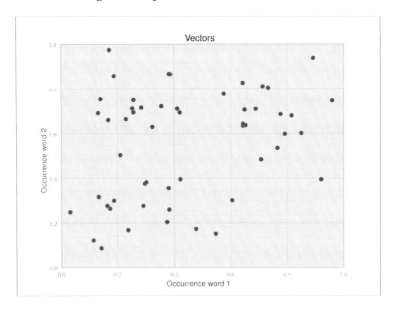

After running one iteration of KMeans, that is, taking any two vectors as starting points, assigning labels to the rest, and updating the cluster centers to be the new center point of all points in that cluster, we get the following clustering:

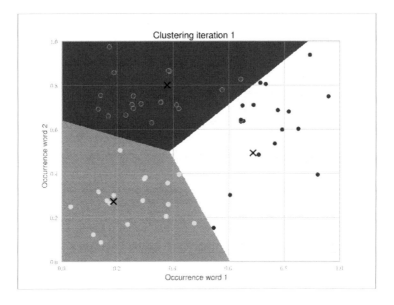

Because the cluster centers are moved, we have to reassign the cluster labels and recalculate the cluster centers. After iteration 2, we get the following clustering:

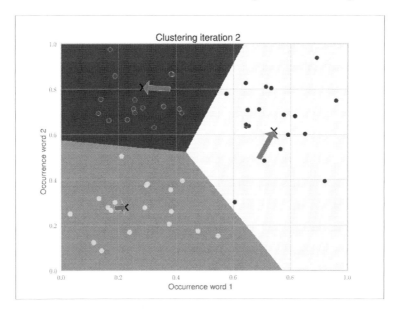

The arrows show the movements of the cluster centers. After five iterations in this example, the cluster centers don't move noticeably any more (Scikit's tolerance threshold is 0.0001 by default).

After the clustering has settled, we just need to note down the cluster centers and their identity. When each new document comes in, we have to vectorize and compare it with all the cluster centers. The cluster center with the smallest distance to our new post vector belongs to the cluster we will assign to the new post.

Getting test data to evaluate our ideas on

In order to test clustering, let us move away from the toy text examples and find a dataset that resembles the data we are expecting in the future so that we can test our approach. For our purpose, we need documents on technical topics that are already grouped together so that we can check whether our algorithm works as expected when we apply it later to the posts we hope to receive.

One standard dataset in machine learning is the 20newsgroup dataset, which contains 18,826 posts from 20 different newsgroups. Among the groups' topics are technical ones such as comp.sys.mac.hardware or sci.crypt as well as more politics- and religion-related ones such as talk.politics.guns or soc.religion. christian. We will restrict ourselves to the technical groups. If we assume each newsgroup is one cluster, we can nicely test whether our approach of finding related posts works.

The dataset can be downloaded from http://people.csail.mit.edu/ jrennie/20Newsgroups. Much more simple, however, is to download it from MLComp at http://mlcomp.org/datasets/379 (free registration required). Scikit already contains custom loaders for that dataset and rewards you with very convenient data loading options.

The dataset comes in the form of a ZIP file, dataset-379-20news-18828_WJQIG. zip, which we have to unzip to get the folder 379, which contains the datasets. We also have to notify Scikit about the path containing that data directory. It contains a metadata file and three directories test, train, and raw. The test and train directories split the whole dataset into 60 percent of training and 40 percent of testing posts. For convenience, the dataset module also contains the function fetch_20newsgroups, which downloads that data into the desired directory.

> The website http://mlcomp.org is used for comparing machine-learning programs on diverse datasets. It serves two purposes: finding the right dataset to tune your machine-learning program and exploring how other people use a particular dataset. For instance, you can see how well other people's algorithms performed on particular datasets and compare them.

Either you set the environment variable MLCOMP_DATASETS_HOME or you specify the path directly with the mlcomp_root parameter when loading the dataset as follows:

```
>>> import sklearn.datasets
>>> MLCOMP_DIR = r"D:\data"
>>> data = sklearn.datasets.load_mlcomp("20news-18828", mlcomp_
root=MLCOMP_DIR)
>>> print(data.filenames)
array(['D:\\data\\379\\raw\\comp.graphics\\1190-38614',
       'D:\\data\\379\\raw\\comp.graphics\\1383-38616',
       'D:\\data\\379\\raw\\alt.atheism\\487-53344',
       ...,
       'D:\\data\\379\\raw\\rec.sport.hockey\\10215-54303',
       'D:\\data\\379\\raw\\sci.crypt\\10799-15660',
```

```
           'D:\\data\\379\\raw\\comp.os.ms-windows.misc\\2732-10871'],
       dtype='|S68')
>>> print(len(data.filenames))
18828
>>> data.target_names
['alt.atheism', 'comp.graphics', 'comp.os.ms-windows.misc', 'comp.sys.
ibm.pc.hardware', 'comp.sys.mac.hardware', 'comp.windows.x', 'misc.
forsale', 'rec.autos', 'rec.motorcycles', 'rec.sport.baseball', 'rec.
sport.hockey', 'sci.crypt', 'sci.electronics', 'sci.med', sci.space',
'soc.religion.christian', 'talk.politics.guns', 'talk.politics.
mideast', 'talk.politics.misc', 'talk.religion.misc']
```

We can choose among training and test sets as follows:

```
>>> train_data = sklearn.datasets.load_mlcomp("20news-18828", "train",
mlcomp_root=MLCOMP_DIR)
>>> print(len(train_data.filenames))
13180
>>> test_data = sklearn.datasets.load_mlcomp("20news-18828",
"test", mlcomp_root=MLCOMP_DIR)
>>> print(len(test_data.filenames))
5648
```

For simplicity's sake, we will restrict ourselves to only some newsgroups so that the overall experimentation cycle is shorter. We can achieve this with the `categories` parameter as follows:

```
>>> groups = ['comp.graphics', 'comp.os.ms-windows.misc', 'comp.sys.
ibm.pc.hardware', 'comp.sys.ma c.hardware', 'comp.windows.x', 'sci.
space']
>>> train_data = sklearn.datasets.load_mlcomp("20news-18828", "train",
mlcomp_root=MLCOMP_DIR, categories=groups)
>>> print(len(train_data.filenames))
3414
```

Clustering posts

You must have already noticed one thing – real data is noisy. The newsgroup dataset is no exception. It even contains invalid characters that will result in `UnicodeDecodeError`.

We have to tell the vectorizer to ignore them:

```
>>> vectorizer = StemmedTfidfVectorizer(min_df=10, max_df=0.5,
...                 stop_words='english', charset_error='ignore')
>>> vectorized = vectorizer.fit_transform(dataset.data)
```

```
>>> num_samples, num_features = vectorized.shape
>>> print("#samples: %d, #features: %d" % (num_samples, num_features))
#samples: 3414, #features: 4331
```

We now have a pool of 3,414 posts and extracted for each of them a feature vector of 4,331 dimensions. That is what KMeans takes as input. We will fix the cluster size to 50 for this chapter and hope you are curious enough to try out different values as an exercise, as shown in the following code:

```
>>> num_clusters = 50
>>> from sklearn.cluster import KMeans
>>> km = KMeans(n_clusters=num_clusters, init='random', n_init=1,
verbose=1)
>>> km.fit(vectorized)
```

That's it. After fitting, we can get the clustering information out of the members of km. For every vectorized post that has been fit, there is a corresponding integer label in km.labels_:

```
>>> km.labels_
array([33, 22, 17, ..., 14, 11, 39])
>>> km.labels_.shape
(3414,)
```

The cluster centers can be accessed via km.cluster_centers_.

In the next section we will see how we can assign a cluster to a newly arriving post using km.predict.

Solving our initial challenge

We now put everything together and demonstrate our system for the following new post that we assign to the variable new_post:

Disk drive problems. Hi, I have a problem with my hard disk.

After 1 year it is working only sporadically now.

I tried to format it, but now it doesn't boot any more.

Any ideas? Thanks.

As we have learned previously, we will first have to vectorize this post before we predict its label as follows:

```
>>> new_post_vec = vectorizer.transform([new_post])
>>> new_post_label = km.predict(new_post_vec)[0]
```

Now that we have the clustering, we do not need to compare new_post_vec to all post vectors. Instead, we can focus only on the posts of the same cluster. Let us fetch their indices in the original dataset:

```
>>> similar_indices = (km.labels_==new_post_label).nonzero()[0]
```

The comparison in the bracket results in a Boolean array, and nonzero converts that array into a smaller array containing the indices of the True elements.

Using similar_indices, we then simply have to build a list of posts together with their similarity scores as follows:

```
>>> similar = []
>>> for i in similar_indices:
...     dist = sp.linalg.norm((new_post_vec - vectorized[i]).toarray())
...     similar.append((dist, dataset.data[i]))
>>> similar = sorted(similar)
>>> print(len(similar))
44
```

We found 44 posts in the cluster of our post. To give the user a quick idea of what kind of similar posts are available, we can now present the most similar post (show_at_1), the least similar one (show_at_3), and an in-between post (show_at_2), all of which are from the same cluster as follows:

```
>>> show_at_1 = similar[0]
>>> show_at_2 = similar[len(similar)/2]
>>> show_at_3 = similar[-1]
```

The following table shows the posts together with their similarity values:

Position	Similarity	Excerpt from post
1	1.018	BOOT PROBLEM with IDE controller
		Hi,
		I've got a Multi I/O card (IDE controller + serial/parallel interface) and two floppy drives (5 1/4, 3 1/2) and a Quantum ProDrive 80AT connected to it. I was able to format the hard disk, but I could not boot from it. I can boot from drive A: (which disk drive does not matter) but if I remove the disk from drive A and press the reset switch, the LED of drive A: continues to glow, and the hard disk is not accessed at all. I guess this must be a problem of either the Multi I/o card\nor floppy disk drive settings (jumper configuration?) Does someone have any hint what could be the reason for it. [...]
2	1.294	IDE Cable
		I just bought a new IDE hard drive for my system to go with the one I already had. My problem is this. My system only had a IDE cable for one drive, so I had to buy cable with two drive connectors on it, and consequently have to switch cables. The problem is, the new hard drive\'s manual refers to matching pin 1 on the cable with both pin 1 on the drive itself and pin 1 on the IDE card. But for the life of me I cannot figure out how to tell which way to plug in the cable to align these. Secondly, the cable has like a connector at two ends and one between them. I figure one end goes in the controller and then the other two go into the drives. Does it matter which I plug into the "master" drive and which into the "Slave"? any help appreciated [...]

Position	Similarity	Excerpt from post
3	1.375	`Conner CP3204F info please`
		`How to change the cluster size Wondering` `if somebody could tell me if we can` `change the cluster size of my IDE drive.` `Normally I can do it with Norton's` `Calibrat on MFM/RLL drives but dunno if` `I can on IDE too. [...]`

It is interesting how the posts reflect the similarity measurement score. The first post contains all the salient words from our new post. The second one also revolves around hard disks, but lacks concepts such as formatting. Finally, the third one is only slightly related. Still, for all the posts, we would say that they belong to the same domain as that of the new post.

Another look at noise

We should not expect a perfect clustering, in the sense that posts from the same newsgroup (for example, `comp.graphics`) are also clustered together. An example will give us a quick impression of the noise that we have to expect:

```
>>> post_group = zip(dataset.data, dataset.target)
>>> z = (len(post[0]), post[0], dataset.target_names[post[1]]) for
post in post_group
>>> print(sorted(z)[5:7])
[(107, 'From: "kwansik kim" <kkim@cs.indiana.edu>\nSubject: Where
is FAQ ?\n\nWhere can I find it ?\n\nThanks, Kwansik\n\n', 'comp.
graphics'), (110, 'From: lioness@maple.circa.ufl.edu\nSubject: What is
3dO?\n\n\nSomeone please fill me in on what 3do.\n\nThanks,\n\nBH\n',
'comp.graphics')]
```

For both of these posts, there is no real indication that they belong to `comp.graphics`, considering only the wording that is left after the preprocessing step:

```
>>> analyzer = vectorizer.build_analyzer()
>>> list(analyzer(z[5][1]))
[u'kwansik', u'kim', u'kkim', u'cs', u'indiana', u'edu', u'subject',
u'faq', u'thank', u'kwansik']
>>> list(analyzer(z[6][1]))
[u'lioness', u'mapl', u'circa', u'ufl', u'edu', u'subject', u'3do',
u'3do', u'thank', u'bh']
```

This is only after tokenization, lower casing, and stop word removal. If we also subtract those words that will be later filtered out via `min_df` and `max_df`, which will be done later in `fit_transform`, it gets even worse:

```
>>> list(set(analyzer(z[5][1])).intersection(
        vectorizer.get_feature_names()))
[u'cs', u'faq', u'thank']
>>> list(set(analyzer(z[6][1])).intersection(
vectorizer.get_feature_names()))
[u'bh', u'thank']
```

Furthermore, most of the words occur frequently in other posts as well, as we can check with the IDF scores. Remember that the higher the TF-IDF, the more discriminative a term is for a given post. And as IDF is a multiplicative factor here, a low value of it signals that it is not of great value in general:

```
>>> for term in ['cs', 'faq', 'thank', 'bh', 'thank']:
...     print('IDF(%s)=%.2f'%(term,
            vectorizer._tfidf.idf_[vectorizer.vocabulary_[term]])
IDF(cs)=3.23
IDF(faq)=4.17
IDF(thank)=2.23
IDF(bh)=6.57
IDF(thank)=2.23
```

So, except for `bh`, which is close to the maximum overall IDF value of 6.74, the terms don't have much discriminative power. Understandably, posts from different newsgroups will be clustered together.

For our goal, however, this is no big deal, as we are only interested in cutting down the number of posts that we have to compare a new post to. After all, the particular newsgroup from where our training data came from is of no special interest.

Tweaking the parameters

So what about all the other parameters? Can we tweak them all to get better results?

Sure. We could, of course, tweak the number of clusters or play with the vectorizer's `max_features` parameter (you should try that!). Also, we could play with different cluster center initializations. There are also more exciting alternatives to KMeans itself. There are, for example, clustering approaches that also let you use different similarity measurements such as Cosine similarity, Pearson, or Jaccard. An exciting field for you to play.

But before you go there, you will have to define what you actually mean by "better". Scikit has a complete package dedicated only to this definition. The package is called `sklearn.metrics` and also contains a full range of different metrics to measure clustering quality. Maybe that should be the first place to go now, right into the sources of the metrics package.

Summary

That was a tough ride, from preprocessing over clustering to a solution that can convert noisy text into a meaningful concise vector representation that we can cluster. If we look at the efforts we had to do to finally be able to cluster, it was more than half of the overall task, but on the way, we learned quite a bit on text processing and how simple counting can get you very far in the noisy real-world data.

The ride has been made much smoother though, because of Scikit and its powerful packages. And there is more to explore. In this chapter we were scratching the surface of its capabilities. In the next chapters we will see more of its powers.

4
Topic Modeling

In the previous chapter we clustered texts into groups. This is a very useful tool, but it is not always appropriate. Clustering results in each text belonging to exactly one cluster. This book is about machine learning and Python. Should it be grouped with other Python-related works or with machine-related works? In the paper book age, a bookstore would need to make this decision when deciding where to stock it. In the Internet store age, however, the answer is that this book is both about machine learning and Python, and the book can be listed in both sections. We will, however, not list it in the food section.

In this chapter, we will learn methods that do not cluster objects, but put them into a small number of groups called topics. We will also learn how to derive between topics that are central to the text and others only that are vaguely mentioned (this book mentions plotting every so often, but it is not a central topic such as machine learning is). The subfield of machine learning that deals with these problems is called **topic modeling**.

Latent Dirichlet allocation (LDA)

LDA and **LDA**: unfortunately, there are two methods in machine learning with the initials LDA: latent Dirichlet allocation, which is a topic modeling method; and linear discriminant analysis, which is a classification method. They are completely unrelated, except for the fact that the initials LDA can refer to either. However, this can be confusing. Scikit-learn has a submodule, `sklearn.lda`, which implements linear discriminant analysis. At the moment, scikit-learn does not implement latent Dirichlet allocation.

The simplest topic model (on which all others are based) is **latent Dirichlet allocation (LDA)**. The mathematical ideas behind LDA are fairly complex, and we will not go into the details here.

For those who are interested and adventurous enough, a Wikipedia search will provide all the equations behind these algorithms
at the following link:

```
http://en.wikipedia.org/wiki/Latent_Dirichlet_allocation
```

However, we can understand that this is at a high level and there is a sort of fable which underlies these models. In this fable, there are topics that are fixed. This lacks clarity. Which documents?

For example, let's say we have only three topics at present:

- Machine learning
- Python
- Baking

Each topic has a list of words associated with it. This book would be a mixture of the first two topics, perhaps 50 percent each. Therefore, when we are writing it, we pick half of our words from the machine learning topic and half from the Python topic. In this model, the order of words does not matter.

The preceding explanation is a simplification of the reality; each topic assigns a probability to each word so that it is possible to use the word "flour" when the topic is either machine learning or baking, but more probable if the topic is baking.

Of course, we do not know what the topics are. Otherwise, this would be a different and much simpler problem. Our task right now is to take a collection of text and reverse engineer this fable in order to discover what topics are out there and also where each document belongs.

Building a topic model

Unfortunately, scikit-learn does not support latent Dirichlet allocation. Therefore, we are going to use the gensim package in Python. Gensim is developed by *Radim Řehůřek*, who is a machine learning researcher and consultant in the Czech Republic. We must start by installing it. We can achieve this by running one of the following commands:

```
pip install gensim
easy_install gensim
```

We are going to use an **Associated Press (AP)** dataset of news reports. This is a standard dataset, which was used in some of the initial work on topic models:

```
>>> from gensim import corpora, models, similarities
>>> corpus = corpora.BleiCorpus('./data/ap/ap.dat',
'/data/ap/vocab.txt')
```

Corpus is just the preloaded list of words:

```
>>> model = models.ldamodel.LdaModel(
    corpus,
    num_topics=100,
    id2word=corpus.id2word)
```

This one-step process will build a topic model. We can explore the topics in many ways. We can see the list of topics a document refers to by using the `model[doc]` syntax:

```
>>> topics = [model[c] for c in corpus]
>>> print topics[0]
[(3, 0.023607255776894751),
 (13, 0.11679936618551275),
 (19, 0.075935855202707139),
 (92, 0.10781541687001292)]
```

I elided some of the output, but the format is a list of pairs `(topic_index, topic_weight)`. We can see that only a few topics are used for each document. The topic model is a sparse model, as although there are many possible topics for each document, only a few of them are used. We can plot a histogram of the number of topics as shown in the following graph:

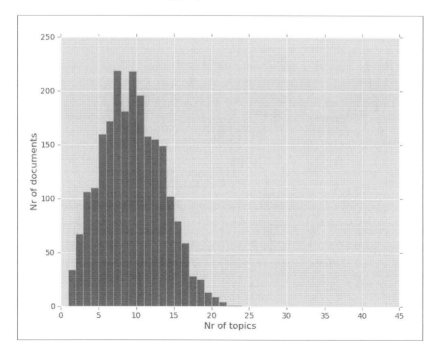

Sparsity means that while you may have large matrices and vectors, in principle, most of the values are zero (or so small that we can round them to zero as a good approximation). Therefore, only a few things are relevant at any given time.

Often problems that seem too big to solve are actually feasible because the data is sparse. For example, even though one webpage can link to any other webpage, the graph of links is actually very sparse as each webpage will link to a very tiny fraction of all other webpages.

In the previous graph, we can see that about **150** documents have **5** topics, while the majority deal with around 10 to 12 of them. No document talks about more than 20 topics.

To a large extent, this is a function of the parameters used, namely the alpha parameter. The exact meaning of alpha is a bit abstract, but bigger values for alpha will result in more topics per document. Alpha needs to be positive, but is typically very small; usually smaller than one. By default, gensim will set alpha equal to 1.0/ len (corpus), but you can set it yourself as follows:

```
>>> model = models.ldamodel.LdaModel(
   corpus,
   num_topics=100,
   id2word=corpus.id2word,
   alpha=1)
```

In this case, this is a larger alpha, which should lead to more topics per document. We could also use a smaller value. As we can see in the combined histogram given next, gensim behaves as we expected:

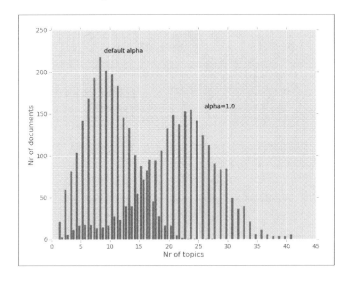

Now we can see that many documents touch upon 20 to 25 different topics.

What are these topics? Technically, they are multinomial distributions over words, which mean that they give each word in the vocabulary a probability. Words with high probability are more associated with that topic than words with lower probability.

Our brains aren't very good at reasoning with probability distributions, but we can readily make sense of a list of words. Therefore, it is typical to summarize topics with a the list of the most highly weighted words. Here are the first ten topics:

- dress military soviet president new state capt carlucci states leader stance government

- koch zambia lusaka one-party orange kochs party i government mayor new political

- human turkey rights abuses royal thompson threats new state wrote garden president

- bill employees experiments levin taxation federal measure legislation senate president whistleblowers sponsor

- ohio july drought jesus disaster percent hartford mississippi crops northern valley virginia

- united percent billion year president world years states people i bush news

- b hughes affidavit states united ounces squarefoot care delaying charged unrealistic bush

- yeutter dukakis bush convention farm subsidies uruguay percent secretary general i told

- Kashmir government people srinagar india dumps city two jammu-kashmir group moslem pakistan

- workers vietnamese irish wage immigrants percent bargaining last island police hutton I

Although daunting at first glance, we can clearly see that the topics are not just random words, but are connected. We can also see that these topics refer to older news items, from when the Soviet union still existed and Gorbachev was its Secretary General. We can also represent the topics as word clouds, making more likely words larger For example, this is the visualization of a topic, which deals with the Middle East and politics:

We can also see that some of the words should perhaps be removed (for example, the word I) as they are not so informative (stop words). In topic modeling, it is important to filter out stop words, as otherwise you might end up with a topic consisting entirely of stop words, which is not very informative. We may also wish to preprocess the text to stems in order to normalize plurals and verb forms. This process was covered in the previous chapter, and you can refer to it for details. If you are interested, you can download the code from the companion website of the book and try all these variations to draw different pictures.

Building a word cloud like the one in the previous screenshot can be done with several different pieces of software. For the previous graphic, I used the online tool wordle (`http://www.wordle.net`), which generates particularly attractive images. Since I only had a few examples, I copy and pasted the list of words manually, but it is possible to use it as a web service and call it directly from Python.

Comparing similarity in topic space

Topics can be useful on their own to build small vignettes with words that are in the previous screenshot. These visualizations could be used to navigate a large collection of documents and, in fact, they have been used in just this way.

However, topics are often just an intermediate tool to another end. Now that we have an estimate for each document about how much of that document comes from each topic, we can compare the documents in topic space. This simply means that instead of comparing word per word, we say that two documents are similar if they talk about the same topics.

This can be very powerful, as two text documents that share a few words may actually refer to the same topic. They may just refer to it using different constructions (for example, one may say the President of the United States while the other will use the name Barack Obama).

 Topic models are useful on their own to build visualizations and explore data. They are also very useful as an intermediate step in many other tasks.

At this point, we can redo the exercise we performed in the previous chapter and look for the most similar post, but by using the topics. Whereas previously we compared two documents by comparing their word vectors, we can now compare two documents by comparing their topic vectors.

For this, we are going to project the documents to the topic space. That is, we want to have a vector of topics that summarizes the document. Since the number of topics (100) is smaller than the number of possible words, we have reduced dimensionality. How to perform these types of dimensionality reduction in general is an important task in itself, and we have a chapter entirely devoted to this task. One additional computational advantage is that it is much faster to compare 100 vectors of topic weights than vectors of the size of the vocabulary (which will contain thousands of terms).

Using gensim, we saw before how to compute the topics corresponding to all documents in the corpus:

```
>>> topics = [model[c] for c in corpus]
>>> print topics[0]
[(3, 0.023607255776894751),
 (13, 0.11679936618551275),
 (19, 0.075935855202707139),
 (92, 0.10781541687001292)]
```

We will store all these topic counts in NumPy arrays and compute all pairwise distances:

```
>>> dense = np.zeros( (len(topics), 100), float)
>>> for ti,t in enumerate(topics):
```

```
...        for tj,v in t:
...            dense[ti,tj] = v
```

Now, `dense` is a matrix of topics. We can use the `pdist` function in SciPy to compute all pairwise distances. That is, with a single function call, we compute all the values of `sum((dense[ti] - dense[tj])**2)`:

```
>>> from scipy.spatial import distance
>>> pairwise = distance.squareform(distance.pdist(dense))
```

Now we employ one last little trick; we set the diagonal elements of the distance matrix to a high value (it just needs to be larger than the other values in the matrix):

```
>>> largest = pairwise.max()
  >>> for ti in range(len(topics)):
    pairwise[ti,ti] = largest+1
```

And we are done! For each document, we can look up the closest element easily:

```
>>> def closest_to(doc_id):
    return pairwise[doc_id].argmin()
```

 The previous code would not work if we had not set the diagonal elements to a large value; the function would always return the same element as it is almost similar to itself (except in the weird case where two elements have exactly the same topic distribution, which is very rare unless they are exactly the same).

For example, here is the second document in the collection (the first document is very uninteresting, as the system returns a post stating that it is the most similar):

```
From: geb@cs.pitt.edu (Gordon Banks)
Subject: Re: request for information on "essential tremor" and Indrol?
In article <1q1tbnINNnfn@life.ai.mit.edu> sundar@ai.mit.edu writes:
Essential tremor is a progressive hereditary tremor that gets worse
when the patient tries to use the effected member. All limbs, vocal
cords, and head can be involved.  Inderal is a beta-blocker and is
usually effective in diminishing the tremor. Alcohol and mysoline are
also effective, but alcohol is too toxic to use as a treatment.
----------------------------------------------------------------Gordon
Banks  N3JXP       | "Skepticism is the chastity of the intellect, and
geb@cadre.dsl.pitt.edu   |  it is shameful to surrender it too soon."
    ----------------------------------------------------------------
```

If we ask for the most similar document, `closest_to(1)`, we receive the following document:

```
From: geb@cs.pitt.edu (Gordon Banks)
```

```
Subject: Re: High Prolactin

In article <93088.112203JER4@psuvm.psu.edu> JER4@psuvm.psu.edu (John
E. Rodway) writes:
>Any comments on the use of the drug Parlodel for high prolactin in
the blood?
>It can suppress secretion of prolactin.  Is useful in cases of
galactorrhea. Some adenomas of the pituitary secret too much.
-----------------------------------------------------------------
Gordon Banks  N3JXP      | "Skepticism is the chastity of the
intellect, and geb@cadre.dsl.pitt.edu   |  it is shameful to surrender
it too soon."
-----------------------------------------------------------------
```

We received a post by the same author discussing medications.

Modeling the whole of Wikipedia

While the initial LDA implementations could be slow, modern systems can work with very large collections of data. Following the documentation of gensim, we are going to build a topic model for the whole of the English language Wikipedia. This takes hours, but can be done even with a machine that is not too powerful. With a cluster of machines, we could make it go much faster, but we will look at that sort of processing in a later chapter.

First we download the whole Wikipedia dump from http://dumps.wikimedia.org. This is a large file (currently just over 9 GB), so it may take a while, unless your Internet connection is very fast. Then, we will index it with a gensim tool:

```
python -m gensim.scripts.make_wiki enwiki-latest-pages-articles.xml.bz2
wiki_en_output
```

Run the previous command on the command line, not on the Python shell. After a few hours, the indexing will be finished. Finally, we can build the final topic model. This step looks exactly like what we did for the small AP dataset. We first import a few packages:

```
>>> import logging, gensim
>>> logging.basicConfig(
    format='%(asctime)s : %(levelname)s : %(message)s',
    level=logging.INFO)
```

Now, we load the data that has been preprocessed:

```
>>> id2word =
gensim.corpora.Dictionary.load_from_text('wiki_en_output_wordids.txt')
>>> mm = gensim.corpora.MmCorpus('wiki_en_output_tfidf.mm')
```

Finally, we build the LDA model as before:

```
>>> model = gensim.models.ldamodel.LdaModel(
    corpus=mm,
    id2word=id2word,
    num_topics=100,
    update_every=1,
    chunksize=10000,
    passes=1)
```

This will again take a couple of hours (you will see the progress on your console, which can give you an indication of how long you still have to wait). Once it is done, you can save it to a file so you don't have to redo it all the time:

```
>>> model.save('wiki_lda.pkl')
```

If you exit your session and come back later, you can load the model again with:

```
>>> model = gensim.models.ldamodel.LdaModel.load('wiki_lda.pkl')
```

Let us explore some `topics`:

```
>>> topics = []
>>> for doc in mm:
    topics.append(model[doc])
```

We can see that this is still a sparse model even if we have many more documents than before (over 4 million as we are writing this):

```
>>> import numpy as np
>>> lens = np.array([len(t) for t in  topics])
>>> print np.mean(lens)
6.55842326445
>>> print np.mean(lens <= 10)
0.932382190219
```

So, the average document mentions 6.5 topics and 93 percent of them mention 10 or fewer.

If you have not seen the idiom before, it may be odd to take the mean of a comparison, but it is a direct way to compute a fraction.

`np.mean(lens <= 10)` is taking the mean of an array of Booleans. The Booleans get interpreted as 0s and 1s in a numeric context. Therefore, the result is a number between 0 and 1, which is the fraction of ones. In this case, it is the fraction of elements of `lens`, which are less than or equal to 10.

We can also ask what the most talked about topic in Wikipedia is. We first collect some statistics on topic usage:

```
>>> counts = np.zeros(100)
>>> for doc_top in topics:
...     for ti,_ in doc_top:
...         counts[ti] += 1
>>> words = model.show_topic(counts.argmax(), 64)
```

Using the same tool as before to build up visualization, we can see that the most talked about topic is fiction and stories, both as books and movies. For variety, we chose a different color scheme. A full 25 percent of Wikipedia pages are partially related to this topic (or alternatively, 5 percent of the words come from this topic):

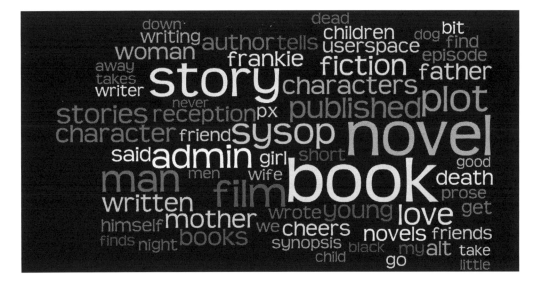

 These plots and numbers were obtained when the book was being written in early 2013. As Wikipedia keeps changing, your results will be different. We expect that the trends will be similar, but the details may vary. Particularly, the least relevant topic is subject to change, while a topic similar to the previous topic is likely to be still high on the list (even if not as the most important).

Alternatively, we can look at the least talked about topic:

```
>>> words = model.show_topic(counts.argmin(), 64)
```

The least talked about are the former French colonies in Central Africa. Just 1.5 percent of documents touch upon it, and it represents 0.08 percent of the words. Probably if we had performed this exercise using the French Wikipedia, we would have obtained a very different result.

Choosing the number of topics

So far, we have used a fixed number of topics, which is 100. This was purely an arbitrary number; we could have just as well done 20 or 200 topics. Fortunately, for many users, this number does not really matter. If you are going to only use the topics as an intermediate step as we did previously, the final behavior of the system is rarely very sensitive to the exact number of topics. This means that as long as you use enough topics, whether you use 100 topics or 200, the recommendations that result from the process will not be very different. One hundred is often a good number (while 20 is too few for a general collection of text documents). The same is true of setting the alpha (α) value. While playing around with it can change the topics, the final results are again robust against this change.

Topic modeling is often an end towards a goal. In that case, it is not always important exactly which parameters you choose. Different numbers of topics or values for parameters such as alpha will result in systems whose end results are almost identical.

If you are going to explore the topics yourself or build a visualization tool, you should probably try a few values and see which gives you the most useful or most appealing results.

However, there are a few methods that will automatically determine the number of topics for you depending on the dataset. One popular model is called the hierarchical Dirichlet process. Again, the full mathematical model behind it is complex and beyond the scope of this book, but the fable we can tell is that instead of having the topics be fixed a priori and our task being to reverse engineer the data to get them back, the topics themselves were generated along with the data. Whenever the writer was going to start a new document, he had the option of using the topics that already existed or creating a completely new one.

This means that the more documents we have, the more topics we will end up with. This is one of those statements that is unintuitive at first, but makes perfect sense upon reflection. We are learning topics, and the more examples we have, the more we can break them up. If we only have a few examples of news articles, then sports will be a topic. However, as we have more, we start to break it up into the individual modalities such as Hockey, Soccer, and so on. As we have even more data, we can start to tell nuances apart articles about individual teams and even individual players. The same is true for people. In a group of many different backgrounds, with a few "computer people", you might put them together; in a slightly larger group, you would have separate gatherings for programmers and systems managers. In the real world, we even have different gatherings for Python and Ruby programmers.

One of the methods for automatically determining the number of topics is called the **hierarchical Dirichlet process (HDP)**, and it is available in `gensim`. Using it is trivial. Taking the previous code for LDA, we just need to replace the call to `gensim. models.ldamodel.LdaModel` with a call to the `HdpModel` constructor as follows:

```
>>> hdp = gensim.models.hdpmodel.HdpModel(mm, id2word)
```

That's it (except it takes a bit longer to compute—there are no free lunches). Now, we can use this model as much as we used the LDA model, except that we did not need to specify the number of topics.

Summary

In this chapter, we discussed a more advanced form of grouping documents, which is more flexible than simple clustering as we allow each document to be present in more than one group. We explored the basic LDA model using a new package, `gensim`, but were able to integrate it easily into the standard Python scientific ecosystem.

Topic modeling was first developed and is easier to understand in the case of text, but in *Chapter 10, Computer Vision – Pattern Recognition,* we will see how some of these techniques may be applied to images as well. Topic models are very important in most of modern computer vision research. In fact, unlike the previous chapters, this chapter was very close to the cutting edge of research in machine learning algorithms. The original LDA algorithm was published in a scientific journal in 2003, but the method that `gensim` uses to be able to handle Wikipedia was only developed in 2010, and the HDP algorithm is from 2011. The research continues and you can find many variations and models with wonderful names such as the Indian buffet process (not to be confused with the Chinese restaurant process, which is a different model), or Pachinko allocation (Pachinko being a type of Japanese game, a cross between a slot-machine and pinball). Currently, they are still in the realm of research. In a few years, though, they might make the jump into the real world.

We have now gone over some of the major machine learning models such as classification, clustering, and topic modeling. In the next chapter, we go back to classification, but this time we will be exploring advanced algorithms and approaches.

5

Classification – Detecting Poor Answers

Now that we are able to extract useful features from text, we can take on the challenge of building a classifier using real data. Let's go back to our imaginary website in *Chapter 3, Clustering – Finding Related Posts*, where users can submit questions and get them answered.

A continuous challenge for owners of these Q&A sites is to maintain a decent level of quality in the posted content. Websites such as `stackoverflow.com` take considerable efforts to encourage users to score questions and answers with badges and bonus points. Higher quality content is the result, as users are trying to spend more energy on carving out the question or crafting a possible answer.

One particular successful incentive is the possibility for the asker to flag one answer to their question as the accepted answer (again, there are incentives for the asker to flag such answers). This will result in more score points for the author of the flagged answer.

Would it not be very useful for the user to immediately see how good their answer is while they are typing it in? This means that the website would continuously evaluate their work-in-progress answer and provide feedback as to whether the answer shows signs of being a poor one or not. This will encourage the user to put more effort into writing the answer (for example, providing a code example, including an image, and so on). So finally, the overall system will be improved.

Let us build such a mechanism in this chapter.

Sketching our roadmap

We will build a system using real data that is very noisy. This chapter is not for the fainthearted, as we will not arrive at the golden solution for a classifier that achieves 100 percent accuracy. This is because even humans often disagree whether an answer was good or not (just look at some of the comments on the `stackoverflow.com` website). Quite the contrary, we will find out that some problems like this one are so hard that we have to adjust our initial goals on the way. But on that way, we will start with the nearest neighbor approach, find out why it is not very good for the task, switch over to logistic regression, and arrive at a solution that will achieve a good prediction quality but on a smaller part of the answers. Finally, we will spend some time on how to extract the winner to deploy it on the target system.

Learning to classify classy answers

While classifying, we want to find the corresponding classes, sometimes also called **labels**, for the given data instances. To be able to achieve this, we need to answer the following two questions:

- How should we represent the data instances?
- Which model or structure should our classifier possess?

Tuning the instance

In its simplest form, in our case, the data instance is the text of the answer and the label is a binary value indicating whether the asker accepted this text as an answer or not. Raw text, however, is a very inconvenient representation to process for most of the machine learning algorithms. They want numbers. It will be our task to extract useful features from raw text, which the machine learning algorithm can then use to learn the right label.

Tuning the classifier

Once we have found or collected enough (text and label) pairs, we can train a **classifier**. For the underlying structure of the classifier, we have a wide range of possibilities, each of them having advantages and drawbacks. Just to name some of the more prominent choices, there is logistic regression, and there are decision trees, SVMs, and Naive Bayes. In this chapter, we will contrast the instance-based method from the previous chapter with model-based logistic regression.

Fetching the data

Luckily for us, the team behind *stackoverflow* provides most of the data behind the *StackExchange* universe to which *stackoverflow* belongs under a CC Wiki license. While writing this, the latest data dump can be found at http://www.clearbits. net/torrents/2076-aug-2012. Most likely, this page will contain a pointer to an updated dump when you read it.

After downloading and extracting it, we have around 37 GB of data in the XML format. This is illustrated in the following table:

File	Size (MB)	Description
badges.xml	309	Badges of users
comments.xml	3,225	Comments on questions or answers
posthistory.xml	18,370	Edit history
posts.xml	12,272	Questions and answers—this is what we need
users.xml	319	General information about users
votes.xml	2,200	Information on votes

As the files are more or less self-contained, we can delete all of them except posts. xml; it contains all the questions and answers as individual row tags within the root tag posts. Refer to the following code:

```
<?xml version="1.0" encoding="utf-8"?>
<posts>
  <row Id="4572748" PostTypeId="2" ParentId="4568987"
    CreationDate="2011-01-01T00:01:03.387" Score="4"
    ViewCount="" Body="&lt;p&gt;IANAL, but &lt;a
    href=&quot;http://support.apple.com/kb/HT2931&quot;
    rel=&quot;nofollow&quot;&gt;this&lt;/a&gt; indicates to me
    that you cannot use the loops in your
    application:&lt;/p&gt;&#xA;&#xA;&lt;blockquote&gt;&#xA;
    &lt;p&gt;...however, individual audio loops may&#xA;  not
    be commercially or otherwise&#xA;  distributed on a
    standalone basis, nor&#xA;  may they be repackaged in whole
    or in&#xA;  part as audio samples, sound effects&#xA;  or
    music beds.&quot;&lt;/p&gt;&#xA;  &#xA;  &lt;p&gt;So don't
    worry, you can make&#xA;  commercial music with GarageBand,
    you&#xA;  just can't distribute the loops as&#xA;
    loops.&lt;/p&gt;&#xA;&lt;/blockquote&gt;&#xA;"
    OwnerUserId="203568" LastActivityDate="2011-01-
    01T00:01:03.387" CommentCount="1" />
```

Name	Type	Description
Id	Integer	This is a unique identifier
PostType	Integer	This describes the category of the post. The following values are of interest to us: • Question • Answer Other values will be ignored
ParentId	Integer	This is a unique identifier of the question to which this answer belongs (missing for questions)
CreationDate	DateTime	This is the date of submission
Score	Integer	This is the score of the post
ViewCount	Integer or empty	This tells us the number of user views for this post
Body	String	This is the complete post as it is encoded in HTML text
OwnerUserId	Id	This is a unique identifier of the poster. If it is 1, it is a wiki question
Title	String	This is the title of the question (missing for answers)
AcceptedAnswerId	Id	This is the ID of the accepted answer (missing for answers)
CommentCount	Integer	This tells us the number of comments for the post

Slimming the data down to chewable chunks

To speed up our experimentation phase, we should not try to evaluate our classification ideas on a 12 GB file. Instead, we should think of how we can trim it down so that we can still keep a representable snapshot of it while being able to quickly test our ideas. If we filter an XML for `row` tags that have a `CreationDate` of 2011 or later, we still end up with over 6 million posts (2,323,184 questions and 4,055,999 answers), which should be enough training data for now. We also do not operate on the XML format as it will slow us down. The simpler the format, the better it is. That's why we parse the remaining XML using Python's `cElementTree` and write it out to a tab-separated file.

Preselection and processing of attributes

We should also only keep those attributes that we think could help the classifier in determining the good from the not-so-good answers. Certainly, we need the identification-related attributes to assign the correct answers to the questions. Read the following attributes:

- The `PostType` attribute, for example, is only necessary to distinguish between questions and answers. Furthermore, we can distinguish between them later by checking for the `ParentId` attribute. So, we keep it for questions too, and set it to 1.

- The `CreationDate` attribute could be interesting to determine the time span between posting the question and posting the individual answers, so we keep it.

- The `Score` attribute is, of course, important as an indicator of the community's evaluation.

- The `ViewCount` attribute, in contrast, is most likely of no use for our task. Even if it is able to help the classifier distinguish between good and bad, we will not have this information at the time when an answer is being submitted. We will ignore it.

- The `Body` attribute obviously contains the most important information. As it is encoded in HTML, we will have to decode it to plain text.

- The `OwnerUserId` attribute is useful only if we will take the user-dependent features into account, which we won't. Although we drop it here, we encourage you to use it (maybe in connection with `users.xml`) to build a better classifier.

- The `Title` attribute is also ignored here, although it could add some more information about the question.

- The `CommentCount` attribute is also ignored. Similar to `ViewCount`, it could help the classifier with posts that were posted a while ago (more comments are equal to more ambiguous posts). It will, however, not help the classifier at the time that an answer is posted.

- The `AcceptedAnswerId` attribute is similar to the `Score` attribute, that is, it is an indicator of a post's quality. As we will access this per answer, instead of keeping this attribute, we will create a new attribute, `IsAccepted`, which will be 0 or 1 for answers and ignored for questions (`ParentId` = 1).

We end up with the following format:

```
Id <TAB> ParentId <TAB> IsAccepted <TAB> TimeToAnswer <TAB> Score
<TAB> Text
```

For concrete parsing details, please refer to so_xml_to_tsv.py and choose_instance.py. It will suffice to say that in order to speed up the process, we will split the data into two files. In meta.json, we store a dictionary, mapping a post's Id to its other data (except Text in the JSON format) so that we can read it in the proper format. For example, the score of a post would reside at meta[Id]['Score']. In data.tsv, we store Id and Text, which we can easily read with the following method:

```python
def fetch_posts():

    for line in open("data.tsv", "r"):

        post_id, text = line.split("\t")

        yield int(post_id), text.strip()
```

Defining what is a good answer

Before we can train a classifier to distinguish between good and bad answers, we have to create the training data. So far, we have only a bunch of data. What we still have to do is to define labels.

We could, of course, simply use the IsAccepted attribute as a label. After all, it marks the answer that answered the question. However, that is only the opinion of the asker. Naturally, the asker wants to have a quick answer and accepts the first best answer. If more answers are submitted over time, some of them will tend to be better than the already accepted one. The asker, however, seldom gets back to the question and changes his/her mind. So we end up with many questions with accepted answers that have not been scored the highest.

At the other extreme, we could take the best and worst scored answer per question as positive and negative examples. However, what do we do with questions that have only good answers, say, one with two and the other with four points? Should we really take the answer with two points as a negative example?

We should settle somewhere between these extremes. If we take all answers that are scored higher than zero as positive and all answers with 0 or less points as negative, we end up with quite reasonable labels as follows:

```python
>>> all_answers = [q for q,v in meta.iteritems() if v['ParentId']!=-1]
>>> Y = np.asarray([meta[aid]['Score']>0 for aid in all_answers])
```

Creating our first classifier

Let us start with the simple and beautiful nearest neighbor method from the previous chapter. Although it is not as advanced as other methods, it is very powerful. As it is not model-based, it can learn nearly any data. However, this beauty comes with a clear disadvantage, which we will find out very soon.

Starting with the k-nearest neighbor (kNN) algorithm

This time, we won't implement it ourselves, but rather take it from the `sklearn` toolkit. There, the classifier resides in `sklearn.neighbors`. Let us start with a simple 2-nearest neighbor classifier:

```
>>> from sklearn import neighbors
>>> knn = neighbors.KNeighborsClassifier(n_neighbors=2)
>>> print(knn)
KNeighborsClassifier(algorithm=auto, leaf_size=30, n_neighbors=2, p=2,
warn_on_equidistant=True, weights=uniform)
```

It provides the same interface as all the other estimators in `sklearn`. We train it using `fit()`, after which we can predict the classes of new data instances using `predict()`:

```
>>> knn.fit([[1],[2],[3],[4],[5],[6]], [0,0,0,1,1,1])
>>> knn.predict(1.5)
array([0])
>>> knn.predict(37)
array([1])
>>> knn.predict(3)
NeighborsWarning: kneighbors: neighbor k+1 and neighbor k have the
same distance: results will be dependent on data order.
  neigh_dist, neigh_ind = self.kneighbors(X)
array([0])
```

To get the class probabilities, we can use `predict_proba()`. In this case, where we have two classes, 0 and 1, it will return an array of two elements as in the following code:

```
>>> knn.predict_proba(1.5)
array([[ 1.,   0.]])
>>> knn.predict_proba(37)
array([[ 0.,   1.]])
>>> knn.predict_proba(3.5)
array([[ 0.5,   0.5]])
```

Engineering the features

So, what kind of features can we provide to our classifier? What do we think will have the most discriminative power?

The `TimeToAnswer` attribute is already present in our `meta` dictionary, but it probably won't provide much value on its own. Then there is only `Text`, but in its raw form, we cannot pass it to the classifier as the features must be in numerical form. We will have to do the dirty work of extracting features from it.

What we could do is check the number of HTML links in the answer as a proxy for quality. Our hypothesis would be that more hyperlinks in an answer indicate better answers, and thus have a higher likelihood of being up-voted. Of course, we want to only count links in normal text and not in code examples:

```
import re
code_match = re.compile('<pre>(.*?)</pre>',
                        re.MULTILINE|re.DOTALL)
link_match = re.compile('<a href="http://.*?".*?>(.*?)</a>',
                        re.MULTILINE|re.DOTALL)

def extract_features_from_body(s):

    link_count_in_code = 0

    # count links in code to later subtract them

    for match_str in code_match.findall(s):

        link_count_in_code +=
        len(link_match.findall(match_str))

    return len(link_match.findall(s)) - link_count_in_code
```

> For production systems, we should not parse HTML content with regular expressions. Instead, we should rely on excellent libraries such as BeautifulSoup that does a marvelous job of robustly handling all the weird things that typically occur in everyday HTML.

With this in place, we can generate one feature per answer. But before we train the classifier, let us first have a look at what we will train it with. We can get a first impression with the frequency distribution of our new feature. This can be done by plotting the percentage of how often each value occurs in the data as shown in the following graph:

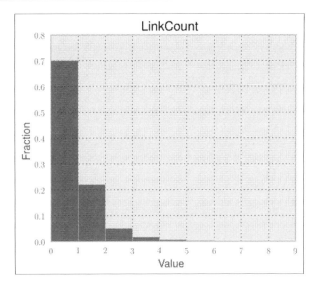

With the majority of posts having no link at all, we now know that this feature alone will not make a good classifier. Let us nevertheless try it out to get a first estimation of where we are.

Training the classifier

We have to pass the feature array together with the previously defined Y labels to the kNN learner to obtain a classifier:

```
X = np.asarray([extract_features_from_body(text) for post_id,
  text in fetch_posts() if post_id in all_answers])
knn = neighbors.KNeighborsClassifier()
knn.fit(X, Y)
```

Using the standard parameters, we just fitted a 5NN (meaning NN with $k = 5$) to our data. Why 5NN? Well, with the current state of our knowledge about the data, we really have no clue what the right k should be. Once we have more insight, we will have a better idea of how to set the value for k.

Measuring the classifier's performance

We have to be clear about what we want to measure. The naive but easiest way is to simply calculate the average prediction quality over the test set. This will result in a value between 0 for incorrectly predicting everything and 1 for perfect prediction. Accuracy can be obtained through knn.score().

But as we learned in the previous chapter, we will not do it just once, but apply cross-validation here using the ready-made `KFold` class from `sklearn.cross_validation`. Finally, we will average the scores on the test set of each fold and see how much it varies using standard deviation. Refer to the following code:

```
from sklearn.cross_validation import KFold
scores = []
cv = KFold(n=len(X), k=10, indices=True)
for train, test in cv:
  X_train, y_train = X[train], Y[train]
  X_test, y_test = X[test], Y[test]
  clf = neighbors.KNeighborsClassifier()
  clf.fit(X, Y)
  scores.append(clf.score(X_test, y_test))

print("Mean(scores)=%.5f\tStddev(scores)=%.5f"%(np.mean(scores,
np.std(scores)))
```

The output is as follows:

```
Mean(scores)=0.49100    Stddev(scores)=0.02888
```

This is far from being usable. With only 49 percent accuracy, it is even worse than tossing a coin. Apparently, the number of links in a post are not a very good indicator of the quality of the post. We say that this feature does not have much discriminative power—at least, not for kNN with $k = 5$.

Designing more features

In addition to using a number of hyperlinks as proxies for a post's quality, using a number of code lines is possibly another good option too. At least it is a good indicator that the post's author is interested in answering the question. We can find the code embedded in the `<pre>...</pre>` tag. Once we have extracted it, we should count the number of words in the post while ignoring the code lines:

```
def extract_features_from_body(s):
  num_code_lines = 0
  link_count_in_code = 0
  code_free_s = s

  # remove source code and count how many lines
  for match_str in code_match.findall(s):
    num_code_lines += match_str.count('\n')
    code_free_s = code_match.sub("", code_free_s)
  # sometimes source code contain links,
```

```
# which we don't want to count
  link_count_in_code += len(link_match.findall(match_str))

  links = link_match.findall(s)
  link_count = len(links)
  link_count -= link_count_in_code
  html_free_s = re.sub(" +", " ", tag_match.sub('',
    code_free_s)).replace("\n", "")
  link_free_s = html_free_s

# remove links from text before counting words
  for anchor in anchors:
    if anchor.lower().startswith("http://"):
    link_free_s = link_free_s.replace(anchor,'')

    num_text_tokens = html_free_s.count(" ")

    return num_text_tokens, num_code_lines, link_count
```

Looking at the following graphs, we can notice that the number of words in a post show higher variability:

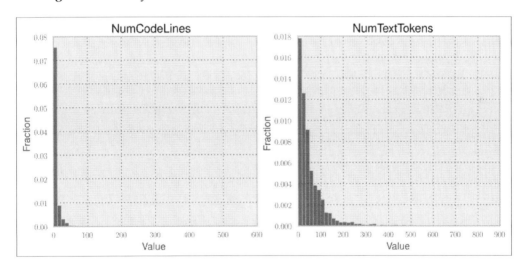

Training on the bigger feature space improves accuracy quite a bit:

```
Mean(scores)=0.58300   Stddev(scores)=0.02216
```

But still, this would mean that we could classify roughly four out of the ten wrong answers. At least we are heading in the right direction. More features lead to higher accuracy, which leads us to adding more features. Therefore, let us extend the feature space with even more features:

- `AvgSentLen`: This feature measures the average number of words in a sentence. Maybe there is a pattern that particularly good posts don't overload the reader's brain with very long sentences.

- `AvgWordLen`: This feature is similar to `AvgSentLen`; it measures the average number of characters in the words of a post.

- `NumAllCaps`: This feature measures the number of words that are written in uppercase, which is considered a bad style.

- `NumExclams`: This feature measures the number of exclamation marks.

The following charts show the value distributions for average sentences and word lengths as well as the number of uppercase words and exclamation marks:

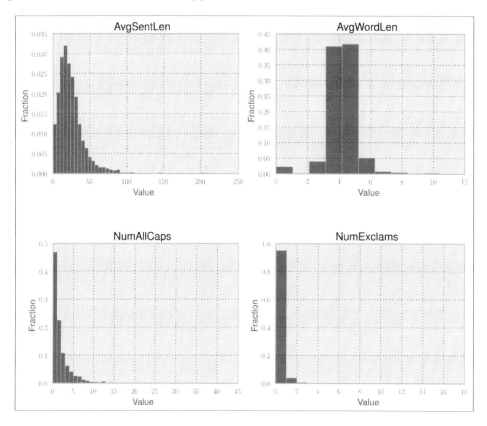

With these four additional features, we now have seven features representing individual posts. Let's see how we have progressed:

```
Mean(scores)=0.57650    Stddev(scores)=0.03557
```

Now that's interesting. We added four more features and got worse classification accuracy. How can that be possible?

To understand this, we have to remind ourselves of how kNN works. Our 5NN classifier determines the class of a new post by calculating the preceding seven described features, namely `LinkCount`, `NumTextTokens`, `NumCodeLines`, `AvgSentLen`, `AvgWordLen`, `NumAllCaps`, and `NumExclams`, and then finds the five nearest other posts. The new post's class is then the majority of the classes of those nearest posts. The nearest posts are determined by calculating the Euclidean distance. As we did not specify it, the classifier was initialized with the default value `p = 2`, which is the parameter in the Minkowski distance. This means that all seven features are treated similarly. kNN does not really learn that, for instance, `NumTextTokens` is good to have but much less important than `NumLinks`. Let us consider the following two posts, A and B, which only differ in the following features, and how they compare to a new post:

Post	NumLinks	NumTextTokens
A	2	20
B	0	25
New	1	23

Although we would think that links provide more value than mere text, post B would be considered more similar to the new post than post A.

Clearly, kNN has a hard time correctly using the available data.

Deciding how to improve

To improve on this, we basically have the following options:

- **Add more data**: It may be that there is just not enough data for the learning algorithm and that we simply need to add more training data.

- **Play with the model complexity**: It may be that the model is not complex enough or is already too complex. In this case, we could either decrease *k* so that it would take less nearest neighbors into account and thus would be better at predicting non-smooth data, or we could increase it to achieve the opposite.

- **Modify the feature space**: It may be that we do not have the right set of features. We could, for example, change the scale of our current features or design even more new features. Or rather, we could remove some of our current features in case some features are aliasing others.

- **Change the model**: It may be that kNN is generally not a good fit for our use case, such that it will never be capable of achieving good prediction performance no matter how complex we allow it to be and how sophisticated the feature space will become.

In real life, at this point, people often try to improve the current performance by randomly picking one of the preceding options and trying them out in no particular order, hoping to find the golden configuration by chance. We could do the same here, but it will surely take longer than making informed decisions. Let's take the informed route, for which we need to introduce the bias-variance tradeoff.

Bias-variance and its trade-off

In *Chapter 1*, *Getting Started with Python Machine Learning*, we tried to fit polynomials of different complexities controlled by the dimensionality parameter, d, to fit the data. We realized that a two-dimensional polynomial, a straight line, did not fit the example data very well because the data was not of a linear nature. No matter how elaborate our fitting procedure would have been, our two-dimensional model will see everything as a straight line. We say that it is too biased for the data at hand; it is under-fitting.

We played a bit with the dimensions and found out that the 100-dimensional polynomial was actually fitting very well into the data on which it was trained (we did not know about train-test splits at the time). However, we quickly found that it was fitting too well. We realized that it was over-fitting so badly that with different samples of the data points, we would have gotten totally different 100-dimensional polynomials. We say that the model has too high a variance for the given data or that it is over-fitting.

These are the extremes between which most of our machine learning problems reside. Ideally, we want to have both low bias and low variance. But, we are in a bad world and have to trade off between them. If we improve on one, we will likely get worse on the other.

Fixing high bias

Let us assume that we are suffering from high bias. In this case, adding more training data clearly will not help. Also, removing features surely will not help as our model is probably already overly simplistic.

The only possibilities we have in this case is to either get more features, make the model more complex, or change the model.

Fixing high variance

If, on the contrary, we suffer from high variance that means our model is too complex for the data. In this case, we can only try to get more data or decrease the complexity. This would mean to increase k so that more neighbors would be taken into account or to remove some of the features.

High bias or low bias

To find out what actually our problem is, we have to simply plot the train and test errors over the data size.

High bias is typically revealed by the test error decreasing a bit at the beginning, but then settling at a very high value with the train error approaching a growing dataset size. High variance is recognized by a big gap between both curves.

Plotting the errors for different dataset sizes for 5NN shows a big gap between the train and test error, hinting at a high variance problem. Refer to the following graph:

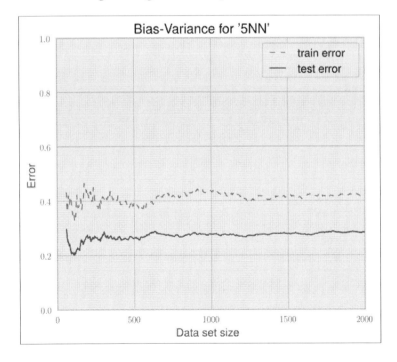

Looking at the previous graph, we immediately see that adding more training data will not help, as the dashed line corresponding to the test error seems to stay above 0.4. The only option we have is to decrease the complexity either by increasing *k* or by reducing the feature space.

Reducing the feature space does not help here. We can easily confirm this by plotting the graph for a simplified feature space of `LinkCount` and `NumTextTokens`. Refer to the following graph:

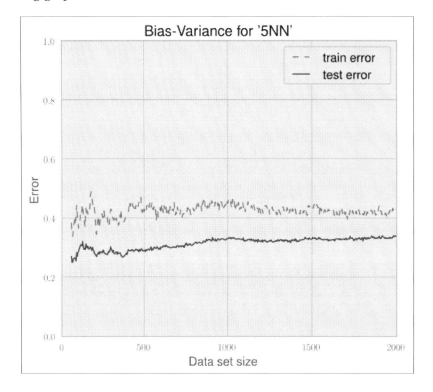

We will get similar graphs for other smaller feature sets as well. No matter what subset of features we take, the graph will look similar.

At least reducing the model complexity by increasing *k* shows some positive impact. This is illustrated in the following table:

k	mean(scores)	stddev(scores)
90	0.6280	0.02777
40	0.6265	0.02748
5	0.5765	0.03557

But this is not enough, and it comes at the price of lower classification runtime performance. Take, for instance, the value of *k = 90*, where we have a very low test error. To classify a new post, we need to find the 90 nearest other posts to decide whether the new post is a good one or not:

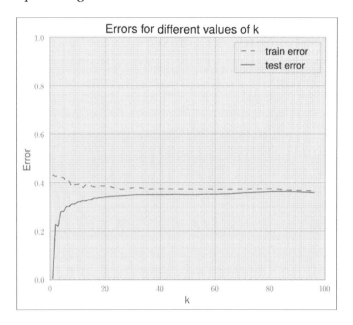

Clearly, we seem to be facing an issue with using the nearest neighbor algorithm for our scenario. It also has another real disadvantage. Over time, we will get more and more posts to our system. As the nearest neighbor method is an instance-based approach, we will have to store all the posts in our system. The more posts we get, the slower the prediction will be. This is different with model-based approaches where you try to derive a model from the data.

So here we are, with enough reasons now to abandon the nearest neighbor approach and look for better places in the classification world. Of course, we will never know whether there is the one golden feature we just did not happen to think of. But for now, let's move on to another classification method that is known to work great in text-based classification scenarios.

Using logistic regression

Contrary to its name, logistic regression is a classification method, and is very powerful when it comes to text-based classification. It achieves this by first performing regression on a logistic function, hence the name.

A bit of math with a small example

To get an initial understanding of the way logistic regression works, let us first take a look at the following example, where we have an artificial **feature value** at the X axis plotted with the corresponding **class** range, either 0 or 1. As we can see, the data is so noisy that classes overlap in the **feature value** range between 1 and 6. Therefore, it is better to not directly model the discrete classes, but rather the probability that a **feature value** belongs to class 1, $P(X)$. Once we possess such a model, we could then predict class 1 if $P(X) > 0.5$ or class 0 otherwise:

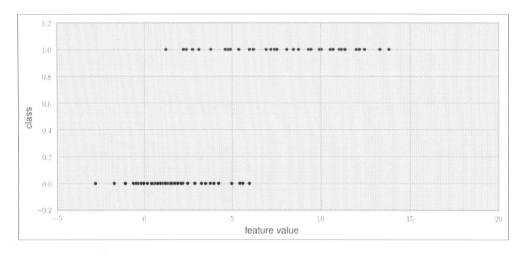

Mathematically, it is always difficult to model something that has a finite range, as is the case here with our discrete labels 0 and 1. We can, however, tweak the probabilities a bit so that they always stay between 0 and 1. For this, we will need the odds ratio and its logarithm.

Let's say a feature has the probability of 0.9 that it belongs to class 1, that is, $P(y=1) = 0.9$. The odds ratio is then $P(y=1)/P(y=0) = 0.9/0.1 = 9$. We could say that the chance is 9:1 that this feature maps to class 1. If $P(y=0.5)$, we would consequently have a 1:1 chance that the instance is of class 1. The odds ratio is bounded by 0, but goes to infinity (the left graph in the following screenshot). If we now take the logarithm of it, we can map all probabilities between 0 and 1 to the full range from negative to positive infinity (the right graph in the following screenshot). The best part is that we still maintain the relationship that higher probability leads to a higher log of odds—it's just not limited to 0 or 1 anymore:

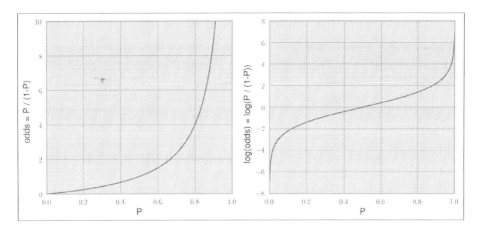

This means that we can now fit linear combinations of our features (ok, we have only one feature and a constant, but that will change soon) to the $\log(\text{odds})$ values. Let's consider the linear equation in *Chapter 1, Getting Started with Python Machine Learning* shown as follows:

$$y_i = c_0 + c_1 x_i$$

This can be replaced with the following equation (by replacing y with p):

$$\log\left(\frac{p_i}{1-p_i}\right) = c_0 + c_1 x_i$$

We can solve the equation for p_i as shown in the following formula:

$$p_i = \frac{1}{1+e^{-(c_0+c_1 x_i)}}$$

We simply have to find the right coefficients such that the formula will give the lowest errors for all our pairs (xi, pi) in the dataset, which will be detected by Scikit-learn.

After fitting the data to the class labels, the formula will give the probability for every new data point, x, that belongs to class 1. Refer to the following code:

```
>>> from sklearn.linear_model import LogisticRegression
>>> clf = LogisticRegression()
>>> print(clf)
LogisticRegression(C=1.0, class_weight=None, dual=False, fit_
intercept=True, intercept_scaling=1, penalty=l2, tol=0.0001)
```

```
>>> clf.fit(X, y)
>>> print(np.exp(clf.intercept_), np.exp(clf.coef_.ravel()))
[ 0.09437188] [ 1.80094112]
>>> def lr_model(clf, X):
return 1 / (1 + np.exp(-(clf.intercept_ + clf.coef_*X)))
>>> print("P(x=-1)=%.2f\tP(x=7)=%.2f"%(lr_model(clf, -1), lr_
model(clf, 7)))
P(x=-1)=0.05      P(x=7)=0.85
```

You might have noticed that Scikit-learn exposes the first coefficient through the special field `intercept_`.

If we plot the fitted model, we see that it makes perfect sense given the data:

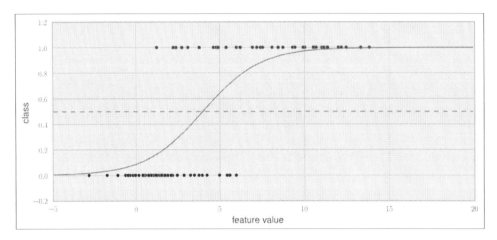

Applying logistic regression to our postclassification problem

Admittedly, the example in the previous section was created to show the beauty of logistic regression. How does it perform on the extremely noisy data?

Comparing it to the best nearest neighbour classifier ($k = 90$) as a baseline, we see that it performs a bit better, but also won't change the situation a whole lot:

Method	mean(scores)	stddev(scores)
LogReg C=0.1	0.6310	0.02791
LogReg C=100.00	0.6300	0.03170
LogReg C=10.00	0.6300	0.03170
LogReg C=0.01	0.6295	0.02752

Method	mean(scores)	stddev(scores)
LogReg C=1.00	0.6290	0.03270
90NN	0.6280	0.02777

We have seen the accuracy for the different values of the regularization parameter C. With it, we can control the model complexity, similar to the parameter k for the nearest neighbor method. Smaller values for C result in a higher penalty, that is, they make the model more complex.

A quick look at the bias-variance chart for our best candidate, $C = 0.1$, shows that our model has high bias—test and train error curves approach closely but stay at unacceptably high values. This indicates that logistic regression with the current feature space is under-fitting and cannot learn a model that captures the data correctly.

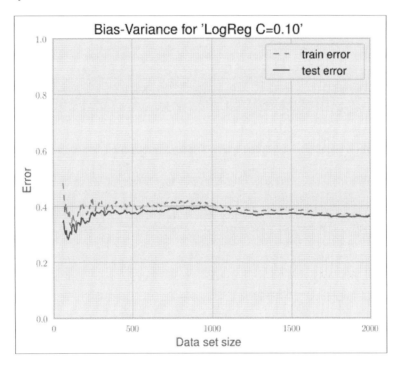

So what now? We switched the model and tuned it as much as we could with our current state of knowledge, but we still have no acceptable classifier.

It seems more and more that either the data is too noisy for this task or that our set of features is still not appropriate to discriminate the classes that are good enough.

Looking behind accuracy – precision and recall

Let us step back and think again what we are trying to achieve here. Actually, we do not need a classifier that perfectly predicts good and bad answers, as we measured it until now using accuracy. If we can tune the classifier to be particularly good in predicting one class, we could adapt the feedback to the user accordingly. If we had a classifier, for example, that was always right when it predicted an answer to be bad, we would give no feedback until the classifier detected the answer to be bad. Contrariwise, if the classifier succeeded in predicting answers to be always good, we could show helpful comments to the user at the beginning and remove them when the classifier said that the answer is a good one.

To find out which situation we are in here, we have to understand how to measure precision and recall. To understand this, we have to look into the four distinct classification results as they are described in the following table:

		Classified as	
		Positive	Negative
In reality it is	Positive	True positive (TP)	False negative (FN)
	Negative	False positive (FP)	True negative (TN)

For instance, if the classifier predicts an instance to be positive and the instance indeed is positive in reality, this is a true positive instance. If on the other hand, the classifier misclassified that instance saying that it is negative while in reality it is positive, that instance is said to be a false negative.

What we want is to have a high success rate when we are predicting a post as either good or bad, but not necessarily both. That is, we want as many true positives as possible. This is what **precision** captures:

$$\text{Precision} = \frac{TP}{TP+FP}$$

If instead our goal would have been to detect as much good or bad answers as possible, we would be more interested in **recall**:

$$\text{Recall} = \frac{\text{TP}}{\text{TP+FN}}$$

The next screenshot shows all the good answers and the answers that have been classified as being good ones:

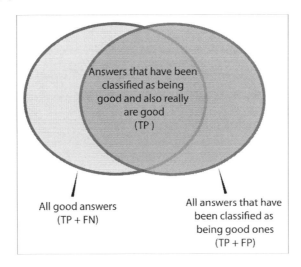

In terms of the previous diagram, precision is the fraction of the intersection of the right circle while recall is the fraction of the intersection of the left circle.

So, how can we optimize for precision? Up to now, we have always used 0.5 as the threshold to decide whether an answer is good or not. What we can do now is to count the number of TP, FP, and FN instances while varying that threshold between 0 and 1. With these counts, we can then plot precision over recall.

The handy function `precision_recall_curve()` from the metrics module does all the calculations for us as shown in the following code:

```
>>> from sklearn.metrics import precision_recall_curve
>>> precision, recall, thresholds = precision_recall_curve(y_test,
clf.predict(X_test)
```

Predicting one class with acceptable performance does not always mean that the classifier will predict the other classes acceptably. This can be seen in the following two graphs where we plot the **Precision/Recall** curves for classifying bad (left graph of the next screenshot) and good (right graph of the next screenshot) answers:

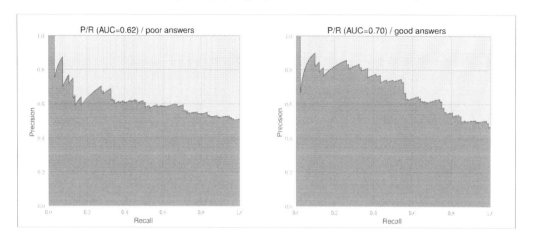

In the previous graphs, we have also included a much better description of a classifier's performance: the **area under curve** (**AUC**). This can be understood as the average precision of the classifier and is a great way of comparing different classifiers.

We see that we can basically forget about predicting bad answers (the left graph of the previous screenshot). This is because the precision for predicting bad answers decreases very quickly, at already very low recall values, and stays at an unacceptably low 60 percent.

Predicting good answers, however, shows that we can get above 80 percent precision at a recall of almost 40 percent. Let us find out what threshold we need for that with the following code:

```
>>> thresholds = np.hstack(([0],thresholds[medium]))
>>> idx80 = precisions>=0.8
>>> print("P=%.2f R=%.2f thresh=%.2f" % \ (precision[idx80][0],
    recall[idx80][0], threshold[idx80][0]))
P=0.81 R=0.37 thresh=0.63
```

Setting the threshold at 0.63, we see that we can still achieve a precision of above 80 percent, detecting good answers when we accept a low recall of 37 percent. This means that we will detect only one in three bad answers, but those answers that we manage to detect we would be reasonably sure of.

To apply this threshold in the prediction process, we have to use `predict_proba()`, which returns per class probabilities, instead of `predict()`, which returns the class itself:

```
>>> thresh80 = threshold[idx80][0]
>>> probs_for_good = clf.predict_proba(answer_features)[:,1]
>>> answer_class = probs_for_good>thresh80
```

We can confirm that we are in the desired precision/recall range using `classification_report`:

```
>>> from sklearn.metrics import classification_report
>>> print(classification_report(y_test, clf.predict_proba [:,1]>0.63,
target_names=['not accepted', 'accepted']))
```

	precision	recall	f1-score	support
not accepted	0.63	0.93	0.75	108
accepted	0.80	0.36	0.50	92
avg / total	0.71	0.67	0.63	200

 Using the threshold will not guarantee that we are always above the precision and recall values that we determined previously together with its threshold.

Slimming the classifier

It is always worth looking at the actual contributions of the individual features. For logistic regression, we can directly take the learned coefficients (`clf.coef_`) to get an impression of the feature's impact. The higher the coefficient of a feature is, the more the feature plays a role in determining whether the post is good or not. Consequently, negative coefficients tell us that the higher values for the corresponding features indicate a stronger signal for the post to be classified as bad:

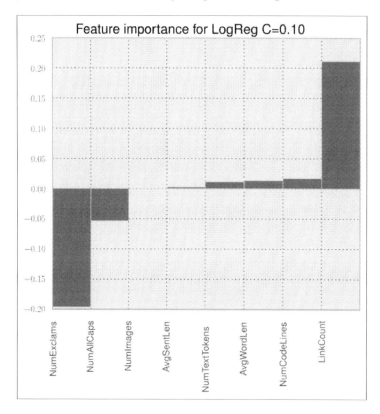

We see that `LinkCount` and `NumExclams` have the biggest impact on the overall classification decision, while `NumImages` and `AvgSentLen` play a rather minor role. While the feature importance overall makes sense intuitively, it is surprising that `NumImages` is basically ignored. Normally, answers containing images are always rated high. In reality, however, answers very rarely have images. So although in principal it is a very powerful feature, it is too sparse to be of any value. We could easily drop this feature and retain the same classification performance.

Ship it!

Let's assume we want to integrate this classifier into our site. What we definitely do not want is to train the classifier each time we start the classification service. Instead, we can simply serialize the classifier after training and then deserialize it on that site:

```
>>> import pickle
>>> pickle.dump(clf, open("logreg.dat", "w"))
>>> clf = pickle.load(open("logreg.dat", "r"))
```

Congratulations, the classifier is now ready to be used as if it had just been trained.

Summary

We made it! For a very noisy dataset, we built a classifier that suits part of our goal. Of course, we had to be pragmatic and adapt our initial goal to what was achievable. But on the way, we learned about the strengths and weaknesses of the nearest neighbor and logistic regression algorithms. We learned how to extract features, such as LinkCount, NumTextTokens, NumCodeLines, AvgSentLen, AvgWordLen, NumAllCaps, NumExclams, and NumImages, and how to analyze their impact on the classifier's performance.

But what is even more valuable is that we learned an informed way of how to debug badly performing classifiers. This will help us in the future to come up with usable systems much faster.

After having looked into the nearest neighbor and logistic regression algorithms, in the next chapter we will get familiar with yet another simple yet powerful classification algorithm: Naive Bayes. Along the way, we will also learn how to use some more convenient tools from Scikit-learn.

6
Classification II – Sentiment Analysis

For companies, it is vital to closely monitor the public reception of key events such as product launches or press releases. With real-time access and easy accessibility of user-generated content on Twitter, it is now possible to do sentiment classification of tweets. Sometimes also called **opinion mining**, it is an active field of research in which several companies are already selling their products. As this shows that a market obviously exists, we have motivation to use our classification muscles built in the previous chapter to build our own home-grown sentiment classifier.

Sketching our roadmap

Sentiment analysis of tweets is particularly hard because of Twitter's size limitation of 140 characters. This leads to a special syntax, creative abbreviations, and seldom well-formed sentences. The typical approach of analyzing sentences, aggregating their sentiment information per paragraph and then calculating the overall sentiment of a document, therefore, does not work here.

Clearly, we will not try to build a state-of-the-art sentiment classifier. Instead, we want to:

- Use this scenario as a vehicle to introduce yet another classification algorithm: Naive Bayes
- Explain how **Part Of Speech** (**POS**) tagging works and how it can help us
- Show some more tricks from the scikit-learn toolbox that come in handy from time to time

Fetching the Twitter data

Naturally, we need tweets and their corresponding labels that tell us whether a tweet contains positive, negative, or neutral sentiment. In this chapter, we will use the corpus from *Niek Sanders*, who has done an awesome job of manually labeling more than 5000 tweets and granted us permission to use it in this chapter.

To comply with Twitter's terms of services, we will not provide any data from Twitter nor show any real tweets in this chapter. Instead, we can use Sanders' hand-labeled data, which contains the tweet IDs and their hand-labeled sentiment, and use his script, `install.py`, to fetch the corresponding Twitter data. As the script is playing nicely with Twitter's servers, it will take quite some time to download all the data for more than 5000 tweets. So it is a good idea to start it now.

The data comes with four sentiment labels:

```
>>> X, Y = load_sanders_data()
>>> classes = np.unique(Y)
>>> for c in classes:
        print("#%s: %i" % (c, sum(Y==c)))
#irrelevant: 543
#negative: 535
#neutral: 2082
#positive: 482
```

We will treat irrelevant and neutral labels together and ignore all non-English tweets, resulting into 3642 tweets. These can be easily filtered using the data provided by Twitter.

Introducing the Naive Bayes classifier

Naive Bayes is probably one of the most elegant machine learning algorithms out there that is of practical use. Despite its name, it is not that naive when you look at its classification performance. It proves to be quite robust to irrelevant features, which it kindly ignores. It learns fast and predicts equally so. It does not require lots of storage. So, why is it then called *naive*?

The *naive* was added to the account for one assumption that is required for Bayes to work optimally: all features must be independent of each other. This, however, is rarely the case for real-world applications. Nevertheless, it still returns very good accuracy in practice even when the independent assumption does not hold.

Getting to know the Bayes theorem

At its core, Naive Bayes classification is nothing more than keeping track of which feature gives evidence to which class. To ease our understanding, let us assume the following meanings for the variables that we will use to explain Naive Bayes:

Variable	Possible values	Meaning
C	"pos", "neg"	Class of a tweet (positive or negative)
F_1	Non-negative integers	Counting the occurrence of *awesome* in the tweet
F_2	Non-negative integers	Counting the occurrence of *crazy* in the tweet

During training, we learn the Naive Bayes model, which is the probability for a class C when we already know features F_1 and F_2. This probability is written as $P(C \mid F_1, F_2)$.

Since we cannot estimate this directly, we apply a trick, which was found out by Bayes:

$$P(A) \cdot P(B|A) = P(B) \cdot P(A|B)$$

If we substitute A with the probability of both features F_1 and F_2 occurring and think of B as being our class C, we arrive at the relationship that helps us to later retrieve the probability for the data instance belonging to the specified class:

$$P(F_1, F_2) \cdot P(C|F_1, F_2) = P(C) \cdot P(F_1, F_2|C)$$

This allows us to express $P(C \mid F_1, F_2)$ by means of the other probabilities:

$$P(C|F_1, F_2) = \frac{P(C) \cdot P(F_1, F_2|C)}{P(F_1, F_2)}$$

We could also say that:

$$posterior = \frac{prior \cdot likelihood}{evidence}$$

The prior and evidence values are easily determined:

- $P(C)$ is the prior probability of class c without knowing about the data. This quantity can be obtained by simply calculating the fraction of all training data instances belonging to that particular class.

- $P(F_1, F_2)$ is the evidence, or the probability of features F_1 and F_2. This can be retrieved by calculating the fraction of all training data instances having that particular feature value.

- The tricky part is the calculation of the likelihood $P(F_1, F_2|C)$. It is the value describing how likely it is to see feature values F_1 and F_2 if we know that the class of the data instance is C. To estimate this we need a bit more thinking.

Being naive

From the probability theory, we also know the following relationship:

$$P(F_1, F_2|C) = P(F_1|C) \cdot P(F_2|C, F_1)$$

This alone, however, does not help much, since we treat one difficult problem (estimating $P(F_1, F_2|C)$) with another one (estimating $P(F_2|C, F_1)$).

However, if we naively assume that F_1 and F_2 are independent from each other, $P(F_2|C, F_1)$ simplifies to $P(F_2|C)$ and we can write it as follows:

$$P(F_1, F_2|C) = P(F_1|C) \cdot P(F_2|C)$$

Putting everything together, we get this quite manageable formula:

$$P(C|F_1, F_2) = \frac{P(C) \cdot P(F_1|C) \cdot P(F_2|C)}{P(F_1, F_2)}$$

The interesting thing is that although it is not theoretically correct to simply tweak our assumptions when we are in the mood to do so, in this case it proves to work astonishingly well in real-world applications.

Using Naive Bayes to classify

Given a new tweet, the only part left is to simply calculate the probabilities:

$$P(C = \text{"pos"}|F_1, F_2) = \frac{P(C=\text{"pos"}) \cdot P(F_1|C=\text{"pos"}) \cdot P(F_2|C=\text{"pos"})}{P(F_1, F_2)}$$
$$P(C = \text{"neg"}|F_1, F_2) = \frac{P(C=\text{"neg"}) \cdot P(F_1|C=\text{"neg"}) \cdot P(F_2|C=\text{"neg"})}{P(F_1, F_2)}$$

We also need to choose the class C_{best} having the higher probability. As for both classes the denominator, $P(F_1, F_2)$, is the same, so we can simply ignore it without changing the winner class.

Note, however, that we don't calculate any real probabilities any more. Instead, we are estimating which class is more likely given the evidence. This is another reason why Naive Bayes is so robust: it is not so much interested in the real probabilities, but only in the information which class is more likely to. In short, we can write it as follows:

$$C_{\text{best}} = \arg\max_{c \in C} P(C = c) \cdot P(F_1|C = c) \cdot P(F_2|C = c)$$

Here we are calculating the part after *argmax* for all classes of C ("pos" and "neg" in our case) and returning the class that results in the highest value.

But for the following example, let us stick to real probabilities and do some calculations to see how Naive Bayes works. For the sake of simplicity, we will assume that Twitter allows only for the two words mentioned earlier, *awesome* and *crazy*, and that we had already manually classified a handful of tweets:

Tweet	Class
awesome	Positive
awesome	Positive
awesome crazy	Positive
crazy	Positive
crazy	Negative
crazy	Negative

In this case, we have six total tweets, out of which four are positive and two negative, which results in the following priors:

$$P(C = "pos") = \tfrac{4}{6} \approx 0.67$$
$$P(C = "neg") = \tfrac{2}{6} \approx 0.33$$

This means, without knowing anything about the tweet itself, we would be wise in assuming the tweet to be positive.

The piece that is still missing is the calculation of $P(F_1|C)$ and $P(F_2|C)$, which are the probabilities for the two features F_1 and F_2 conditioned on class C.

This is calculated as the number of tweets in which we have seen that the concrete feature is divided by the number of tweets that have been labeled with the class of C. Let's say we want to know the probability of seeing *awesome* occurring once in a tweet knowing that its class is "positive"; we would have the following:

$$P(F_1 = 1|C = "pos") = \frac{\text{\# pos tweets containing awesome once}}{\text{\# pos tweets}} = \tfrac{3}{4} = 0.75$$

Since out of the four positive tweets three contained the word awesome, obviously the probability for not having *awesome* in a positive tweet is its inverse as we have seen only tweets with the counts 0 or 1:

$$P(F_1 = 0|C = "pos") = 1 - P(F_1 = 1|C = "pos") = 0.25$$

Similarly for the rest (omitting the case that a word is not occurring in a tweet):

$$P(F_2 = 1|C = "pos") = \tfrac{2}{4} = 0.25$$
$$P(F_1 = 1|C = "neg") = \tfrac{0}{2} = 0$$
$$P(F_2 = 1|C = "neg") = \tfrac{2}{2} = 1$$

For the sake of completeness, we will also compute the evidence so that we can see real probabilities in the following example tweets. For two concrete values of F_1 and F_2, we can calculate the evidence as follows:

$$P(F_1, F_2) = P(F_1, F_2|C = "pos") \cdot P(C = "pos") + ""$$
$$"" P(F_1, F_2|C = "neg") \cdot P(C = "neg")$$

This denotation " " leads to the following values:

$$P(F_1 = 1, F_2 = 1) = \frac{1}{3} \cdot \frac{4}{6} + 0 \cdot \frac{2}{6} = 0.22$$
$$P(F_1 = 1, F_2 = 0) = \frac{2}{3} \cdot \frac{4}{6} + 0 \cdot \frac{2}{6} = 0.44$$
$$P(F_1 = 0, F_2 = 1) = 0 \cdot \frac{4}{6} + 1 \cdot \frac{2}{6} = 0.33$$
$$P(F_1 = 0, F_2 = 0) = 0$$

Now we have all the data to classify new tweets. The only work left is to parse the tweet and give features to it.

Tweet	F_1	F_2	Class probabilities	Classification
awesome	1	0	$P(C = \text{"pos"}\|F_1, F_2) = \frac{0.67 \cdot 0.75 \cdot 0.5}{0.44} = 0.57$ $P(C = \text{"neg"}\|F_1, F_2) = \frac{0.33 \cdot 0 \cdot 0}{0.44} = 0$	Positive
crazy	0	1	$P(C = \text{"pos"}\|F_1, F_2) = \frac{0.67 \cdot 0.25 \cdot 0.5}{0.33} = 0.25$ $P(C = \text{"neg"}\|F_1, F_2) = \frac{0.33 \cdot 1 \cdot 1}{0.33} = 1$	Negative
awesome crazy	1	1	$P(C = \text{"pos"}\|F_1, F_2) = \frac{0.67 \cdot 0.75 \cdot 0.5}{0.33} = 0.76$ $P(C = \text{"neg"}\|F_1, F_2) = \frac{0.33 \cdot 0 \cdot 1}{0.33} = 0$	Positive
awesome text	0	0	$P(C = \text{"pos"}\|F_1, F_2) = \frac{0.67 \cdot 0.75 \cdot 0}{0} = ?$ $P(C = \text{"neg"}\|F_1, F_2) = \frac{0.33 \cdot 0 \cdot 0}{0} = ?$	Undefined, because we have never seen these words in this tweet before

So far, so good. The classification of trivial tweets makes sense except for the last one, which results in a division by zero. How can we handle that?

Accounting for unseen words and other oddities

When we calculated the preceding probabilities, we actually cheated ourselves. We were not calculating the real probabilities, but only rough approximations by means of the fractions. We assumed that the training corpus would tell us the whole truth about the real probabilities. It did not. A corpus of only six tweets obviously cannot give us all the information about every tweet that has ever been written. For example, there certainly are tweets containing the word "text", it is just that we have never seen them. Apparently, our approximation is very rough, so we should account for that. This is often done in practice with "add-one smoothing".

Add-one smoothing is sometimes also referred to as *additive smoothing* or *Laplace smoothing*. Note that Laplace smoothing has nothing to do with *Laplacian smoothing*, which is related to smoothing of polygon meshes. If we do not smooth by one but by an adjustable parameter alpha greater than zero, it is called **Lidstone smoothing**.

It is a very simple technique, simply adding one to all counts. It has the underlying assumption that even if we have not seen a given word in the whole corpus, there is still a chance that our sample of tweets happened to not include that word. So, with add-one smoothing we pretend that we have seen every occurrence once more than we actually did. That means that instead of calculating the following:

$$P(F_1 = 1 | C = "pos") = \tfrac{3}{4} = 0.75$$

We now calculate:

$$P(F_1 = 1 | C = "pos") = \tfrac{3+1}{4+2} = 0.67$$

Why do we add 2 in the denominator? We have to make sure that the end result is again a probability. Therefore, we have to normalize the counts so that all probabilities sum up to one. As in our current dataset *awesome*, can occur either zero or one time, we have two cases. And indeed, we get 1 as the total probability:

$$P(F_1 = 1 | C = "pos") + P(F_1 = 0 | C = "pos") = \tfrac{3+1}{4+2} + \tfrac{1+1}{4+2} = 1$$

Similarly, we do this for the prior probabilities:

$$P(C = \text{"pos"}) = \frac{4+1}{6+2} \approx 0.625$$

Accounting for arithmetic underflows

There is yet another roadblock. In reality, we work with probabilities much smaller than the ones we have dealt with in the toy example. In reality, we also have more than two features, which we multiply with each other. This will quickly lead to the point where the accuracy provided by NumPy does not suffice anymore:

```
>>> import numpy as np
>>> np.set_printoptions(precision=20) # tell numpy to print out more
digits (default is 8)
>>> np.array([2.48E-324])
array([ 4.94065645841246544177e-324])
>>> np.array([2.47E-324])
array([ 0.])
```

So, how probable is it that we will ever hit a number like `2.47E-324`? To answer this, we just have to imagine a likelihood for the conditional probabilities of 0.0001 and then multiply 65 of them together (meaning that we have 65 low probable feature values) and you've been hit by the arithmetic underflow:

```
>>> x=0.00001
>>> x**64 # still fine
1e-320
>>> x**65 # ouch
0.0
```

A `float` in Python is typically implemented using `double` in C. To find out whether it is the case for your platform, you can check it as follows:

```
>>> import sys
>>> sys.float_info
sys.float_info(max=1.7976931348623157e+308, max_exp=1024, max_10_
exp=308, min=2.2250738585072014e-308, min_exp=-1021, min_10_exp=-307,
dig=15, mant_dig=53, epsilon=2.220446049250313e-16, radix=2, rounds=1)
```

To mitigate this, you could switch to math libraries such as mpmath (http://code. google.com/p/mpmath/) that allow arbitrary accuracy. However, they are not fast enough to work as a NumPy replacement.

Fortunately, there is a better way to take care of this, and it has to do with a nice relationship that we maybe still know from school:

$$\log(x \cdot y) = \log(x) + \log(y)$$

If we apply it to our case, we get the following:

$$\log \left[P(C) \cdot P(F_1|C) \cdot P(F_2|C) \right] = \log P(C) + \log P(F_1|C) + \log P(F_2|C)$$

As the probabilities are in the interval between 0 and 1, the log of the probabilities lies in the interval -∞ and 0. Don't get irritated with that. Higher numbers are still a stronger indicator for the correct class — it is only that they are negative now.

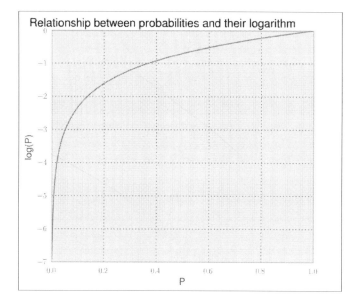

There is one caveat though: we actually don't have *log* in the formula's nominator (the part preceding the fraction). We only have the product of the probabilities. In our case, luckily we are not interested in the actual value of the probabilities. We simply want to know which class has the highest posterior probability. We are lucky because if we find this:

$$P(C = \text{"pos"}|F_1, F_2) > P(C = \text{"neg"}|F_1, F_2)$$

Then we also have the following:

$$\log P(C = \text{"pos"}|F_1, F_2) > \log P(C = \text{"neg"}|F_1, F_2)$$

A quick look at the previous graph shows that the curve never goes down when we go from left to right. In short, applying the logarithm does not change the highest value. So, let us stick this into the formula we used earlier:

$$C_{\text{best}} = \arg\max_{c \in C} P(C = c) \cdot P(F_1|C = c) \cdot P(F_2|C = c)$$

We will use this to retrieve the formula for two features that will give us the best class for real-world data that we will see in practice:

$$C_{\text{best}} = \arg\max_{c \in C} \log P(C = c) + P(F_1|C = c) + \log P(F_2|C = c)$$

Of course, we will not be very successful with only two features, so let us rewrite it to allow the arbitrary number of features:

$$C_{\text{best}} = \arg\max_{c \in C} \left(\log P(C = c) + \sum_k P(F_k|C = c)\right)$$

There we are, ready to use our first classifier from the scikit-learn toolkit.

Creating our first classifier and tuning it

The Naive Bayes classifiers reside in the `sklearn.naive_bayes` package. There are different kinds of Naive Bayes classifiers:

- `GaussianNB`: This assumes the features to be normally distributed (Gaussian). One use case for it could be the classification of sex according to the given height and width of a person. In our case, we are given tweet texts from which we extract word counts. These are clearly not Gaussian distributed.

- `MultinomialNB`: This assumes the features to be occurrence counts, which is relevant to us since we will be using word counts in the tweets as features. In practice, this classifier also works well with TF-IDF vectors.

- `BernoulliNB`: This is similar to `MultinomialNB`, but more suited when using binary word occurrences and not word counts.

As we will mainly look at the word occurrences, for our purpose, `MultinomialNB` is best suited.

Solving an easy problem first

As we have seen when we looked at our tweet data, the tweets are not just positive or negative. The majority of tweets actually do not contain any sentiment, but are neutral or irrelevant, containing, for instance, raw information (New book: Building Machine Learning ... http://link). This leads to four classes. To avoid complicating the task too much, let us for now only focus on the positive and negative tweets:

```
>>> pos_neg_idx=np.logical_or(Y=="positive", Y=="negative")
>>> X = X[pos_neg_idx]
>>> Y = Y[pos_neg_idx]
>>> Y = Y=="positive"
```

Now, we have in X the raw tweet texts and in Y the binary classification; we assign 0 for negative and 1 for positive tweets.

As we have learned in the chapters before, we can construct TfidfVectorizer to convert the raw tweet text into the TF-IDF feature values, which we then use together with the labels to train our first classifier. For convenience, we will use the Pipeline class, which allows us to join the vectorizer and the classifier together and provides the same interface:

```
from sklearn.feature_extraction.text import TfidfVectorizer
from sklearn.naive_bayes import MultinomialNB
from sklearn.pipeline import Pipeline

def create_ngram_model():
    tfidf_ngrams = TfidfVectorizer(ngram_range=(1, 3),
                    analyzer="word", binary=False)
    clf = MultinomialNB()
    pipeline = Pipeline([('vect', tfidf_ngrams), ('clf', clf)])
    return pipeline
```

The Pipeline instance returned by create_ngram_model() can now be used for fit() and predict() as if we had a normal classifier.

Since we do not have that much data, we should do cross-validation. This time, however, we will not use KFold, which partitions the data in consecutive folds, but instead we use ShuffleSplit. This shuffles the data for us, but does not prevent the same data instance to be in multiple folds. For each fold, then, we keep track of the area under the Precision-Recall curve and the accuracy.

To keep our experimentation agile, let us wrap everything together in a `train_model()` function, which takes a function as a parameter that creates the classifier:

```
from sklearn.metrics import precision_recall_curve, auc
from sklearn.cross_validation import ShuffleSplit

def train_model(clf_factory, X, Y):
    # setting random_state to get deterministic behavior
    cv = ShuffleSplit(n=len(X), n_iter=10, test_size=0.3,
        indices=True, random_state=0)

    scores = []
    pr_scores = []

    for train, test in cv:
        X_train, y_train = X[train], Y[train]
        X_test, y_test = X[test], Y[test]

        clf = clf_factory()
        clf.fit(X_train, y_train)

        train_score = clf.score(X_train, y_train)
        test_score = clf.score(X_test, y_test)

        scores.append(test_score)
        proba = clf.predict_proba(X_test)

        precision, recall, pr_thresholds = precision_recall_curve
(y_test, proba[:,1])

        pr_scores.append(auc(recall, precision))

    summary = (np.mean(scores), np.std(scores),
               np.mean(pr_scores), np.std(pr_scores))
    print "%.3f\t%.3f\t%.3f\t%.3f"%summary

>>> X, Y = load_sanders_data()
>>> pos_neg_idx=np.logical_or(Y=="positive", Y=="negative")
>>> X = X[pos_neg_idx]
>>> Y = Y[pos_neg_idx]
>>> Y = Y=="positive"
>>> train_model(create_ngram_model)
0.805    0.024    0.878    0.016
```

With our first try of using Naive Bayes on vectorized TF-IDF trigram features, we get an accuracy of 80.5 percent and a P/R AUC of 87.8 percent. Looking at the P/R chart shown in the following screenshot, it shows a much more encouraging behavior than the plots we saw in the previous chapter:

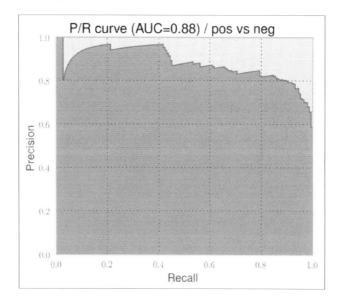

For the first time, the results are quite encouraging. They get even more impressive when we realize that 100 percent accuracy is probably never achievable in a sentiment classification task. For some tweets, even humans often do not really agree on the same classification label.

Using all the classes

But again, we simplified our task a bit, since we used only positive or negative tweets. That means we assumed a perfect classifier that classified upfront whether the tweet contains a sentiment and forwarded that to our Naive Bayes classifier.

So, how well do we perform if we also classify whether a tweet contains any sentiment at all? To find that out, let us first write a convenience function that returns a modified class array that provides a list of sentiments that we would like to interpret as positive

```
def tweak_labels(Y, pos_sent_list):
    pos = Y==pos_sent_list[0]
    for sent_label in pos_sent_list[1:]:
pos |= Y==sent_label
```

```
Y = np.zeros(Y.shape[0])
Y[pos] = 1
Y = Y.astype(int)

return Y
```

Note that we are talking about two different *positives* now. The sentiment of a tweet can be positive, which is to be distinguished from the class of the training data. If, for example, we want to find out how good we can separate the tweets having sentiment from neutral ones, we could do this as follows:

```
>>> Y = tweak_labels(Y, ["positive", "negative"])
```

In Y we now have a 1 (positive class) for all tweets that are either positive or negative and a 0 (negative class) for neutral and irrelevant ones.

```
>>> train_model(create_ngram_model, X, Y, plot=True)
0.767    0.014    0.670    0.022
```

As expected, the P/R AUC drops considerably, being only 67 percent now. The accuracy is still high, but that is only due to the fact that we have a highly imbalanced dataset. Out of 3,642 total tweets, only 1,017 are either positive or negative, which is about 28 percent. This means that if we created a classifier that always classified a tweet as not containing any sentiments, we would already have an accuracy of 72 percent. This is another example of why you should always look at precision and recall if the training and test data is unbalanced.

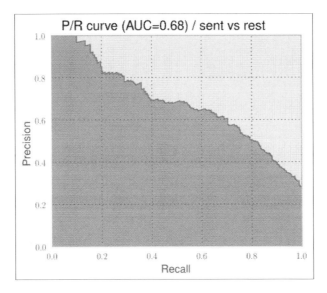

So, how would the Naive Bayes classifier perform on classifying positive tweets versus the rest and negative tweets versus the rest? One word: bad.

```
== Pos vs. rest ==
0.866    0.010    0.327    0.017
== Neg vs. rest ==
0.861    0.010    0.560    0.020
```

Pretty unusable if you ask me. Looking at the P/R curves shown in the following screenshots, we also find no usable precision/recall tradeoff as we were able to do in the previous chapter.

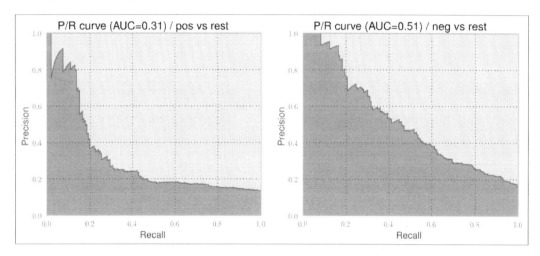

Tuning the classifier's parameters

Certainly, we have not explored the current setup enough and should investigate more. There are roughly two areas where we could play with the knobs: `TfidfVectorizer` and `MultinomialNB`. As we have no real intuition as to which area we should explore, let us try to distribute the parameters' values:

- `TfidfVectorizer`
    - Use different settings for NGrams: unigrams (1,1), bigrams (1,2), and trigrams (1,3)
    - Play with `min_df`: 1 or 2
    - Explore the impact of IDF within `TF-IDF` using `use_idf` and `smooth_idf`: False or True
    - Play with the idea of whether to remove stop words or not by setting `stop_words` to English or None

- ○ Experiment with whether or not to use the logarithm of the word counts (`sublinear_tf`)
- ○ Experiment with whether or not to track word counts or simply track whether words occur or not by setting `binary` to `True` or `False`

- `MultinomialNB`

  - ○ Decide which of the following smoothing methods to use by setting `alpha`:
  - ○ Add-one or Laplace smoothing: `1`
  - ○ Lidstone smoothing: `0.01`, `0.05`, `0.1`, or `0.5`
  - ○ No smoothing: `0`

A simple approach could be to train a classifier for all those reasonable exploration values while keeping the other parameters constant and checking the classifier's results. As we do not know whether those parameters affect each other, doing it right would require that we train a classifier for every possible combination of all parameter values. Obviously, this is too tedious for us to do.

Because this kind of parameter exploration occurs frequently in machine learning tasks, scikit-learn has a dedicated class for it called `GridSearchCV`. It takes an estimator (an instance with a classifier-like interface), which would be the pipeline instance in our case, and a dictionary of parameters with their potential values.

`GridSearchCV` expects the dictionary's keys to obey a certain format so that it is able to set the parameters of the correct estimator. The format is as follows:

```
<estimator>__<subestimator>__...__<param_name>
```

Now, if we want to specify the desired values to explore for the `min_df` parameter of `TfidfVectorizer` (named `vect` in the `Pipeline` description), we would have to say:

```
Param_grid={"vect__ngram_range"=[(1, 1), (1, 2), (1, 3)]}
```

This would tell `GridSearchCV` to try out unigrams, bigrams, and trigrams as parameter values for the `ngram_range` parameter of `TfidfVectorizer`.

Then it trains the estimator with all possible parameter/value combinations. Finally, it provides the best estimator in the form of the member variable `best_estimator_`.

As we want to compare the returned best classifier with our current best one, we need to evaluate it the same way. Therefore, we can pass the `ShuffleSplit` instance using the `CV` parameter (this is the reason `CV` is present in `GridSearchCV`).

The only missing thing is to define how `GridSearchCV` should determine the best estimator. This can be done by providing the desired score function to (surprise!) the `score_func` parameter. We could either write one ourselves or pick one from the `sklearn.metrics` package. We should certainly not take `metric.accuracy` because of our class imbalance (we have a lot less tweets containing sentiment than neutral ones). Instead, we want to have good precision and recall on both the classes: the tweets with sentiment and the tweets without positive or negative opinions. One metric that combines both precision and recall is the `F-measure` metric, which is implemented as `metrics.f1_score`:

$$F = \frac{2 \cdot \text{precision} \cdot \text{recall}}{\text{precision} + \text{recall}}$$

Putting everything together, we get the following code:

```
from sklearn.grid_search import GridSearchCV
from sklearn.metrics import f1_score

def grid_search_model(clf_factory, X, Y):
    cv = ShuffleSplit(
        n=len(X), n_iter=10, test_size=0.3, indices=True, random_
state=0)

    param_grid = dict(vect__ngram_range=[(1, 1), (1, 2), (1, 3)],
                      vect__min_df=[1, 2],
                      vect__stop_words=[None, "english"],
                      vect__smooth_idf=[False, True],
                      vect__use_idf=[False, True],
                      vect__sublinear_tf=[False, True],
                      vect__binary=[False, True],
                      clf__alpha=[0, 0.01, 0.05, 0.1, 0.5, 1],
                      )

    grid_search = GridSearchCV(clf_factory(),
                               param_grid=param_grid,
                               cv=cv,
                               score_func=f1_score,
                               verbose=10)
    grid_search.fit(X, Y)

    return grid_search.best_estimator_
```

We have to be patient when executing the following code:

```
clf = grid_search_model(create_ngram_model, X, Y)
print clf
```

This is because we have just requested a parameter sweep over the
$3 \cdot 2 \cdot 2 \cdot 2 \cdot 2 \cdot 2 \cdot 2 \cdot 6 = 1152$ parameter combinations—each being trained on 10 folds:

```
... waiting some hours   ...
Pipeline(clf=MultinomialNB(
            alpha=0.01, class_weight=None,
         fit_prior=True),
        clf__alpha=0.01,
        clf__class_weight=None,
        clf__fit_prior=True,
        vect=TfidfVectorizer(
            analyzer=word, binary=False,
                charset=utf-8, charset_error=strict,
            dtype=<type 'long'>, input=content,
            lowercase=True, max_df=1.0,
            max_features=None, max_n=None,
            min_df=1, min_n=None, ngram_range=(1, 2),
            norm=l2, preprocessor=None, smooth_idf=False,
            stop_words=None,strip_accents=None,
            sublinear_tf=True, token_pattern=(?u)\b\w\w+\b,
            token_processor=None, tokenizer=None,
            use_idf=False, vocabulary=None),
        vect__analyzer=word, vect__binary=False,
        vect__charset=utf-8,
        vect__charset_error=strict,
        vect__dtype=<type 'long'>,
        vect__input=content, vect__lowercase=True,
        vect__max_df=1.0, vect__max_features=None,
        vect__max_n=None, vect__min_df=1,
        vect__min_n=None, vect__ngram_range=(1, 2),
        vect__norm=l2, vect__preprocessor=None,
        vect__smooth_idf=False, vect__stop_words=None,
        vect__strip_accents=None, vect__sublinear_tf=True,
        vect__token_pattern=(?u)\b\w\w+\b,
        vect__token_processor=None, vect__tokenizer=None,
        vect__use_idf=False, vect__vocabulary=None)
    0.795    0.007    0.702    0.028
```

The best estimator indeed improves the P/R AUC by nearly 3.3 percent to 70.2 with
the setting that was printed earlier.

The devastating results for positive tweets against the rest and negative tweets against the rest will improve if we configure the vectorizer and classifier with those parameters that we have just found out:

```
== Pos vs. rest ==
0.883     0.005     0.520     0.028
== Neg vs. rest ==
0.888     0.009     0.631     0.031
```

Indeed, the P/R curves look much better (note that the graphs are from the medium of the fold classifiers, thus have slightly diverging AUC values):

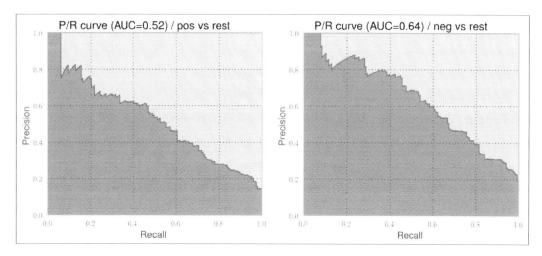

Nevertheless, we probably still wouldn't use those classifiers. Time for something completely different!

Cleaning tweets

New constraints lead to new forms. Twitter is no exception in this regard. Because text has to fit into 140 characters, people naturally develop new language shortcuts to say the same in less characters. So far, we have ignored all the diverse emoticons and abbreviations. Let's see how much we can improve by taking that into account. For this endeavor, we will have to provide our own `preprocessor()` to `TfidfVectorizer`.

First, we define a range of frequent emoticons and their replacements in a dictionary. Although we could find more distinct replacements, we go with obvious positive or negative words to help the classifier:

```
emo_repl = {
    # positive emoticons
    "&lt;3": " good ",
    ":d": " good ", # :D in lower case
    ":dd": " good ", # :DD in lower case
    "8)": " good ",
    ":-)": " good ",
    ":)": " good ",
    ";)": " good ",
    "(-:": " good ",
    "(:": " good ",

    # negative emoticons:
    ":/": " bad ",
    ":&gt;": " sad ",
    ":')": " sad ",
    ":-(": " bad ",
    ":(": " bad ",
    ":S": " bad ",
    ":-S": " bad ",
    }

# make sure that e.g. :dd is replaced before :d
emo_repl_order = [k for (k_len,k) in reversed(sorted([(len(k),k) for k
in emo_repl.keys()]))]
```

Then, we define abbreviations as regular expressions together with their expansions (\b marks the word boundary):

```
re_repl = {
    r"\br\b": "are",
    r"\bu\b": "you",
    r"\bhaha\b": "ha",
    r"\bhahaha\b": "ha",
    r"\bdon't\b": "do not",
    r"\bdoesn't\b": "does not",
    r"\bdidn't\b": "did not",
    r"\bhasn't\b": "has not",
    r"\bhaven't\b": "have not",
    r"\bhadn't\b": "had not",
    r"\bwon't\b": "will not",
```

```
        r"\bwouldn't\b": "would not",
        r"\bcan't\b": "can not",
        r"\bcannot\b": "can not",
        }

def create_ngram_model(params=None):
    def preprocessor(tweet):
        global emoticons_replaced
        tweet = tweet.lower()

        #return tweet.lower()
        for k in emo_repl_order:
            tweet = tweet.replace(k, emo_repl[k])
        for r, repl in re_repl.iteritems():
            tweet = re.sub(r, repl, tweet)

        return tweet

    tfidf_ngrams = TfidfVectorizer(preprocessor=preprocessor,
                                   analyzer="word")
    # ...
```

Certainly, there are many more abbreviations that could be used here. But already with this limited set, we get an improvement for sentiment versus not sentiment of half a point, which comes to 70.7 percent:

```
== Pos vs. neg ==
0.804     0.022     0.886     0.011
== Pos/neg vs. irrelevant/neutral ==
0.797     0.009     0.707     0.029
== Pos vs. rest ==
0.884     0.005     0.527     0.025
== Neg vs. rest ==
0.886     0.011     0.640     0.032
```

Taking the word types into account

So far our hope was to simply use the words independent of each other with the hope that a bag-of-words approach would suffice. Just from our intuition, however, neutral tweets probably contain a higher fraction of nouns, while positive or negative tweets are more colorful, requiring more adjectives and verbs. What if we could use this linguistic information of the tweets as well? If we could find out how many words in a tweet were nouns, verbs, adjectives, and so on, the classifier could maybe take that into account as well.

Determining the word types

Determining the word types is what **part of speech** (POS) tagging is all about. A POS tagger parses a full sentence with the goal to arrange it into a dependence tree, where each node corresponds to a word and the parent-child relationship determines which word it depends on. With this tree, it can then make more informed decisions; for example, whether the word "book" is a noun ("This is a good book.") or a verb ("Could you please book the flight?").

You might have already guessed that NLTK will also play a role also in this area. And indeed, it comes readily packaged with all sorts of parsers and taggers. The POS tagger we will use, `nltk.pos_tag()`, is actually a full-blown classifier trained using manually annotated sentences from the Penn Treebank Project (http://www.cis.upenn.edu/~treebank). It takes as input a list of word tokens and outputs a list of tuples, each element of which contains the part of the original sentence and its part of speech tag:

```
>>> import nltk
>>> nltk.pos_tag(nltk.word_tokenize("This is a good book."))
[('This', 'DT'), ('is', 'VBZ'), ('a', 'DT'), ('good', 'JJ'), ('book',
'NN'), ('.', '.')]
>>> nltk.pos_tag(nltk.word_tokenize("Could you please book the
flight?"))
[('Could', 'MD'), ('you', 'PRP'), ('please', 'VB'), ('book', 'NN'),
('the', 'DT'), ('flight', 'NN'), ('?', '.')]
```

The POS tag abbreviations are taken from the Penn Treebank Project (adapted from http://americannationalcorpus.org/OANC/penn.html):

POS tag	Description	Example
CC	coordinating conjunction	or
CD	cardinal number	2 second
DT	determiner	the
EX	existential there	there are
FW	foreign word	kindergarten
IN	preposition/subordinating conjunction	on, of, like
JJ	adjective	cool
JJR	adjective, comparative	cooler
JJS	adjective, superlative	coolest
LS	list marker	1)
MD	modal	could, will

POS tag	Description	Example
NN	noun, singular or mass	book
NNS	noun plural	books
NNP	proper noun, singular	Sean
NNPS	proper noun, plural	Vikings
PDT	predeterminer	both the boys
POS	possessive ending	friend's
PRP	personal pronoun	I, he, it
PRP$	possessive pronoun	my, his
RB	adverb	however, usually, naturally, here, good
RBR	adverb, comparative	better
RBS	adverb, superlative	best
RP	particle	give up
TO	to	to go, to him
UH	interjection	uhhuhhuhh
VB	verb, base form	take
VBD	verb, past tense	took
VBG	verb, gerund/present participle	taking
VBN	verb, past participle	taken
VBP	verb, singular, present, non-3D	take
VBZ	verb, third person singular, present	takes
WDT	wh-determiner	which
WP	wh-pronoun	who, what
WP$	possessive wh-pronoun	whose
WRB	wh-abverb	where, when

With these tags it is pretty easy to filter the desired tags from the output of `pos_tag()`. We simply have to count all the words whose tags start with NN for nouns, VB for verbs, JJ for adjectives, and RB for adverbs.

Successfully cheating using SentiWordNet

While the linguistic information that we discussed earlier will most likely help us, there is something better we can do to harvest it: SentiWordNet (http://sentiwordnet.isti.cnr.it). Simply put, it is a 13 MB file that assigns most of the English words a positive and negative value. In more complicated words, for every synonym set, it records both the positive and negative sentiment values. Some examples are as follows:

POS	ID	PosScore	NegScore	SynsetTerms	Description
a	00311354	0.25	0.125	studious#1	Marked by care and effort; "made a studious attempt to fix the television set"
a	00311663	0	0.5	careless#1	Marked by lack of attention or consideration or forethought or thoroughness; not careful
n	03563710	0	0	implant#1	A prosthesis placed permanently in tissue
v	00362128	0	0	kink#2 curve#5 curl#1	Form a curl, curve, or kink; "the cigar smoke curled up at the ceiling"

With the information in the POS column, we will be able to distinguish between the noun "book" and the verb "book". PosScore and NegScore together will help us to determine the neutrality of the word, which is 1-PosScore-NegScore. SynsetTerms lists all words in the set that are synonyms. The ID and Description can be safely ignored for our purpose.

The synset terms have a number appended, because some occur multiple times in different synsets. For example, "fantasize" conveys two quite different meanings, also leading to different scores:

POS	ID	PosScore	NegScore	SynsetTerms	Description
v	01636859	0.375	0	fantasize#2 fantasise#2	Portray in the mind; "he is fantasizing the ideal wife"
v	01637368	0	0.125	fantasy#1 fantasize#1 fantasise#1	Indulge in fantasies; "he is fantasizing when he says that he plans to start his own company"

To find out which of the synsets to take, we would have to really understand the meaning of the tweets, which is beyond the scope of this chapter. The field of research that focuses on this challenge is called **word sense disambiguation**. For our task, we take the easy route and simply average the scores over all the synsets in which a term is found. For "fantasize", `PosScore` would be `0.1875` and `NegScore` would be `0.0625`.

The following function, `load_sent_word_net()`, does all that for us, and returns a dictionary where the keys are strings of the form "word type/word", for example "n/ implant", and the values are the positive and negative scores:

```
import csv, collections
def load_sent_word_net():

    sent_scores = collections.defaultdict(list)

    with open(os.path.join(DATA_DIR,
      SentiWordNet_3.0.0_20130122.txt"), "r") as csvfile:

        reader = csv.reader(csvfile, delimiter='\t',
                quotechar='"')
        for line in reader:
            if line[0].startswith("#"):
                continue
            if len(line)==1:
                continue

            POS,ID,PosScore,NegScore,SynsetTerms,Gloss = line
            if len(POS)==0 or len(ID)==0:
                continue
            #print POS,PosScore,NegScore,SynsetTerms
            for term in SynsetTerms.split(" "):
                # drop number at the end of every term
                term = term.split("#")[0]
                term = term.replace("-", " ").replace("_", " ")
                key = "%s/%s"%(POS,term.split("#")[0])
                sent_scores[key].append((float(PosScore),
                float(NegScore)))
    for key, value in sent_scores.iteritems():
        sent_scores[key] = np.mean(value, axis=0)

    return sent_scores
```

Our first estimator

Now we have everything in place to create our first vectorizer. The most conveni
way to do it is to inherit it from BaseEstimator. It requires us to implement the
following three methods:

- get_feature_names(): This returns a list of strings of the features that we
will return in transform().

- fit(document, y=None): As we are not implementing a classifier, we can
ignore this one and simply return self.

- transform(documents): This returns numpy.array(), containing an array of
shape (len(documents), len(get_feature_names)). This means that for
every document in documents, it has to return a value for every feature name
in get_feature_names().

Let us now implement these methods:

```
sent_word_net = load_sent_word_net()

class LinguisticVectorizer(BaseEstimator):
    def get_feature_names(self):
        return np.array(['sent_neut', 'sent_pos', 'sent_neg',
            'nouns', 'adjectives', 'verbs', 'adverbs',
            'allcaps', 'exclamation', 'question', 'hashtag',
            'mentioning'])

    # we don't fit here but need to return the reference
    # so that it can be used like fit(d).transform(d)
    def fit(self, documents, y=None):
        return self

    def _get_sentiments(self, d):

        sent = tuple(d.split())
        tagged = nltk.pos_tag(sent)

        pos_vals = []
        neg_vals = []

        nouns = 0.
        adjectives = 0.
        verbs = 0.
        adverbs = 0.
```

```
for w,t in tagged:
    p, n = 0,0
    sent_pos_type = None
    if t.startswith("NN"):
        sent_pos_type = "n"
        nouns += 1
    elif t.startswith("JJ"):
        sent_pos_type = "a"
        adjectives += 1
    elif t.startswith("VB"):
        sent_pos_type = "v"
        verbs += 1
    elif t.startswith("RB"):
        sent_pos_type = "r"
        adverbs += 1

    if sent_pos_type is not None:
        sent_word = "%s/%s"%(sent_pos_type, w)

        if sent_word in sent_word_net:
            p,n = sent_word_net[sent_word]

    pos_vals.append(p)
    neg_vals.append(n)

l = len(sent)
avg_pos_val = np.mean(pos_vals)
avg_neg_val = np.mean(neg_vals)
return [1-avg_pos_val-avg_neg_val,
        avg_pos_val, avg_neg_val,
        nouns/l, adjectives/l, verbs/l, adverbs/l]


def transform(self, documents):
    obj_val, pos_val, neg_val, nouns, adjectives, \
    verbs, adverbs = np.array([self._get_sentiments(d) \
                    for d in documents]).T

    allcaps = []
    exclamation = []
    question = []
    hashtag = []
    mentioning = []
```

```
for d in documents:
    allcaps.append(np.sum([t.isupper() \
        for t in d.split() if len(t)>2]))

    exclamation.append(d.count("!"))
    question.append(d.count("?"))
    hashtag.append(d.count("#"))
    mentioning.append(d.count("@"))

result = np.array([obj_val, pos_val, neg_val,
                   nouns, adjectives, verbs, adverbs,
                   allcaps, exclamation, question,
                   hashtag, mentioning]).T

return result
```

Putting everything together

Nevertheless, using these linguistic features in isolation without the words themselves will not take us very far. Therefore, we have to combine TfidfVectorizer with the linguistic features. This can be done with scikit-learn's FeatureUnion class. It is initialized the same way as Pipeline, but instead of evaluating the estimators in a sequence and each passing the output of the previous one to the next one, FeatureUnion does it in parallel and joins the output vectors afterwards:

```
def create_union_model(params=None):
    def preprocessor(tweet):
        tweet = tweet.lower()

        for k in emo_repl_order:
            tweet = tweet.replace(k, emo_repl[k])
        for r, repl in re_repl.iteritems():
            tweet = re.sub(r, repl, tweet)

        return tweet.replace("-", " ").replace("_", " ")

    tfidf_ngrams = TfidfVectorizer(preprocessor=preprocessor,
                                   analyzer="word")
    ling_stats = LinguisticVectorizer()
    all_features = FeatureUnion([('ling', ling_stats), ('tfidf',
                                 tfidf_ngrams)])
    clf = MultinomialNB()
```

```
pipeline = Pipeline([('all', all_features), ('clf', clf)])

if params:
    pipeline.set_params(**params)

return pipeline
```

Training and testing on the combined featurizers gives another 0.6 percent improvement on positive versus negative:

```
== Pos vs. neg ==
0.808    0.016    0.892    0.010
== Pos/neg vs. irrelevant/neutral ==
0.794    0.009    0.707    0.033
== Pos vs. rest ==
0.886    0.006    0.533    0.026
== Neg vs. rest ==
0.881    0.012    0.629    0.037
```

With these results, we probably do not want to use the positive versus rest and negative versus rest classifiers, but instead use first the classifier determining whether the tweet contains sentiment at all ("pos/neg versus irrelevant/neutral") and then, when it does, use the positive versus negative classifier to determine the actual sentiment.

Summary

Congratulations for sticking with us until the end! Together we have learned how Naive Bayes work and why they are not that naive at all. For training sets where we don't have enough data to learn all the niches in the class probability space, Naive Bayes do a great job of generalizing. We learned how to apply them to tweets and that cleaning the rough tweets' text helps a lot. Finally, we realized that a bit of "cheating" (only after we have done our fair share of work) is OK, especially, when it gives another improvement of the classifier's performance, as we have experienced with the use of SentiWordNet.

7
Regression – Recommendations

You have probably learned about regression already in high school mathematics class, this was probably called **ordinary least squares** (**OLS**) regression then. This centuries old technique is fast to run and can be effectively used for many real-world problems. In this chapter, we will start by reviewing OLS regression and showing you how it is available in both NumPy and scikit-learn.

In various modern problems, we run into limitations of the classical methods and start to benefit from more advanced methods, which we will see later in this chapter. This is particularly true when we have many features, including when we have more features than examples (which is something that ordinary least squares cannot handle correctly). These techniques are much more modern, with major developments happening in the last decade. They go by names such as lasso, ridge, or elastic nets. We will go into these in detail.

Finally, we will start looking at recommendations. This is an important area in many applications as it is a significant added-value to many applications. This is a topic that we will start exploring here and will see in more detail in the next chapter.

Predicting house prices with regression

Let us start with a simple problem, predicting house prices in Boston.

We can use a publicly available dataset. We are given several demographic and geographical attributes, such as the crime rate or the pupil-teacher ratio, and the goal is to predict the median value of a house in a particular area. As usual, we have some training data, where the answer is known to us.

We start by using scikit-learn's methods to load the dataset. This is one of the built-in datasets that scikit-learn comes with, so it is very easy:

```
from sklearn.datasets import load_boston
boston = load_boston()
```

The `boston` object is a composite object with several attributes, in particular, `boston.data` and `boston.target` will be of interest to us.

We will start with a simple one-dimensional regression, trying to regress the price on a single attribute according to the average number of rooms per dwelling, which is stored at position 5 (you can consult `boston.DESCR` and `boston.feature_names` for detailed information on the data):

```
from matplotlib import pyplot as plt
plt.scatter(boston.data[:,5], boston.target, color='r')
```

The `boston.target` attribute contains the average house price (our target variable). We can use the standard least squares regression you probably first saw in high school. Our first attempt looks like this:

```
import numpy as np
```

We import NumPy, as this basic package is all we need. We will use functions from the `np.linalg` submodule, which performs basic linear algebra operations:

```
x = boston.data[:,5]
x = np.array([[v] for v in x])
```

This may seem strange, but we want x to be two dimensional: the first dimension is the different examples, while the second dimension is the attributes. In our case, we have a single attribute, the mean number of rooms per dwelling, so the second dimension is 1:

```
y = boston.target
slope,_,_,_ = np.linalg.lstsq(x,y)
```

Finally, we use least squares regression to obtain the slope of the regression. The `np.linalg.lstsq` function also returns some internal information on how well the regression fits the data, which we will ignore for the moment.

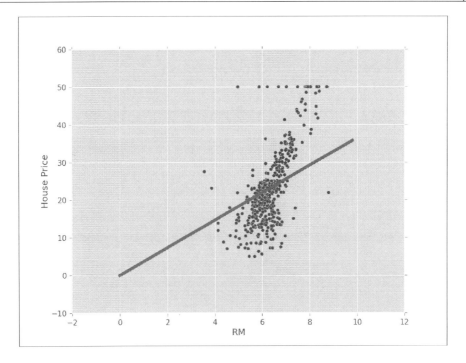

The preceding graph shows all the points (as dots) and our fit (the solid line). This does not look very good. In fact, using this one-dimensional model, we understand that House Price is a multiple of the RM variable (the number of rooms).

This would mean that, on average, a house with two rooms would be double the price of a single room and with three rooms would be triple the price. We know that these are false assumptions (and are not even approximately true).

One common step is to add a bias term to the previous expression so that the price is a multiple of RM plus a bias. This bias is the base price for a zero-bedroom apartment. The trick to implement this is to add 1 to every element of x:

```
x = boston.data[:,5]
x = np.array([[v,1] for v in x]) # we now use [v,1] instead of [v]
    y = boston.target
(slope,bias),_,_,_ = np.linalg.lstsq(x,y)
```

In the following screenshot, we can see that visually it looks better (even though a few outliers may be having a disproportionate impact on the result):

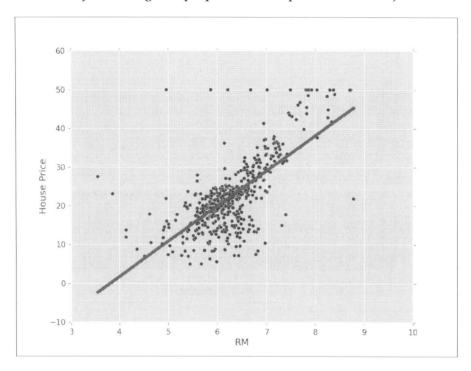

Ideally, though, we would like to measure how good of a fit this is quantitatively. In order to do so, we can ask how close our prediction is. For this, we now look at one of those other returned values from the `np.linalg.lstsq` function, the second element:

```
(slope,bias),total_error,_,_ = np.linalg.lstsq(x,y)
rmse = np.sqrt(total_error[0]/len(x))
```

The `np.linalg.lstsq` function returns the total squared error. For each element, it checks the error (the difference between the line and the true value), squares it, and returns the sum of all these. It is more understandable to measure the average error, so we divide by the number of elements. Finally, we take the square root and print out the **root mean squared error** (RMSE). For the first unbiased regression, we get an error of 7.6, while adding the bias improves it to 6.6. This means that we can expect the price to be different from the real price by at the most 13 thousand dollars.

Root mean squared error and prediction

The root mean squared error corresponds approximately to an estimate of the standard deviation. Since most of the data is at the most two standard deviations from the mean, we can double our RMSE to obtain a rough confident interval. This is only completely valid if the errors are normally distributed, but it is roughly correct even if they are not.

Multidimensional regression

So far, we have only used a single variable for prediction, the number of rooms per dwelling. We will now use all the data we have to fit a model using multidimensional regression. We now try to predict a single output (the average house price) based on multiple inputs.

The code looks very much like before:

```
x = boston.data
       # we still add a bias term, but now we must use np.concatenate,
which
       # concatenates two arrays/lists because we
       # have several input variables in v
x = np.array([np.concatenate(v,[1]) for v in boston.data])
  y = boston.target
  s,total_error,_,_ = np.linalg.lstsq(x,y)
```

Now, the root mean squared error is only 4.7! This is better than what we had before, which indicates that the extra variables did help. Unfortunately, we can no longer easily display the results as we have a 14-dimensional regression.

Cross-validation for regression

If you remember when we first introduced classification, we stressed the importance of cross-validation for checking the quality of our predictions. In regression, this is not always done. In fact, we only discussed the training error model earlier. This is a mistake if you want to confidently infer the generalization ability. Since ordinary least squares is a very simple model, this is often not a very serious mistake (the amount of overfitting is slight). However, we should still test this empirically, which we will do now using scikit-learn. We will also use its linear regression classes as they will be easier to replace for more advanced methods later in the chapter:

```
from sklearn.linear_model import LinearRegression
```

The `LinearRegression` class implements OLS regression as follows:

```
lr = LinearRegression(fit_intercept=True)
```

We set the `fit_intercept` parameter to `True` in order to add a bias term. This is exactly what we had done before, but in a more convenient interface:

```
lr.fit(x,y)
p = map(lr.predict, x)
```

Learning and prediction are performed for classification as follows:

```
e = p-y
total_error = np.sum(e*e) # sum of squares
rmse_train = np.sqrt(total_error/len(p))
print('RMSE on training: {}'.format(rmse_train))
```

We have used a different procedure to compute the root mean square error on the training data. Of course, the result is the same as we had before: 4.6 (it is always good to have these sanity checks to make sure we are doing things correctly).

Now, we will use the `KFold` class to build a 10-fold cross-validation loop and test the generalization ability of linear regression:

```
from sklearn.cross_validation import Kfold
kf = KFold(len(x), n_folds=10)
err = 0
for train,test in kf:
    lr.fit(x[train],y[train])
    p = map(lr.predict, x[test])
    e = p-y[test]
    err += np.sum(e*e)
rmse_10cv = np.sqrt(err/len(x))
print('RMSE on 10-fold CV: {}'.format(rmse_10cv))
```

With cross-validation, we obtain a more conservative estimate (that is, the error is greater): 5.6. As in the case of classification, this is a better estimate of how well we could generalize to predict prices.

Ordinary least squares is fast at learning time and returns a simple model, which is fast at prediction time. For these reasons, it should often be the first model that you use in a regression problem. However, we are now going to see more advanced methods.

Penalized regression

The important variations of OLS regression fall under the theme of penalized regression. In ordinary regression, the returned fit is the best fit on the training data, which can lead to overfitting. Penalizing means that we add a penalty for overconfidence in the parameter values.

Penalized regression is about tradeoffs

Penalized regression is another example of the bias-variance tradeoff. When using a penalty, we get a worse fit in the training data as we are adding bias. On the other hand, we reduce the variance and tend to avoid overfitting. Therefore, the overall result might be generalized in a better way.

L1 and L2 penalties

There are two types of penalties that are typically used for regression: L1 and L2 penalties. The L1 penalty means that we penalize the regression by the sum of the absolute values of the coefficients, and the L2 penalty penalizes by the sum of squares.

Let us now explore these ideas formally. The OLS optimization is given as follows:

$$\vec{b}^* = \arg\min_{\vec{b}} (y - X\vec{b})^2$$

In the preceding formula, we find the vector b that results in the minimum squared distance to the actual target y.

When we add an L1 penalty, we instead optimize the following formula:

$$\vec{b}^* = \arg\min_{\vec{b}} (y - X\vec{b})^2 + \lambda \sum_i |b_i|$$

Here, we are trying to simultaneously make the error small, but also make the values of the coefficients small (in absolute terms). Using L2 penalty means that we use the following formula:

$$\vec{b}^* = \arg\min_{\vec{b}} (y - X\vec{b})^2 + \lambda \sum_i b_i^2$$

The difference is rather subtle: we now penalize by the square of the coefficient rather than its absolute value. However, the difference in the results is dramatic.

Ridge, Lasso, and Elastic nets

These penalized models often go by rather interesting names. The L1 penalized model is often called the **Lasso**, while an L2 penalized model is known as **Ridge** regression. Of course, we can combine the two and we obtain an **Elastic net** model.

Both the Lasso and the Ridge result in smaller coefficients than unpenalized regression. However, the Lasso has the additional property that it results in more coefficients being set to zero! This means that the final model does not even use some of its input features, the model is sparse. This is often a very desirable property as the model performs both feature selection and regression in a single step.

You will notice that whenever we add a penalty, we also add a weight λ, which governs how much penalization we want. When λ is close to zero, we are very close to OLS (in fact, if you set λ to zero, you are just performing OLS), and when λ is large, we have a model which is very different from the OLS one.

The Ridge model is older as the Lasso is hard to compute manually. However, with modern computers, we can use the Lasso as easily as Ridge, or even combine them to form Elastic nets. An Elastic net has two penalties, one for the absolute value and another for the squares.

Using Lasso or Elastic nets in scikit-learn

Let us adapt the preceding example to use elastic nets. Using scikit-learn, it is very easy to swap in the Elastic net regressor for the least squares one that we had before:

```
from sklearn.linear_model import ElasticNet
en = ElasticNet(fit_intercept=True, alpha=0.5)
```

Now we use `en` whereas before we had used `lr`. This is the only change that is needed. The results are exactly what we would have expected. The training error increases to 5.0 (which was 4.6 before), but the cross-validation error decreases to 5.4 (which was 5.6 before). We have a larger error on the training data, but we gain better generalization. We could have tried an L1 penalty using the `Lasso` class or L2 using the `Ridge` class with the same code.

The next plot shows what happens when we switch from unpenalized regression (shown as a dotted line) to a Lasso regression, which is closer to a flat line. The benefits of a Lasso regression are, however, more apparent when we have many input variables and we consider this setting next:

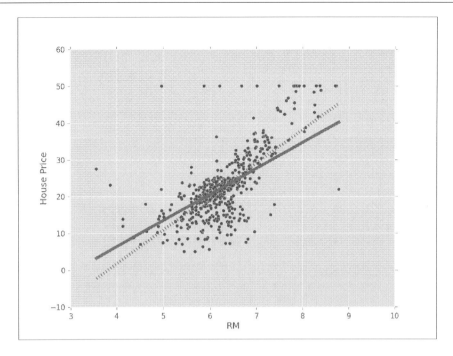

P greater than N scenarios

The title of this section is a bit of inside jargon, which you will now learn. Starting in the 1990s, first in the biomedical domain and then on the Web, problems started to appear when P was greater than N. What this means is that the number of features, P, was greater than the number of examples, N (these letters were the conventional statistical shorthand for these concepts). These became known as "P greater than N" problems.

For example, if your input is a set of written text, a simple way to approach it is to consider each possible word in the dictionary as a feature and regress on those (we will later work on one such problem ourselves). In the English language, you have over 20,000 words (this is if you perform some stemming and only consider common words; it is more than ten times that if you keep trademarks). If you only have a few hundred or a few thousand examples, you will have more features than examples.

In this case, as the number of features is greater than the number of examples, it is possible to have a perfect fit on the training data. This is a mathematical fact: you are, in effect, solving a system of equations with fewer equations than variables. You can find a set of regression coefficients with zero training error (in fact, you can find more than one perfect solution, infinitely many).

'ever, and this is a major problem, zero training error does not mean that your
'ion will generalize well. In fact, it may generalize very poorly. Whereas before
regularization could give you a little extra boost, it is now completely required for a
meaningful result.

An example based on text

We will now turn to an example which comes from a study performed at Carnegie
Mellon University by Prof. Noah Smith's research group. The study was based on
mining the so-called "10-K reports" that companies file with the **Securities and
Exchange Commission** (SEC) in the United States. This filing is mandated by the
law for all publicly-traded companies. The goal is to predict, based on this piece
of public information, what the future volatility of the company's stock will be. In
the training data, we are actually using historical data for which we already know
what happened.

There are 16,087 examples available. The features correspond to different words,
150,360 in total, which have already been preprocessed for us. Thus, we have many
more features than examples.

The dataset is available in SVMLight format from multiple sources, including the
book's companion website. This is a format which scikit-learn can read. SVMLight is,
as the name says, a support vector machine implementation, which is also available
through scikit-learn; right now, we are only interested in the file format.

```
from sklearn.datasets import load_svmlight_file
data,target = load_svmlight_file('E2006.train')
```

In the preceding code, `data` is a sparse matrix (that is, most of its entries are zeros
and, therefore, only the non-zero entries are saved in memory), while `target` is a
simple one-dimensional vector. We can start by looking at some attributes of `target`:

```
print('Min target value: {}'.format(target.min()))
print('Max target value: {}'.format(target.max()))
print('Mean target value: {}'.format(target.mean()))
print('Std. dev. target: {}'.format(target.std()))
```

This prints out the following values:

```
Min target value: -7.89957807347
Max target value: -0.51940952694
Mean target value: -3.51405313669
Std. dev. target: 0.632278353911
```

So, we can see that the data lies between -7.9 and -0.5. Now that we have an estimate data, we can check what happens when we use OLS to predict. Note that we can use exactly the same classes and methods as before:

```
from sklearn.linear_model import LinearRegression
lr = LinearRegression(fit_intercept=True)
lr.fit(data,target)
p = np.array(map(lr.predict, data))
p = p.ravel() # p is a (1,16087) array, we want to flatten it
e = p-target # e is 'error': difference of prediction and reality
total_sq_error = np.sum(e*e)
rmse_train = np.sqrt(total_sq_error/len(p))
print(rmse_train)
```

The error is not exactly zero because of the rounding error, but it is very close: 0.0025 (much smaller than the standard deviation of the target, which is the natural comparison value).

When we use cross-validation (the code is very similar to what we used before in the Boston example), we get something very different: 0.78. Remember that the standard deviation of the data is only 0.6. This means that if we always "predict" the mean value of -3.5, we have a root mean square error of 0.6! So, with OLS, in training, the error is insignificant. When generalizing, it is very large and the prediction is actually harmful: we would have done better (in terms of root mean square error) by simply predicting the mean value every time!

> **Training and generalization error**
>
> When the number of features is greater than the number of examples, you always get zero training error with OLS, but this is rarely a sign that your model will do well in terms of generalization. In fact, you may get zero training error and have a completely useless model.

One solution, naturally, is to use regularization to counteract the overfitting. We can try the same cross-validation loop with an elastic net learner, having set the penalty parameter to 1. Now, we get 0.4 RMSE, which is better than just "predicting the mean". In a real-life problem, it is hard to know when we have done all we can as perfect prediction is almost always impossible.

Setting hyperparameters in a smart way

In the preceding example, we set the penalty parameter to 1. We could just as well have set it to 2 (or half, or 200, or 20 million). Naturally, the results vary each time. If we pick an overly large value, we get underfitting. In extreme case, the learning system will just return every coefficient equal to zero. If we pick a value that is too small, we overfit and are very close to OLS, which generalizes poorly.

How do we choose a good value? This is a general problem in machine learning: setting parameters for our learning methods. A generic solution is to use cross-validation. We pick a set of possible values, and then use cross-validation to choose which one is best. This performs more computation (ten times more if we use 10 folds), but is always applicable and unbiased.

We must be careful, though. In order to obtain an estimate of generalization, we have to use two levels of cross-validation: one level is to estimate the generalization, while the second level is to get good parameters. That is, we split the data in, for example, 10 folds. We start by holding out the first fold and will learn on the other nine. Now, we split these again into 10 folds in order to choose the parameters. Once we have set our parameters, we test on the first fold. Now, we repeat this nine other times.

The preceding figure shows how you break up a single training fold into subfolds. We would need to repeat it for all the other folds. In this case, we are looking at five outer folds and five inner folds, but there is no reason to use the same number of outer and inner folds; you can use any numbers you want as long as you keep them separate.

This leads to a lot of computation, but it is necessary in order to do things correctly. The problem is that if you use a piece of data to make any decisions about your model (including which parameters to set), you have contaminated it and you can no longer use it to test the generalization ability of your model. This is a subtle point and it may not be immediately obvious. In fact, it is still the case that many users of machine learning get this wrong and overestimate how well their systems are doing because they do not perform cross-validation correctly!

Fortunately, scikit-learn makes it very easy to do the right thing: it has classes named `LassoCV`, `RidgeCV`, and `ElasticNetCV`, all of which encapsulate a cross-validation check for the inner parameter. The code is 100 percent like the previous one, except that we do not need to specify any value for alpha

```
from sklearn.linear_model import ElasticNetCV
met = ElasticNetCV(fit_intercept=True)
kf = KFold(len(target), n_folds=10)
for train,test in kf:
    met.fit(data[train],target[train])
    p = map(met.predict, data[test])
    p = np.array(p).ravel()
    e = p-target[test]
    err += np.dot(e,e)
rmse_10cv = np.sqrt(err/len(target))
```

This results in a lot of computation, so you may want to get some coffee while you are waiting (depending on how fast your computer is).

Rating prediction and recommendations

If you have used any commercial online system in the last 10 years, you have probably seen these recommendations. Some are like Amazon's "costumers who bought X also bought Y." These will be dealt with in the next chapter under the topic of basket analysis. Others are based on predicting the rating of a product, such as a movie.

This last problem was made famous with the Netflix Challenge; a million-dollar machine learning public challenge by Netflix. Netflix (well-known in the U.S. and U.K., but not available elsewhere) is a movie rental company. Traditionally, you would receive DVDs in the mail; more recently, the business has focused on online streaming of videos. From the start, one of the distinguishing features of the service was that it gave every user the option of rating films they had seen, using these ratings to then recommend other films. In this mode, you not only have the information about which films the user saw, but also their impression of them (including negative impressions).

In 2006, Netflix made available a large number of customer ratings of films in its database and the goal was to improve on their in-house algorithm for ratings prediction. Whoever was able to beat it by 10 percent or more would win 1 million dollars. In 2009, an international team named *BellKor's Pragmatic Chaos* was able to beat that mark and take the prize. They did so just 20 minutes before another team, *The Ensemble*, passed the 10 percent mark as well! An exciting photo-finish for a competition that lasted several years.

Unfortunately, for legal reasons, this dataset is no longer available (although the data was anonymous, there were concerns that it might be possible to discover who the clients were and reveal the private details of movie rentals). However, we can use an academic dataset with similar characteristics. This data comes from GroupLens, a research laboratory at the University of Minnesota.

Machine learning in the real world

Much has been written about the Netflix Prize and you may learn a lot reading up on it (this book will have given you enough to start to understand the issues). The techniques that won were a mix of advanced machine learning with a lot of work in the preprocessing of the data. For example, some users like to rate everything very highly, others are always more negative; if you do not account for this in preprocessing, your model will suffer. Other not so obvious normalizations were also necessary for a good result: how old the film is, how many ratings did it receive, and so on. Good algorithms are a good thing, but you always need to "get your hands dirty" and tune your methods to the properties of the data you have in front of you.

We can formulate this as a regression problem and apply the methods that we learned in this chapter. It is not a good fit for a classification approach. We could certainly attempt to learn the five class classifiers, one class for each possible grade. There are two problems with this approach:

- Errors are not all the same. For example, mistaking a 5-star movie for a 4-star one is not as serious of a mistake as mistaking a 5-star movie for a 1-star one.

- Intermediate values make sense. Even if our inputs are only integer values, it is perfectly meaningful to say that the prediction is 4.7. We can see that this is a different prediction than 4.2.

These two factors together mean that classification is not a good fit to the problem. The regression framework is more meaningful.

We have two choices: we can build movie-specific or user-specific models. In our case, we are going to first build user-specific models. This means that, for each user, we take the movies, it has rated as our target variable. The inputs are the ratings of other old users. This will give a high value to users who are similar to our user (or a negative value to users who like more or less the same movies that our user dislikes).

The system is just an application of what we have developed so far. You will find a copy of the dataset and code to load it into Python on the book's companion website. There you will also find pointers to more information, including the original MovieLens website.

The loading of the dataset is just basic Python, so let us jump ahead to the learning. We have a sparse matrix, where there are entries from 1 to 5 whenever we have a rating (most of the entries are zero to denote that this user has not rated these movies). This time, as a regression method, for variety, we are going to be using the `LassoCV` class:

```
from sklearn.linear_model import LassoCV
reg = LassoCV(fit_intercept=True, alphas=[.125,.25,.5,1.,2.,4.])
```

By passing the constructor an explicit set of alphas, we can constrain the values that the inner cross-validation will use. You may note that the values are multiples of two, starting with 1/8 up to 4. We will now write a function which learns a model for the user `i`:

```
# isolate this user
u = reviews[i]
```

We are only interested in the movies that the user `u` rated, so we must build up the index of those. There are a few NumPy tricks in here: `u.toarray()` to convert from a sparse matrix to a regular array. Then, we `ravel()` that array to convert from a row array (that is, a two-dimensional array with a first dimension of 1) to a simple one-dimensional array. We compare it with zero and ask where this comparison is true. The result, `ps`, is an array of indices; those indices correspond to movies that the user has rated:

```
u = u.array().ravel()
ps, = np.where(u > 0)

# Build an array with indices [0...N] except i
us = np.delete(np.arange(reviews.shape[0]), i)

x = reviews[us][:,ps].T
```

Finally, we select only the movies that the user has rated:

```
y = u[ps]
```

Cross-validation is set up as before. Because we have many users, we are going to only use four folds (more would take a long time and we have enough training data with just 80 percent of the data):

```
err = 0
kf = KFold(len(y), n_folds=4)
for train,test in kf:
        # Now we perform a per-movie normalization
        # this is explained below
        xc,x1 = movie_norm(x[train])
```

```
reg.fit(xc, y[train]-x1)
# We need to perform the same normalization while testing
xc,x1 = movie_norm(x[test])
p = np.array(map(reg.predict, xc)).ravel()
e = (p+x1)-y[test]
err += np.sum(e*e)
```

We did not explain the `movie_norm` function. This function performs per-movie normalization: some movies are just generally better and get higher average marks:

```
def movie_norm(x):
    xc = x.copy().toarray()
```

We cannot use `xc.mean(1)` because we do not want to have the zeros counting for the mean. We only want the mean of the ratings that were actually given:

```
x1 = np.array([xi[xi > 0].mean() for xi in xc])
```

In certain cases, there were no ratings and we got a NaN value, so we replace it with zeros using `np.nan_to_num`, which does exactly this task:

```
x1 = np.nan_to_num(x1)
```

Now we normalize the input by removing the mean value from the non-zero entries:

```
for i in xrange(xc.shape[0]):
    xc[i] -= (xc[i] > 0) * x1[i]
```

Implicitly, this also makes the movies that the user did not rate have a value of zero, which is average. Finally, we return the normalized array and the means:

```
return x,x1
```

You might have noticed that we converted to a regular (dense) array. This has the added advantage that it makes the optimization much faster: while scikit-learn works well with the sparse values, the dense arrays are much faster (if you can fit them in memory; when you cannot, you are forced to use sparse arrays).

When compared with simply guessing the average value for that user, this approach is 80 percent better. The results are not spectacular, but it is a start. On one hand, this is a very hard problem and we cannot expect to be right with every prediction: we perform better when the users have given us more reviews. On the other hand, regression is a blunt tool for this job. Note how we learned a completely separate model for each user. In the next chapter, we will look at other methods that go beyond regression for approaching this problem. In those models, we integrate the information from all users and all movies in a more intelligent manner.

Summary

In this chapter, we started with the oldest trick in the book, ordinary least squares. It is still sometimes good enough. However, we also saw that more modern approaches that avoid overfitting can give us better results. We used Ridge, Lasso, and Elastic nets; these are the state-of-the-art methods for regression.

We once again saw the danger of relying on training error to estimate generalization: it can be an overly optimistic estimate to the point where our model has zero training error, but we can know that it is completely useless. When thinking through these issues, we were led into two-level cross-validation, an important point that many in the field still have not completely internalized. Throughout, we were able to rely on scikit-learn to support all the operations we wanted to perform, including an easy way to achieve correct cross-validation.

At the end of this chapter, we started to shift gears and look at recommendation problems. For now, we approached these problems with the tools we knew: penalized regression. In the next chapter, we will look at new, better tools for this problem. These will improve our results on this dataset.

This recommendation setting also has a disadvantage that it requires that users have rated items on a numeric scale. Only a fraction of users actually perform this operation. There is another type of information that is often easier to obtain: which items were purchased together. In the next chapter, we will also see how to leverage this information in a framework called basket analysis.

8
Regression – Recommendations Improved

At the end of the last chapter, we used a very simple method to build a recommendation engine: we used regression to guess a ratings value. In the first part of this chapter, we will continue this work and build a more advanced (and better) rating estimator. We start with a few ideas that are helpful and then combine all of them. When combining, we use regression again to learn the best way to combine them.

In the second part of this chapter, we will look at a different way of learning called **basket analysis**, where we will learn how to make recommendations. Unlike the case in which we had numeric ratings, in the basket analysis setting, all we have is information about shopping baskets, that is, what items were bought together. The goal is to learn recommendations. You have probably already seen features of the form "people who bought X also bought Y" in online shopping. We will develop a similar feature of our own.

Improved recommendations

Remember where we stopped in the previous chapter: with a very basic, but not very good, recommendation system that gave better than random predictions. We are now going to start improving it. First, we will go through a couple of ideas that will capture some part of the problem. Then, what we will do is combine multiple approaches rather than using a single approach in order to be able to achieve a better final performance.

We will be using the same movie recommendation dataset that we started off with in the last chapter; it consists of a matrix with users on one axis and movies on the other. It is a sparse matrix, as each user has only reviewed a small fraction of the movies.

Using the binary matrix of recommendations

One of the interesting conclusions from the Netflix Challenge was one of those obvious-in-hindsight ideas: we can learn a lot about you just from knowing which movies you rated, even without looking at which rating was given! Even with a binary matrix where we have a rating of *1* where a user rated a movie and *0* where they did not, we can make useful predictions. In hindsight, this makes perfect sense; we do not choose movies to watch completely randomly, but instead pick those where we already have an expectation of liking them. We also do not make random choices of which movies to rate, but perhaps only rate those we feel most strongly about (naturally, there are exceptions, but on an average this is probably true).

We can visualize the values of the matrix as an image where each rating is depicted as a little square. Black represents the absence of a rating and the grey levels represent the rating value. We can see that the matrix is sparse—most of the squares are black. We can also see that some users rate a lot more movies than others and that some movies are the target of many more ratings than others.

The code to visualize the data is very simple (you can adapt it to show a larger fraction of the matrix than is possible to show in this book), as follows:

```
from matplotlib import pyplot as plt
imagedata = reviews[:200, :200].todense()
plt.imshow(imagedata, interpolation='nearest')
```

The following screenshot is the output of this code:

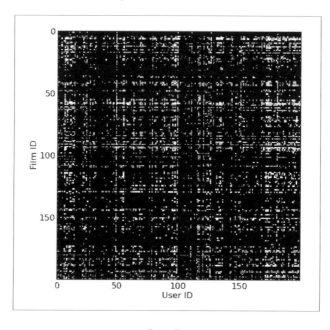

We are now going to use this binary matrix to make predictions of movie ratings. The general algorithm will be (in pseudocode) as follows:

1. For each user, rank every other user in terms of closeness. For this step, we will use the binary matrix and use correlation as the measure of closeness (interpreting the binary matrix as zeros and ones allows us to perform this computation).

2. When we need to estimate a rating for a user-movie pair, we look at the neighbors of the user sequentially (as defined in step 1). When we first find a rating for the movie in question, we report it.

Implementing the code first, we are going to write a simple NumPy function. NumPy ships with `np.corrcoeff`, which computes correlations. This is a very generic function and computes *n*-dimensional correlations even when only a single, traditional correlation is needed. Therefore, to compute the correlation between two users, we need to call the following:

```
corr_between_user1_and_user2 = np.corrcoef(user1, user2)[0,1]
```

In fact, we will be wishing to compute the correlation between a user and all the other users. This will be an operation we will use a few times, so we wrap it in a function named `all_correlations`:

```
import numpy as np
def all_correlations(bait, target):
    '''
    corrs = all_correlations(bait, target)

    corrs[i] is the correlation between bait and target[i]
    '''
    return np.array(
            [np.corrcoef(bait, c)[0,1]
                for c in target])
```

Now we can use this in several ways. A simple one is to select the nearest neighbors of each user. These are the users that most resemble it. We will use the measured correlation discussed earlier:

```python
def estimate(user, rest):
    '''
    estimate movie ratings for 'user' based on the 'rest' of the
universe.
    '''
    # binary version of user ratings
    bu = user > 0
    # binary version of rest ratings
    br = rest > 0
    ws = all_correlations(bu,br)
    # select 100 highest values
    selected = ws.argsort()[-100:]
    # estimate based on the mean:
    estimates = rest[selected].mean(0)
    # We need to correct estimates
    # based on the fact that some movies have more ratings than others:
    estimates /= (.1+br[selected].mean(0))
```

When compared to the estimate obtained over all the users in the dataset, this reduces the RMSE by 20 percent. As usual, when we look only at those users that have more predictions, we do better: there is a 25 percent error reduction if the user is in the top half of the rating activity.

Looking at the movie neighbors

In the previous section, we looked at the users that were most similar. We can also look at which movies are most similar. We will now build recommendations based on a nearest neighbor rule for movies: when predicting the rating of a movie M for a user U, the system will predict that U will rate M with the same points it gave to the movie most similar to M.

Therefore, we proceed with two steps: first, we compute a similarity matrix (a matrix that tells us which movies are most similar); second, we compute an estimate for each (user-movie) pair.

We use the NumPy zeros and ones functions to allocate arrays (initialized to zeros and ones respectively):

```python
movie_likeness = np.zeros((nmovies,nmovies))
allms = np.ones(nmovies, bool)
cs = np.zeros(nmovies)
```

Now, we iterate over all the movies:

```
for i in range(nmovies):
    movie_likeness[i] = all_correlations(reviews[:,i], reviews.T)
    movie_likeness[i,i] = -1
```

We set the diagonal to -1; otherwise, the most similar movie to any movie is itself, which is true, but very unhelpful. This is the same trick we used in *Chapter 2*, *Learning How to Classify with Real-world Examples*, when we first introduced the nearest neighbor classification. Based on this matrix, we can easily write a function that estimates a rating:

```
def nn_movie(movie_likeness, reviews, uid, mid):
    likes = movie_likeness[mid].argsort()
  # reverse the sorting so that most alike are in
  # beginning
    likes = likes[::-1]
  # returns the rating for the most similar movie available
    for ell in likes:
        if reviews[u,ell] > 0:
            return reviews[u,ell]
```

How well does the preceding function do? Fairly well: its RMSE is only 0.85.

The preceding code does not show you all of the details of the cross-validation. While it would work well in production as it is written, for testing, we need to make sure we have recomputed the likeness matrix afresh without using the user that we are currently testing on (otherwise, we contaminate the test set and we have an inflated estimate of generalization). Unfortunately, this takes a long time, and we do not need the full matrix for each user. You should compute only what you need. This makes the code slightly more complex than the preceding examples. On the companion website for this book, you will find code with all the hairy details. There you will also find a much faster implementation of the `all_correlations` function.

Combining multiple methods

We can now combine the methods given in the earlier section into a single prediction. For example, we could average the predictions. This is normally good enough, but there is no reason to think that both predictions are similarly good and should thus have the exact same weight of 0.5. It might be that one is better.

We can try a weighted average, multiplying each prediction by a given weight before summing it all up. How do we find the best weights though? We learn them from the data of course!

Ensemble learning

We are using a general technique in machine learning called **ensemble learning**; this is not only applicable in regression. We learn an ensemble (that is, a set) of predictors. Then, we combine them. What is interesting is that we can see each prediction as being a new feature, and we are now just combining features based on training data, which is what we have been doing all along. Note that we are doing so for regression here, but the same reasoning is applicable during classification: you learn how to create several classifiers and a master classifier, which takes the output of all of them and gives a final prediction. Different forms of ensemble learning differ on how you combine the base predictors. In our case, we reuse the training data that learned the predictors.

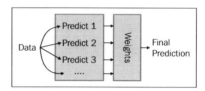

By having a flexible way to combine multiple methods, we can simply try any idea we wish by adding it into the mix of learners and letting the system give it a weight. We can also use the weights to discover which ideas are good: if they get a high weight, this means that it seems they are adding useful information. Ideas with very low weights can even be dropped for better performance.

The code for this is very simple, and is as follows:

```
# We import the code we used in the previous examples:
import similar_movie
import corrneighbors
import usermodel
from sklearn.linear_model import LinearRegression

es = [
  usermodel.estimate_all()
  corrneighbors.estimate_all(),
  similar_movie.estimate_all(),
]
```

```
coefficients = []
# We are now going to run a leave-1-out cross-validation loop
for u in xrange(reviews.shape[0]): # for all user ids
  es0 = np.delete(es,u,1) # all but user u
  r0 = np.delete(reviews, u, 0)
      P0,P1 = np.where(r0 > 0) # we only care about actual
predictions
      X = es[:,P0,P1]
      y = r0[r0 > 0]
      reg.fit(X.T,y)
      coefficients.append(reg.coef_)
  prediction = reg.predict(es[:,u,reviews[u] > 0].T)
  # measure error as before
```

The result is an RMSE of almost exactly 1. We can also analyze the coefficients variable to find out how well our predictors fare:

```
print coefficients.mean(0) # the mean value across all users
```

The values of the array are [0.25164062,   0.01258986,   0.60827019]. The estimate of the most similar movie has the highest weight (it was the best individual prediction, so it is not surprising), and we can drop the correlation-based method from the learning process as it has little influence on the final result.

What this setting does is it makes it easy to add a few extra ideas; for example, if the single most similar movie is a good predictor, how about we use the five most similar movies in the learning process as well? We can adapt the earlier code to generate the *k-th* most similar movie and then use the stacked learner to learn the weights:

```
es = [
    usermodel.estimate_all()
    similar_movie.estimate_all(k=1),
    similar_movie.estimate_all(k=2),
    similar_movie.estimate_all(k=3),
    similar_movie.estimate_all(k=4),
    similar_movie.estimate_all(k=5),
  ]
# the rest of the code remains as before!
```

We gained a lot of freedom in generating new machine learning systems. In this case, the final result is not better, but it was easy to test this new idea.

However, we do have to be careful to not overfit our dataset. In fact, if we randomly try too many things, some of them will work well on this dataset but will not generalize. Even though we are using cross-validation, we are not cross-validating our design decisions. In order to have a good estimate, and if data is plentiful, you should leave a portion of the data untouched until you have your final model that is about to go into production. Then, testing your model gives you an unbiased prediction of how well you should expect it to work in the real world.

Basket analysis

The methods we have discussed so far work well when you have numeric ratings of how much a user liked a product. This type of information is not always available.

Basket analysis is an alternative mode of learning recommendations. In this mode, our data consists only of what items were bought together; it does not contain any information on whether individual items were enjoyed or not. It is often easier to get this data rather than ratings data as many users will not provide ratings, while the basket data is generated as a side effect of shopping. The following screenshot shows you a snippet of Amazon.com's web page for the book *War and Peace*, *Leo Tolstoy*, which is a classic way to use these results:

This mode of learning is not only applicable to actual shopping baskets, naturally. It is applicable in any setting where you have groups of objects together and need to recommend another. For example, recommending additional recipients to a user writing an e-mail is done by Gmail and could be implemented using similar techniques (we do not know what Gmail uses internally; perhaps they combine multiple techniques as we did earlier). Or, we could use these methods to develop an application to recommend webpages to visit based on your browsing history. Even if we are handling purchases, it may make sense to group all purchases by a customer into a single basket independently of whether the items where bought together or on separate transactions (this depends on the business context).

The beer and diapers story

One of the stories that is often mentioned in the context of basket analysis is the "diapers and beer" story. It states that when supermarkets first started to look at their data, they found that diapers were often bought together with beer. Supposedly, it was the father who would go out to the supermarket to buy diapers and then would pick up some beer as well. There has been much discussion of whether this is true or just an urban myth. In this case, it seems that it is true. In the early 1990s, Osco Drug did discover that in the early evening beer and diapers were bought together, and it did surprise the managers who had, until then, never considered these two products to be similar. What is not true is that this led the store to move the beer display closer to the diaper section. Also, we have no idea whether it was really that fathers were buying beer and diapers together more than mothers (or grandparents).

Obtaining useful predictions

It is not just "customers who bought X also bought Y", even though that is how many online retailers phrase it (see the Amazon.com screenshot given earlier); a real system cannot work like this. Why not? Because such a system would get fooled by very frequently bought items and would simply recommend that which is popular without any personalization.

For example, at a supermarket, many customers buy bread (say 50 percent of customers buy bread). So if you focus on any particular item, say dishwasher soap, and look at what is frequently bought with dishwasher soap, you might find that bread is frequently bought with soap. In fact, 50 percent of the times someone buys dishwasher soap, they buy bread. However, bread is frequently bought with anything else just because everybody buys bread very often.

What we are really looking for is *customers who bought X are statistically more likely to buy Y than the baseline*. So if you buy dishwasher soap, you are likely to buy bread, but not more so than the baseline. Similarly, a bookstore that simply recommended bestsellers no matter which books you had already bought would not be doing a good job of personalizing recommendations.

Analyzing supermarket shopping baskets

As an example, we will look at a dataset consisting of anonymous transactions at a supermarket in Belgium. This dataset was made available by *Tom Brijs* at Hasselt University. The data is anonymous, so we only have a number for each product and a basket that is a set of numbers. The datafile is available from several online sources (including the book's companion website) as `retail.dat`.

We begin by loading the dataset and looking at some statistics:

```
    from collections import defaultdict
from itertools import chain
# file format is a line per transaction
# of the form '12 34 342 5...'
dataset = [[int(tok) for tok in ,line.strip().split()]
        for line in open('retail.dat')]
# count how often each product was purchased:
counts = defaultdict(int)
for elem in chain(*dataset):
    counts[elem] += 1
```

We can plot a small histogram as follows:

# of times bought	# of products
Just once	2224
Twice or thrice	2438
Four to seven times	2508
Eight to 15 times	2251
16 to 31 times	2182
32 to 63 times	1940
64 to 127 times	1523
128 to 511 times	1225
512 times or more	179

There are many products that have only been bought a few times. For example, 33 percent of products were bought four or less times. However, this represents only 1 percent of purchases. This phenomenon that many products are only purchased a small number of times is sometimes labeled "the long tail", and has only become more prominent as the Internet made it cheaper to stock and sell niche items. In order to be able to provide recommendations for these products, we would need a lot more data.

There are a few open source implementations of basket analysis algorithms out there, but none that are well-integrated with scikit-learn or any of the other packages we have been using. Therefore, we are going to implement one classic algorithm ourselves. This algorithm is called the **Apriori** algorithm, and it is a bit old (it was published in 1994 by *Rakesh Agrawal* and *Ramakrishnan Srikant*), but it still works (algorithms, of course, never stop working; they just get superceded by better ideas).

Formally, Apriori takes a collection of sets (that is, your shopping baskets) and returns sets that are very frequent as subsets (that is, items that together are part of many shopping baskets).

The algorithm works according to the bottom-up approach: starting with the smallest candidates (those composed of one single element), it builds up, adding one element at a time. We need to define the minimum support we are looking for:

```
minsupport = 80
```

Support is the number of times that a set of products was purchased together. The goal of Apriori is to find itemsets with high support. Logically, any itemset with more than minimal support can only be composed of items that themselves have at least minimal support:

```
valid = set(k for k,v in counts.items()
        if (v >= minsupport))
```

Our initial itemsets are singletons (sets with a single element). In particular, all singletons that have at least minimal support are frequent itemsets.

```
itemsets = [frozenset([v]) for v in valid]
```

Now our iteration is very simple and is given as follows:

```
new_itemsets = []
for iset in itemsets:
    for v in valid:
        if v not in iset:
        # we create a new possible set
        # which is the same as the previous,
        #with the addition of v
            newset = (ell|set([v_]))
            # loop over the dataset to count the number
            # of times newset appears. This step is slow
            # and not used proper implementation
            c_newset = 0
            for d in dataset:
                if d.issuperset(c):
                    c_newset += 1
            if c_newset > minsupport:
                newsets.append(newset)
```

This works correctly, but is very slow. A better implementation has more infrastructure so you can avoid having to loop over all the datasets to get the count (`c_newset`). In particular, we keep track of which shopping baskets have which frequent itemsets. This accelerates the loop but makes the code harder to follow. Therefore, we will not show it here. As usual, you can find both implementations on the book's companion website. The code there is also wrapped into a function that can be applied to other datasets.

The Apriori algorithm returns frequent itemsets, that is, small baskets that are not in any specific quantity (`minsupport` in the code).

Association rule mining

Frequent itemsets are not very useful by themselves. The next step is to build **association rules**. Because of this final goal, the whole field of basket analysis is sometimes called **association rule mining**.

An association rule is a statement of the "if X then Y" form; for example, *if a customer bought War and Peace, they will buy Anna Karenina*. Note that the rule is not deterministic (not all customers who buy X will buy Y), but it is rather cumbersome to always spell it out. So if a customer bought X, he is more likely to buy Y according to the baseline; thus, we say *if X then Y*, but we mean it in a probabilistic sense.

Interestingly, the antecedent and conclusion may contain multiple objects: costumers who bought X, Y, and Z also bought A, B, and C. Multiple antecedents may allow you to make more specific predictions than are possible from a single item.

You can get from a frequent set to a rule by just trying all possible combinations of X implies Y. It is easy to generate many of these rules. However, you only want to have valuable rules. Therefore, we need to measure the value of a rule. A commonly used measure is called the **lift**. The lift is the ratio between the probability obtained by applying the rule and the baseline:

$$\text{lift}(X \rightarrow Y) = \frac{P(Y|X)}{P(Y)}$$

In the preceding formula, `P(Y)` is the fraction of all transactions that include Y while `P(Y|X)` is the fraction of transactions that include `Y` and `X` both. Using the lift helps you avoid the problem of recommending bestsellers; for a bestseller, both `P(Y)` and `P(X|Y)` will be large. Therefore, the lift will be close to one and the rule will be deemed not very relevant. In practice, we wish to have at least 10, perhaps even 100, values of a lift.

Refer to the following code:

```
def rules_from_itemset(itemset, dataset):
    itemset = frozenset(itemset)
    nr_transactions = float(len(dataset))
    for item in itemset:
            antecendent = itemset-consequent
        base = 0.0
        # acount: antecedent count
        acount = 0.0

        # ccount : consequent count
        ccount = 0.0
        for d in dataset:
            if item in d: base += 1
            if d.issuperset(itemset): ccount += 1
            if d.issuperset(antecedent): acount += 1
        base /= nr_transactions
        p_y_given_x = ccount/acount
        lift = p_y_given_x / base
        print('Rule {0} -> {1} has lift {2}'
                .format(antecedent, consequent,lift))
```

This is slow-running code: we iterate over the whole dataset repeatedly. A better implementation would cache the counts for speed. You can download such an implementation from the book's website, and it does indeed run much faster.

Some of the results are shown in the following table:

Antecedent	Consequent	Consequent count	Antecedent count	Antecedent and consequent count	Lift
1378, 13791, 1380	1269	279 (0.3%)	80	57	225
48, 41, 976	117	1026 (1.1%)	122	51	35
48, 41, 16011	16010	1316 (1.5%)	165	159	64

Counts are the number of transactions; they include the following:

- The consequent alone (that is, the base rate at which that product is bought)
- All the items in the antecedent
- All the items in the antecedent and the consequent

We can see, for example, that there were 80 transactions of which 1378, 13791, and 1380 were bought together. Of these, 57 also included 1269, so the estimated conditional probability is $57/80 \approx 71\%$. Compared to the fact that only 0.3% of all transactions included 1269 , this gives us a lift of 255.

The need to have a decent number of transactions in these counts in order to be able to make relatively solid inferences is why we must first select frequent itemsets. If we were to generate rules from an infrequent itemset, the counts would be very small; due to this, the relative values would be meaningless (or subject to very large error bars).

Note that there are many more association rules that have been discovered from this dataset: 1030 datasets are required to support at least 80 minimum baskets and a minimum lift of 5. This is still a small dataset when compared to what is now possible with the Web; when you perform millions of transactions, you can expect to generate many thousands, even millions, of rules.

However, for each customer, only a few of them will be relevant at any given time, and so each costumer only receives a small number of recommendations.

More advanced basket analysis

There are now other algorithms for basket analysis that run faster than Apriori. The code we saw earlier was simple, and was good enough for us as we only had circa 100 thousand transactions. If you have had many millions, it might be worthwhile to use a faster algorithm (although note that for most applications, learning association rules can be run offline).

There are also methods to work with temporal information leading to rules that take into account the order in which you have made your purchases. To take an extreme example of why this may be useful, consider that someone buying supplies for a large party may come back for trash bags. Therefore it may make sense to propose trash bags on the first visit. However, it would not make sense to propose party supplies to everyone who buys a trash bag.

You can find Python open source implementations (a new BSD license as scikit-learn) of some of these in a package called **pymining**. This package was developed by *Barthelemy Dagenais* and is available at https://github.com/bartdag/pymining.

Summary

In this chapter, we started by improving our rating predictions from the previous chapter. We saw a couple of different ways in which to do so and then combined them all in a single prediction by learning how to use a set of weights. These techniques, ensemble or stacked learning, are general techniques that can be used in many situations and not just for regression. They allow you to combine different ideas even if their internal mechanics are completely different; you can combine their final outputs.

In the second half of the chapter, we switched gears and looked at another method of recommendation: shopping basket analysis or association rule mining. In this mode, we try to discover (probabilistic) association rules of the *customers who bought X are likely to be interested in Y* form. This takes advantage of the data that is generated from sales alone without requiring users to numerically rate items. This is not available in scikit-learn (yet), so we wrote our own code (for a change).

Association rule mining needs to be careful to not simply recommend bestsellers to every user (otherwise, what is the point of personalization?). In order to do this, we learned about measuring the value of rules in relation to the baseline as the lift of a rule. In the next chapter, we will build a music genre classifier.

Classification III – Music Genre Classification

So far, we have had the luxury that every training data instance could easily be described by a vector of feature values. In the Iris dataset, for example, the flowers are represented by vectors containing values for the length and width of certain aspects of a flower. In the text-based examples, we could transform the text into a bag-of-words representation and manually craft our own features that captured certain aspects of the texts.

It will be different in this chapter, however, when we try to classify songs by their genre. Or how would we, for instance, represent a three-minute long song? Should we take the individual bits of its MP3 representation? Probably not, since treating it like text and creating something such as a "bag of sound bites" would certainly be way too complex. Somehow, we will nevertheless have to convert a song into a number of values that describes it sufficiently.

Sketching our roadmap

This chapter will show us how we can come up with a decent classifier in a domain that is outside our comfort zone. For one, we will have to use sound-based features, which are much more complex than the text-based ones that we have used before. And then we will have to learn how to deal with multiple classes, whereas we have only encountered binary-classification problems up to now. In addition, we will get to know new ways of measuring classification performance.

Let us assume a scenario where we find a bunch of randomly named MP3 files on our hard disk, which are assumed to contain music. Our task is to sort them according to the music genre into different folders such as `jazz`, `classical`, `country`, `pop`, `rock`, and `metal`.

Fetching the music data

We will use the GTZAN dataset, which is frequently used to benchmark music genre classification tasks. It is organized into 10 distinct genres, of which we will use only six for the sake of simplicity: classical, jazz, country, pop, rock, and metal. The dataset contains the first 30 seconds of 100 songs per genre. We can download the dataset at `http://opihi.cs.uvic.ca/sound/genres.tar.gz`. The tracks are recorded at 22,050 Hz (22,050 readings per second) mono in the WAV format.

Converting into a wave format

Sure enough, if we would want to test our classifier later on our private MP3 collection, we would not be able to extract much meaning. This is because MP3 is a lossy music compression format that cuts out parts that the human ear cannot perceive. This is nice for storing because with MP3, you can fit ten times as many songs on your device. For our endeavor, however, it is not so nice. For classification, we will have an easier time with WAV files, so we will have to convert our MP3 files in case we would want to use them with our classifier.

> In case you don't have a conversion tool nearby, you might want to check out sox: `http://sox.sourceforge.net`. It claims to be the Swiss Army Knife of sound processing, and we agree with this bold claim.

One advantage of having all our music files in the WAV format is that it is directly readable by the SciPy toolkit:

```
>>> sample_rate, X = scipy.io.wavfile.read(wave_filename)
```

Here, X contains the samples and `sample_rate` is the rate at which they were taken. Let us use this information to peek into some music files to get a first impression of what the data looks like.

Looking at music

A very convenient way to get a quick impression of how the songs of the diverse genres "look" like is to draw a spectrogram for a set of songs of a genre. A spectrogram is a visual representation of the frequencies that occur in a song. It shows the intensity of the frequencies on the y axis in the specified time intervals on the x axis; that is, the darker the color, the stronger the frequency is in the particular time window of the song.

Matplotlib provides the convenient function `specgram()` that performs most of the under-the-hood calculation and plotting for us:

```
>>> import scipy
>>> from matplotlib.pyplot import specgram
>>> sample_rate, X = scipy.io.wavfile.read(wave_filename)
>>> print sample_rate, X.shape
22050, (661794,)
>>> specgram(X, Fs=sample_rate, xextent=(0,30))
```

The wave file we just read was sampled at a sample rate of 22,050 Hz and contains 661,794 samples.

If we now plot the spectrogram for these first 30 seconds of diverse wave files, we can see that there are commonalities between songs of the same genre:

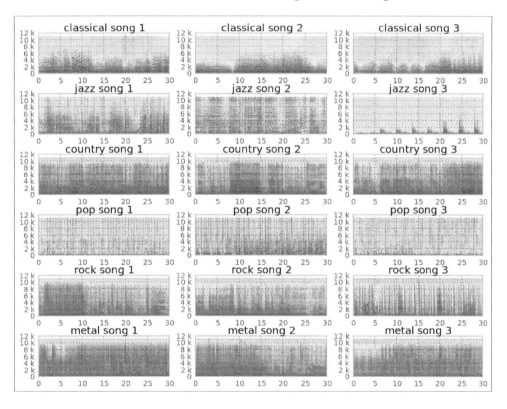

Just glancing at it, we immediately see the difference in the spectrum between, for example, metal and classical songs. While metal songs have high intensity over most of the frequency spectrum all the time (energize!), classical songs show a more diverse pattern over time.

It should be possible to train a classifier that discriminates at least between metal and classical songs with an accuracy that is high enough. Other genre pairs such as country and rock could pose a bigger challenge, though. This looks like a real challenge to us, as we need to discriminate not just between two classes, but between six. We need to be able to discriminate between all six reasonably well.

Decomposing music into sine wave components

Our plan is to extract individual frequency intensities from the raw sample readings (stored in x earlier) and feed them into a classifier. These frequency intensities can be extracted by applying the **Fast Fourier Transform** (**FFT**). As the theory behind FFT is outside the scope of this chapter, let us just look at an example to get an intuition of what it accomplishes. Later on, we will then treat it as a black box feature extractor.

For example, let us generate two wave files, sine_a.wav and sine_b.wav, which contain the sound of 400 Hz and 3,000 Hz sine waves. The Swiss Army Knife, sox, mentioned earlier is one way to achieve this:

```
$ sox --null -r 22050 sine_a.wav synth 0.2 sine 400
$ sox --null -r 22050 sine_b.wav synth 0.2 sine 3000
```

The charts in the following screenshot show the plotting of the first 0.008 seconds. We can also see the FFT of the sine waves. Not surprisingly, we see a spike at 400 and 3,000 Hz below the corresponding sine waves.

Now let us mix them both, giving the 400 Hz sound half the volume of the 3,000 Hz one:

```
$ sox --combine mix --volume 1 sine_b.wav --volume 0.5 sine_a.wav
sine_mix.wav
```

We see two spikes in the FFT plot of the combined sound, of which the 3,000 Hz spike is almost double the size of the 400 Hz one:

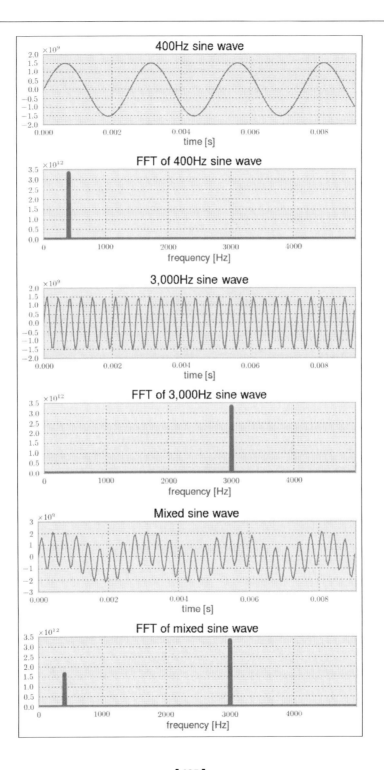

For real music, we can quickly see that the FFT looks not as beautiful as in the preceding toy example:

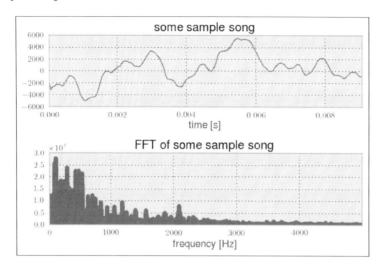

Using FFT to build our first classifier

Nevertheless, we can now create some kind of musical fingerprint of a song using FFT. If we do this for a couple of songs, and manually assign their corresponding genres as labels, we have the training data that we can feed into our first classifier.

Increasing experimentation agility

Before we dive into the classifier training, let us first spend some time on experimentation agility. Although we have the word "fast" in FFT, it is much slower than the creation of the features in our text-based chapters, and because we are still in the experimentation phase, we might want to think about how we could speed up the whole feature-creation process.

Of course, the creation of the FFT for each file will be the same each time we run the classifier. We could therefore cache it and read the cached FFT representation instead of the wave file. We do this with the `create_fft()` function, which in turn uses `scipy.fft()` to create the FFT. For the sake of simplicity (and speed!), let us fix the number of FFT components to the first 1,000 in this example. With our current knowledge, we do not know whether these are the most important ones with regard to music genre classification—only that they show the highest intensities in the earlier FFT example. If we would later want to use more or less FFT components, we would of course have to recreate the cached FFT files.

```
def create_fft(fn):
    sample_rate, X = scipy.io.wavfile.read(fn)
    fft_features = abs(scipy.fft(X)[:1000])
    base_fn, ext = os.path.splitext(fn)
    data_fn = base_fn + ".fft"
    np.save(data_fn, fft_features)
```

We save the data using NumPy's `save()` function, which always appends `.npy` to the filename. We only have to do this once for every wave file needed for training or predicting.

The corresponding FFT reading function is `read_fft()`:

```
def read_fft(genre_list, base_dir=GENRE_DIR):
    X = []
    y = []
    for label, genre in enumerate(genre_list):
        genre_dir = os.path.join(base_dir, genre, "*.fft.npy")
        file_list = glob.glob(genre_dir)
        for fn in file_list:
            fft_features = np.load(fn)

            X.append(fft_features[:1000])
            y.append(label)

    return np.array(X), np.array(y)
```

In our scrambled music directory, we expect the following music genres:

```
genre_list = ["classical", "jazz", "country", "pop", "rock", "metal"]
```

Training the classifier

Let us use the logistic regression classifier, which has already served us well in the chapter on sentiment analysis. The added difficulty is that we are now faced with a multiclass classification problem, whereas up to now we have had to discriminate only between two classes.

One aspect that which is surprising the first time one switches from binary to multiclass classification is the evaluation of accuracy rates. In binary classification problems, we have learned that an accuracy of 50 percent is the worst case as it could have been achieved by mere random guessing. In multiclass settings, 50 percent can already be very good. With our six genres, for instance, random guessing would result in only 16.7 percent (equal class sizes assumed).

Using the confusion matrix to measure accuracy in multiclass problems

With multiclass problems, we should also not limit our interest to how well we manage to correctly classify the genres. In addition, we should also look at which genres we actually confuse with each other. This can be done with the so-called confusion matrix:

```
>>> from sklearn.metrics import confusion_matrix
>>> cm = confusion_matrix(y_test, y_pred)
>>> print(cm)
[[26  1  2  0  0  2]
 [ 4  7  5  0  5  3]
 [ 1  2 14  2  8  3]
 [ 5  4  7  3  7  5]
 [ 0  0 10  2 10 12]
 [ 1  0  4  0 13 12]]
```

It prints the distribution of labels that the classifier predicted for the test set for every genre. Since we have six genres, we have a six by six matrix. The first row in the matrix says that for 31 classical songs (sum of the first row), it predicted 26 to belong to the genre classical, one to be a jazz song, two to belong to the country genre, and two to be metal. The diagonal shows the correct classifications. In the first row, we see that out of 31 songs (*26 + 1 + 2 + 2 = 31*), 26 have been correctly classified as classical and 5 were misclassifications. This is actually not that bad. The second row is more sobering: only 4 out of 24 jazz songs have been correctly classified—that is only 16 percent.

Of course, we follow the train/test split setup from the previous chapters, so that we actually have to record the confusion matrices per cross-validation fold. We also have to average and normalize later on so that we have a range between 0 (total failure) to 1 (everything classified correctly).

A graphical visualization is often much easier to read than NumPy arrays. Matplotlib's matshow() is our friend:

```
from matplotlib import pylab

def plot_confusion_matrix(cm, genre_list, name, title):
    pylab.clf()
    pylab.matshow(cm, fignum=False, cmap='Blues', vmin=0, vmax=1.0)
    ax = pylab.axes()
    ax.set_xticks(range(len(genre_list)))
    ax.set_xticklabels(genre_list)
    ax.xaxis.set_ticks_position("bottom")
```

```
ax.set_yticks(range(len(genre_list)))
ax.set_yticklabels(genre_list)
pylab.title(title)
pylab.colorbar()
pylab.grid(False)
pylab.xlabel('Predicted class')
pylab.ylabel('True class')
pylab.grid(False)
pylab.show()
```

When you create a confusion matrix, be sure to choose a color map (the cmap parameter of matshow()) with an appropriate color ordering, so that it is immediately visible what a lighter or darker color means. Especially discouraged for these kind of graphs are rainbow color maps, such as Matplotlib's default "jet" or even the "Paired" color map.

The final graph looks like the following screenshot:

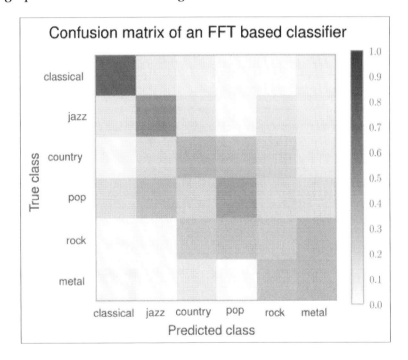

For a perfect classifier, we would have expected a diagonal of dark squares from the left-upper corner to the right-lower one, and light colors for the remaining area. In the graph, we immediately see that our FFT-based classifier is far away from being perfect. It only predicts **classical** songs correctly (dark square). For **rock**, for instance, it prefers the label **metal** most of the time.

Obviously, using FFT points to the right direction (the **classical** genre was not that bad), but it is not enough to get a decent classifier. Surely, we can play with the number of FFT components (fixed to 1,000). But before we dive into parameter tuning, we should do our research. There we find that FFT is indeed not a bad feature for genre classification—it is just not refined enough. Shortly, we will see how we can boost our classification performance by using a processed version of it.

Before we do that, however, we will learn another method of measuring classification performance.

An alternate way to measure classifier performance using receiver operator characteristic (ROC)

We have already learned that measuring accuracy is not enough to truly evaluate a classifier. Instead, we relied on precision-recall curves to get a deeper understanding of how our classifiers perform.

There is a sister of precision-recall curves, called **receiver operator characteristic (ROC)** that measures similar aspects of the classifier's performance, but provides another view on the classification performance. The key difference is that P/R curves are more suitable for tasks where the positive class is much more interesting than the negative one, or where the number of positive examples is much less than the number of negative ones. Information retrieval or fraud detection are typical application areas. On the other hand, ROC curves provide a better picture on how well the classifier behaves in general.

To better understand the differences, let us consider the performance of the trained classifier described earlier in classifying country songs correctly:

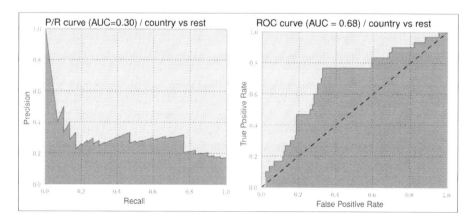

On the left-hand side graph, we see the **P/R curve**. For an ideal classifier, we would have the curve going from the top-left corner directly to the top-right corner and then to the bottom-right corner, resulting in an **area under curve** (**AUC**) of 1.0.

The right-hand side graph depicts the corresponding ROC curve. It plots the true positive rate over the false positive rate. Here, an ideal classifier would have a curve going from the lower-left to top-left corner and then to the top-right corner. A random classifier would be a straight line from the lower-left to upper-right corner, as shown by the dashed line having an AUC of 0.5. Therefore, we cannot compare the AUC of a P/R curve with that of an ROC curve.

When comparing two different classifiers on the same dataset, we are always safe to assume that a higher AUC of a P/R curve for one classifier also means a higher AUC of the corresponding ROC curve and vice versa. Therefore, we never bother to generate both. More on this can be found in the very insightful paper *The Relationship Between Precision-Recall and ROC Curves, Jesse Davis* and *Mark Goadrich, ICML 2006*.

The definitions of both the curves' x and y axes are given in the following table:

	x axis	y axis
P/R	$\text{Recall} = \frac{TP}{TP+FN}$	$\text{Precision} = \frac{TP}{TP+FP}$
ROC	$\text{FPR} = \frac{FP}{FP+TN}$	$\text{TPR} = \frac{TP}{TP+FN}$

Looking at the definitions of both curves' x axes and y axes, we see that the true positive rate in the ROC curve's y axis is the same as `Recall` of the P/R graph's x axis.

The false positive rate measures the fraction of true negative examples that were falsely identified as positive ones, giving a 0 in a perfect case (no false positives) and 1 otherwise. Contrast this to the `Precision` curve, where we track exactly the opposite, namely the fraction of true positive examples that we correctly classified as such.

Going forward, let us use ROC curves to measure our classifier's performance to get a better feeling for it. The only challenge for our multiclass problem is that both ROC and P/R curves assume a binary classification problem. For our purpose, let us therefore create one chart per genre that shows how the classifier performed a "one versus rest" classification:

```
y_pred = clf.predict(X_test)

for label in labels:
```

```
y_label_test = np.asarray(y_test==label, dtype=int)
proba = clf.predict_proba(X_test)
proba_label = proba[:,label]
fpr, tpr, roc_thresholds = roc_curve(y_label_test, proba_
label)
# plot tpr over fpr
# ...
```

The outcome will be the six ROC plots shown in the following screenshot. As we have already found out, our first version of a classifier only performs well on classical songs. Looking at the individual ROC curves, however, tells us that we are really underperforming for most of the other genres. Only jazz and country provide some hope. The remaining genres are clearly not usable:

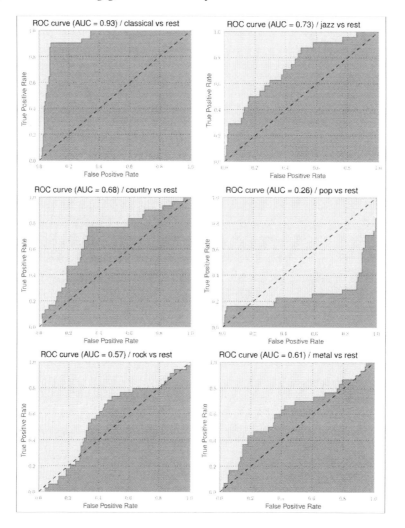

Improving classification performance with Mel Frequency Cepstral Coefficients

We have already learned that FFT is pointing us in the right direction, but in itself it will not be enough to finally arrive at a classifier that successfully manages to organize our scrambled directory containing songs of diverse music genres into individual genre directories. We somehow need a more advanced version of it.

At this point, it is always wise to acknowledge that we have to do more research. Other people might have had similar challenges in the past and already found out new ways that might also help us. And indeed, there is even a yearly conference only dedicated to music genre classification organized by the **International Society for Music Information Retrieval (ISMIR)**. Apparently, **Automatic Music Genre Classification (AMGC)** is an established subfield of **Music Information Retrieval (MIR)**. Glancing over some of the AMGC papers, we see that there is a bunch of work targeting automatic genre classification that might help us.

One technique that seems to be successfully applied in many of those works is called **Mel Frequency Cepstral Coefficients (MFCC)**. The **Mel Frequency Cepstrum (MFC)** encodes the power spectrum of a sound. It is calculated as the Fourier transform of the logarithm of the signal's spectrum. If that sounds too complicated, simply remember that the name "cepstrum" originates from "spectrum", with the first four characters reversed. MFC has been successfully used in speech and speaker recognition. Let's see whether it also works in our case.

We are in a lucky situation where someone else has already needed exactly what we need and published an implementation of it as the Talkbox SciKit. We can install it from `https://pypi.python.org/pypi/scikits.talkbox`. Afterwards, we can call the `mfcc()` function, which calculates the MFC coefficients as follows:

```
>>>from scikits.talkbox.features import mfcc
>>>sample_rate, X = scipy.io.wavfile.read(fn)
>>>ceps, mspec, spec = mfcc(X)
>>> print(ceps.shape)
(4135, 13)
```

The data we would want to feed into our classifier is stored in `ceps`, which contains `13` coefficients (the default value for the `nceps` parameter of the `mfcc()` function) for each of the `4135` frames for the song with the filename `fn`. Taking all of the data would overwhelm our classifier. What we could do instead is to do an averaging per coefficient over all the frames. Assuming that the start and end of each song are possibly less genre-specific than the middle part of it, we also ignore the first and last 10 percent:

```
x = np.mean(ceps[int(num_ceps*1/10):int(num_ceps*9/10)], axis=0)
```

Sure enough, the benchmark dataset that we will be using contains only the first 30 seconds of each song, so that we would not need to cut off the last 10 percent. We do it nevertheless, so that our code works on other datasets as well, which are most likely not truncated.

Similar to our work with FFT, we certainly would also want to cache the once-generated MFCC features and read them instead of recreating them each time we train our classifier.

This leads to the following code:

```
def write_ceps(ceps, fn):
    base_fn, ext = os.path.splitext(fn)
    data_fn = base_fn + ".ceps"
    np.save(data_fn, ceps)
    print("Written %s" % data_fn)

def create_ceps(fn):
    sample_rate, X = scipy.io.wavfile.read(fn)
    ceps, mspec, spec = mfcc(X)
    write_ceps(ceps, fn)

def read_ceps(genre_list, base_dir=GENRE_DIR):
    X, Y = [], []
    for label, genre in enumerate(genre_list):
        for fn in glob.glob(os.path.join(
base_dir, genre, "*.ceps.npy")):
            ceps = np.load(fn)
            num_ceps = len(ceps)
X.append(np.mean(
ceps[int(num_ceps*1/10):int(num_ceps*9/10)], axis=0))
y.append(label)

    return np.array(X), np.array(y)
```

We get the following promising results, as shown in the next screenshot, with a classifier that uses only 13 features per song:

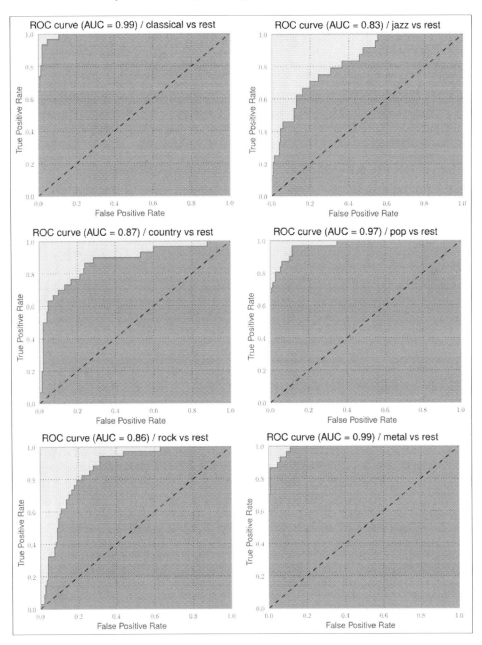

The classification performance for all genres has improved. Jazz and metal are even at almost 1.0 AUC. And indeed, the confusion matrix in the following plot also looks much better now. We can clearly see the diagonal showing that the classifier manages to classify the genres correctly in most of the cases. This classifier is actually quite usable to solve our initial task:

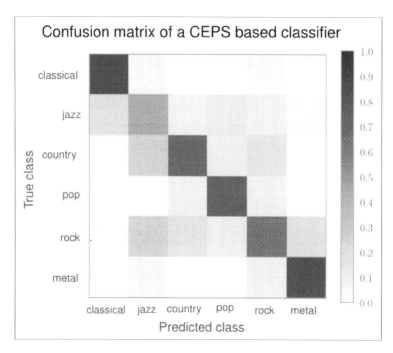

If we would want to improve on this, this confusion matrix quickly tells us where to focus on: the non-white spots on the non-diagonal places. For instance, we have a darker spot where we mislabel `jazz` songs as being `rock` with considerable probability. To fix this, we would probably need to dive deeper into the songs and extract things, for instance, drum patterns and similar genre-specific characteristics. Also, while glancing over the ISMIR papers, you may have also read about so-called **Auditory Filterbank Temporal Envelope (AFTE)** features, which seem to outperform the MFCC features in certain situations. Maybe we should have a look at them as well?

The nice thing is that being equipped with only ROC curves and confusion matrices, we are free to pull in other experts' knowledge in terms of feature extractors, without requiring ourselves to fully understand their inner workings. Our measurement tools will always tell us when the direction is right and when to change it. Of course, being a machine learner who is eager to learn, we will always have the dim feeling that there is an exciting algorithm buried somewhere in a black box of our feature extractors, which is just waiting for us to be understood.

Summary

In this chapter, we stepped out of our comfort zone when we built a music genre classifier. Not having a deep understanding of music theory, at first we failed to train a classifier that predicts the music genre of songs with reasonable accuracy using FFT. But then we created a classifier that showed really usable performance using MFC features.

In both cases, we used features that we understood only so much as to know how and where to put them into our classifier setup. The one failed, the other succeeded. The difference between them is that in the second case, we relied on features that were created by experts in the field.

And that is totally OK. If we are mainly interested in the result, we sometimes simply have to take shortcuts—we only have to make sure to take these shortcuts from experts in the specific domains. And because we had learned how to correctly measure the performance in this new multiclass classification problem, we took these shortcuts with confidence.

In the next chapter, we will look at how to apply techniques you have learned in the rest of the book to this specific type of data. We will learn how to use the mahotas computer vision package to preprocess images using traditional image processing functions.

10

Computer Vision – Pattern Recognition

Image analysis and computer vision has always been important in industrial applications. With the popularization of cell phones with powerful cameras and Internet connections, they are also increasingly being generated by the users. Therefore, there are opportunities to make use of this to provide a better user experience.

In this chapter, we will look at how to apply techniques you have learned in the rest of the book to this specific type of data. In particular, we will learn how to use the **mahotas computer vision** package to preprocess images using traditional image-processing functions. These can be used for preprocessing, noise removal, cleanup, contrast stretching, and many other simple tasks.

We will also look at how to extract features from images. These can be used as input to the same classification methods we have learned about in other chapters. We will apply these techniques to publicly available datasets of photographs.

Introducing image processing

From the point of view of the computer, an image is a large rectangular array of pixel values. We wish to either process this image to generate a new or better image (perhaps with less noise, or with a different look). This is typically the area of image processing. We may also want to go from this array to a decision that is relevant to our application, which is better known as computer vision. Not everybody agrees with this distinction of the two fields, but its description is almost exactly how the terms are typically used.

The first step will be to load the image from the disk, where it is typically stored in an image-specific format such as PNG or JPEG, the former being a lossless compression format and the latter a lossy compression one that is optimized for subjective appreciation of photographs. Then, we may wish to perform preprocessing on the images (for example, normalizing them for illumination variations).

We will have a classification problem as a driver for this chapter. We want to be able to learn a support vector machine (or other) classifier that can learn from images. Therefore, we will use an intermediate representation for extracting numeric features from the images before applying machine learning.

Finally, at the end of the chapter, we will learn about using local features. These are relatively new methods (**SIFT** (**Scale-invariant feature transform**), the first element in this new family, was introduced in 1999) and achieve very good results in many tasks.

Loading and displaying images

In order to manipulate images, we will use a package called mahotas. This is an open source package (MIT license, so it can be used in any project) that was developed by one of the authors of the book you are reading. Fortunately, it is based on **NumPy**. The NumPy knowledge you have acquired so far can be used for image processing. There are other image packages such as **scikit-image (Skimage)**, the **ndimage** (n-dimensional image) module in **SciPy**, and the **Python** bindings for OpenCV. All of these work natively with NumPy, so you can even mix and match functionalities from different packages to get your result.

We start by importing mahotas with the mh abbreviation, which we will use throughout this chapter:

```
import mahotas as mh
```

Now we can load an image file using imread:

```
image = mh.imread('imagefile.png')
```

If imagefile.png contains a color image of height h and width w, then image will be an array of shape (h, w, 3). The first dimension is the height, the second the width, and the third is red/green/blue. Other systems put the width on the first dimension, but this is the mathematical convention and is used by all NumPy-based packages. The type of array will typically be np.uint8 (an unsigned integer of 8 bits). These are the images that your camera takes or that your monitor can fully display.

However, some specialized equipment (mostly in scientific fields) can take images with more bit resolution. 12 or 16 bits are common. Mahotas can deal with all these types, including `floating point` images (not all operations make sense with `floating point` numbers, but when they do, mahotas supports them). In many computations, even if the original data is composed of `unsigned` integers, it is advantageous to convert to `floating point` numbers in order to simplify handling of rounding and overflow issues.

 Mahotas can use a variety of different input/output backends. Unfortunately, none of them can load all existing image formats (there are hundreds, with several variations of each). However, loading PNG and JPEG images is supported by all of them. We will focus on these common formats and refer you to the mahotas documentation on how to read uncommon formats.

The return value of `mh.imread` is a NumPy array. This means that you can use standard NumPy functionalities to work with images. For example, it is often useful to subtract the mean value of the image from it. This can help to normalize images taken under different lighting conditions and can be accomplished with the standard `mean` method:

```
image = image - image.mean()
```

We can display the image on screen using `maplotlib`, the plotting library we have already used several times:

```
from matplotlib import pyplot as plt
plt.imshow(image)
plt.show()
```

This shows the image using the convention that the first dimension is the height and the second the width. It correctly handles color images as well. When using Python for numerical computation, we benefit from the whole ecosystem working well together.

Basic image processing

We will start with a small dataset that was collected especially for this book. It has three classes: buildings, natural scenes (landscapes), and pictures of texts. There are 30 images in each category, and they were all taken using a cell phone camera with minimal composition, so the images are similar to those that would be uploaded to a modern website. This dataset is available from the book's website. Later in the chapter, we will look at a harder dataset with more images and more categories.

This screenshot of a building is one of the images in the dataset. We will use this screenshot as an example.

As you may be aware, image processing is a large field. Here we will only be looking at some very basic operations we can perform on our images. Some of the most basic operations can be performed using NumPy only, but otherwise we will use mahotas.

Thresholding

Thresholding is a very simple operation: we transform all pixel values above a certain threshold to 1 and all those below to 0 (or by using Booleans, transform it to `True` and `False`):

```
binarized = (image > threshold_value)
```

The value of the threshold width (`threshold_value` in the code) needs to be chosen. If the images are all very similar, we can pick one statically and use it for all images. Otherwise, we must compute a different threshold for each image based on its pixel values.

Mahotas implements a few methods for choosing a threshold value. One is called **Otsu**, after its inventor. The first necessary step is to convert the image to grayscale with `rgb2gray`.

Instead of `rgb2gray`, we can also have just the mean value of the red, green, and blue channels by calling `image.mean(2)`. The result, however, will not be the same because `rgb2gray` uses different weights for the different colors to give a subjectively more pleasing result. Our eyes are not equally sensitive to the three basic colors.

```
image = mh.colors.rgb2gray(image, dtype=np.uint8)
plt.imshow(image) # Display the image
```

By default, `matplotlib` will display this single-channel image as a false color image, using red for high values and blue for low. For natural images, grayscale is more appropriate. You can select it with the following:

```
plt.gray()
```

Now the screenshot is shown in grayscale. Note that only the way in which the pixel values are interpreted and shown has changed and the screenshot is untouched. We can continue our processing by computing the threshold value.

```
thresh = mh.thresholding.otsu(image)
print(thresh)
imshow(image > thresh)
```

When applied to the previous screenshot, this method finds the `threshold 164` value, which separates the building and parked cars from the sky above.

The result may be useful on its own (if you are measuring some properties of the thresholded image) or it can be useful for further processing. The result is a binary image that can be used to select a region of interest.

The result is still not very good. We can use operations on this screenshot to further refine it. For example, we can run the `close` operator to get rid of some of the noise in the upper corners.

```
otsubin =   (image <= thresh)
otsubin =   mh.close(otsubin, np.ones((15,15)))
```

In this case, we are closing the region that is below the threshold, so we reversed the threshold operator. We could, alternatively, have performed an `open` operation on the negative of the image.

```
otsubin =   (image > thresh)
otsubin =   mh.open(otsubin, np.ones((15,15)))
```

In either case, the operator takes a structuring element that defines the type of region we want to close. In our case, we used a 15x15 square.

This is still not perfect as there are a few bright objects in the parking lot that are not picked up. We will improve it a bit later in the chapter.

The Otsu threshold was able to identify the region of the sky as brighter than the building. An alternative thresholding method is the **Ridley-Calvard** method (also named after its inventors):

```
thresh = mh.thresholding.rc(image)
print(thresh)
```

This method returns a smaller threshold, 137.7, and tells apart the building details.

Whether this is better or worse depends on what you are trying to distinguish.

Gaussian blurring

Blurring your image may seem odd, but it often serves to reduce noise, which helps with further processing. With mahotas, it is just a function call:

```
image = mh.colors.rgb2gray(image)
im8 = mh.gaussian_filter(image,8)
```

Notice how we did not convert the gray screenshot to `unsigned` integers; we just made use of the `floating point` result as it is. The second argument to the `gaussian_filter` function is the size of the filter (the standard deviation of the filter). Larger values result in more blurring, as can be seen in the following screenshot (shown are filtering with sizes `8`, `16`, and `32`):

We can use the screenshot on the left and threshold it with Otsu (using the same code seen previously). Now the result is a perfect separation of the building region and the sky. While some of the details have been smoothed over, the bright regions in the parking lot have also been smoothed over. The result is an approximate outline of the sky without any artifacts. By blurring, we got rid of the detail that didn't matter to the broad picture. Have a look at the following screenshot:

Filtering for different effects

The use of image processing to achieve pleasing effects in images dates back to the beginning of digital images, but it has recently been the basis of a number of interesting applications, the most well-known of which is probably Instagram.

We are going to use a traditional image in image processing, the screenshot of the Lenna image, which is shown and can be downloaded from the book's website (or many other image-processing websites):

```
im = mh.imread('lenna.jpg', as_grey=True)
```

Adding salt and pepper noise

We can perform many further manipulations on this result if we want to. For example, we will now add a bit of salt and pepper noise to the image to simulate a few scanning artifacts. We generate random arrays of the same width and height as the original image. Only 1 percent of these values will be true.

```
salt = np.random.random(lenna.shape) > .975
pepper = np.random.random(lenna.shape) > .975
```

We now add the salt (which means some values will be almost white) and pepper noise (which means some values will be almost black):

```
lenna = mh.stretch(lenna)
lenna = np.maximum(salt*170, sep)
lenna = np.minimum(pepper*30 + lenna*(~pepper), lenna)
```

We used the values 170 and 30 as white and black. This is slightly smoother than the more extreme choices of 255 and 0. However, all of these are choices that need to be made by subjective preferences and style.

Putting the center in focus

The final example shows how to mix NumPy operators with a tiny bit of filtering to get an interesting result. We start with the Lenna image and split it into the color channels:

```
im = mh.imread('lenna.jpg')
r,g,b = im.transpose(2,0,1)
```

Now we filter the 3 channels separately and build a composite image out of it with `mh.as_rgb`. This function takes 3 two-dimensional arrays, performs contrast stretching to make each an 8-bit integer array, and then stacks them:

```
r12 = mh.gaussian_filter(r, 12.)
g12 = mh.gaussian_filter(g, 12.)
b12 = mh.gaussian_filter(b, 12.)
im12 = mh.as_rgb(

r12,g12,b12)
```

We then blend the two images from the center away to the edges. First we need to build a weights array, w, that will contain at each pixel a normalized value, which is its distance to the center:

```
h,w = r.shape # height and width
Y,X = np.mgrid[:h,:w]
```

We used the `np.mgrid` object, which returns arrays of size (h, w) with values corresponding to the y and x coordinates respectively:

```
Y = Y-h/2. # center at h/2
Y = Y / Y.max() # normalize to -1 .. +1
X = X-w/2.
X = X / X.max()
```

We now use a `gaussian` function to give the center region a high value:

```
W = np.exp(-2.*(X**2+ Y**2))
# Normalize again to 0..1
W = W - C.min()
W = W / C.ptp()
W = C[:,:,None] # This adds a dummy third dimension to W
```

Notice how all of these manipulations are performed using NumPy arrays and not some mahotas-specific methodology. This is one advantage of the Python NumPy ecosystem: the operations you learned to perform when you were learning about pure machine learning now become useful in a completely different context.

Finally, we can combine the two images to have the center in sharp focus and the edges softer.

```
ringed = mh.stretch(im*C + (1-C)*im12)
```

Now that you know some of the basic techniques of filtering images, you can build upon this to generate new filters. It is more of an art than a science after this point.

Pattern recognition

When classifying images, we start with a large rectangular array of numbers (pixel values). Nowadays, millions of pixels are common.

We could try to feed all these numbers as features into the learning algorithm. This is not a very good idea. This is because the relationship of each pixel (or even each small group of pixels) to the final result is very indirect. Instead, a traditional approach is to compute features from the image and use those features for classification.

There are a few methods that do work directly from the pixel values. They have feature computation submodules inside them. They may even attempt to learn what good features are automatically. These are the topics of current research.

We previously used an example of the buildings class. Here are examples of the text and scene classes:

Pattern recognition is just classification of images

For historical reasons, the classification of images has been called **pattern recognition**. However, this is nothing more than the application of classification methods to images. Naturally, images have their own specific issues, which is what we will be dealing with in this chapter.

Computing features from images

With mahotas, it is very easy to compute features from images. There is a submodule named `mahotas.features` where feature computation functions are available.

A commonly used set of features are the **Haralick texture** features. As with many methods in image processing, this method was named after its inventor. These features are texture-based: they distinguish between images that are smooth and those that are patterned and have between different patterns. With mahotas, it is very easy to compute them:

```
haralick_features = np.mean(mh.features.haralick(image),0)
```

The function `mh.features.haralick` returns a 4x13 array. The first dimension refers to four possible directions in which to compute the features (up, down, left, and right). If we are not interested in the direction, we can use the mean overall directions. Based on this function, it is very easy to classify a system.

There are a few other feature sets implemented in mahotas. **Linear binary patterns** is another texture-based feature set that is very robust against illumination changes. There are other types of features, including local features, that we will discuss later in this chapter.

Features are not just for classification

The feature-based approach of reducing a million pixel image can also be applied in other machine learning contexts, such as clustering, regression, or dimensionality reduction. By computing a few hundred features and then running a dimensionality reduction algorithm on the result, you will be able to go from an object with a million pixel values to a few dimensions, even to two-dimensions as you build a visualization tool.

With these features, we use a standard classification method such as support vector machines:

```
images = glob('simple-dataset/*.jpg')
features = []
labels = []
for im in images:
  features.append(mh.features.haralick(im).mean(0))
  labels.append(im[:-len('00.jpg')])
features = np.array(features)
labels = np.array(labels)
```

The three classes have very different textures. Buildings have sharp edges and big blocks where the color is similar (the pixel values are rarely exactly the same, but the variation is slight). Text is made of many sharp dark-light transitions, with small black areas in a sea of white. Natural scenes have smoother variations with fractal-like transitions. Therefore, a classifier based on texture is expected to do well. Since our dataset is small, we only get 79 percent accuracy using logistic regression.

Writing your own features

A feature is nothing magical. It is simply a number that we computed from an image. There are several feature sets already defined in the literature. These often have the added advantage that they have been designed and studied to be invariant to many unimportant factors. For example, linear binary patterns are completely invariant to multiplying all pixel values by a number or adding a constant to all these values. This makes it robust against illumination changes of images.

However, it is also possible that your particular use case would benefit from a few specially designed features. For example, we may think that in order to distinguish text from natural images, it is an important defining feature of text that it is "edgy." We do not mean what the text says (that may be edgy or square), but rather that images of text have many edges. Therefore, we may want to introduce an "edginess feature". There are a few ways in which to do so (infinitely many). One of the advantages of machine learning systems is that we can just write up a few of these ideas and let the system figure out which ones are good and which ones are not.

We start with introducing another traditional image-processing operation: edge finding. In this case, we will use **sobel filtering**. Mathematically, we filter (convolve) our image with two matrices; the vertical one is shown in the following screenshot:

$$\begin{pmatrix} 1 & 0 & 1 \\ -2 & 0 & -2 \\ 1 & 0 & 1 \end{pmatrix}$$

And the horizontal one is shown here:

$$\begin{pmatrix} 1 & -2 & 1 \\ 0 & 0 & 0 \\ 1 & -2 & 1 \end{pmatrix}$$

We then sum up the squared result for an overall measure of edginess at each point (in other uses, you may want to distinguish horizontal from vertical edges and use these in another way; as always, this depends on the underlying application). Mahotas supports sobel filtering as follows:

```
filtered = mh.sobel(image, just_filter=True)
```

The `just_filter=True` argument is necessary, otherwise thresholding is performed and you get an estimate of where the edges are. The following screenshot shows the result of applying the filter (so that lighter areas are edgier) on the left and the result of thresholding on the right:

Based on this operator, we may want to define a global feature as the overall edginess of the result:

```
def edginess_sobel(image):
    edges = mh.sobel(image, just_filter=True)
    edges = edges.ravel()
    return np.sqrt(np.dot(edges, edges))
```

In the last line, we used a trick to compute the root mean square—using the inner product function `np.dot` is equivalent to writing `np.sum(edges ** 2)`, but much faster (we just need to make sure we unraveled the array first). Naturally, we could have thought up many different ways to achieve similar results. Using the thresholding operation and counting the fraction of pixels above threshold would be another obvious example.

We can add this feature to the previous pipeline very easily:

```
features = []
for im in images:
    image = mh.imread(im)
    features.append(np.concatenate(
            mh.features.haralick(im).mean(0),
              # Build a 1-element list with our feature to match
expectations
            # of np.concatenate
            [edginess_sobel(im)],
        ))
```

Feature sets may be combined easily using this structure. By using all of these features, we get 84 percent accuracy.

This is a perfect illustration of the principle that good algorithms are the easy part. You can always use an implementation of a state-of-the-art classification. The real secret and added value often comes in feature design and engineering. This is where knowledge of your dataset is valuable.

Classifying a harder dataset

The previous dataset was an easy dataset for classification using texture features. In fact, many of the problems that are interesting from a business point of view are relatively easy. However, sometimes we may be faced with a tougher problem and need better and more modern techniques to get good results.

We will now test a public dataset that has the same structure: several photographs of the same class. The classes are animals, cars, transportation, and natural scenes.

When compared to the three classes' problem we discussed previously, these classes are harder to tell apart. Natural scenes, buildings, and texts have very different textures. In this dataset, however, the texture is a clear marker of the class. The following is an example from the animal class:

And here is another from the cars class:

Both objects are against natural backgrounds and with large smooth areas inside the objects. We therefore expect that textures will not be very good.

When we use the same features as before, we achieve 55 percent accuracy in cross-validation using logistic regression. This is not too bad on four classes, but not spectacular either. Let's see if we can use a different method to do better. In fact, we will see that we need to combine texture features with other methods to get the best possible results. But, first things first—we look at local features.

Local feature representations

A relatively recent development in the computer vision world has been the development of local-feature-based methods. **Local features** are computed on a small region of the image, unlike the previous features we considered, which had been computed on the whole image. Mahotas supports computing a type of these features; **Speeded Up Robust Features**, also known as **SURF** (there are several others, the most well-known being the original proposal of **Scale-Invariant Feature Transform** (**SIFT**)). These local features are designed to be robust against rotational or illumination changes (that is, they only change their value slightly when illumination changes).

When using these features, we have to decide where to compute them. There are three possibilities that are commonly used:

- Randomly
- In a grid
- Detecting interesting areas of the image (a technique known as **keypoint detection** or **interest point detection**)

All of these are valid and will, under the right circumstances, give good results. Mahotas supports all three. Using interest point detection works best if you have a reason to expect that your interest point will correspond to areas of importance in the image. This depends, naturally, on what your image collection consists of. Typically, this is found to work better in man-made images rather than natural scenes. Man-made scenes have stronger angles, edges, or regions of high contrast, which are the typical regions marked as interesting by these automated detectors.

Since we are using photographs of mostly natural scenes, we are going to use the interest point method. Computing them with mahotas is easy; import the right submodule and call the `surf.surf` function:

```
from mahotas.features import surf
descriptors = surf.surf(image, descriptors_only=True)
```

The `descriptors_only=True` flag means that we are only interested in the descriptors themselves, and not in their pixel location, size, and other method information. Alternatively, we could have used the dense sampling method, using the `surf.dense` function:

```
from mahotas.features import surf
descriptors = surf.dense(image, spacing=16)
```

This returns the value of the descriptors computed on points that are at a distance of `16` pixels from each other. Since the position of the points is fixed, the meta-information on the interest points is not very interesting and is not returned by default. In either case, the result (descriptors) is an *n*-times-64 array, where *n* is the number of points sampled. The number of points depends on the size of your images, their content, and the parameters you pass to the functions. We used defaults previously, and this way we obtain a few hundred descriptors per image.

We cannot directly feed these descriptors to a support vector machine, logistic regressor, or similar classification system. In order to use the descriptors from the images, there are several solutions. We could just average them, but the results of doing so are not very good as they throw away all location-specific information. In that case, we would have just another global feature set based on edge measurements.

The solution we will use here is the **bag-of-words** model, which is a very recent idea. It was published in this form first in 2004. This is one of those "obvious in hindsight" ideas: it is very simple and works very well.

It may seem strange to say "words" when dealing with images. It may be easier to understand if you think that you have not written words, which are easy to distinguish from each other, but orally spoken audio. Now, each time a word is spoken, it will sound slightly different, so its waveform will not be identical to the other times it was spoken. However, by using clustering on these waveforms, we can hope to recover most of the structure so that all the instances of a given word are in the same cluster. Even if the process is not perfect (and it will not be), we can still talk of grouping the waveforms into words.

This is the same thing we do with visual words: we group together similar-looking regions from all images and call these visual words. Grouping is a form of clustering that we first encountered in *Chapter 3, Clustering – Finding Related Posts*.

The number of words used does not usually have a big impact on the final performance of the algorithm. Naturally, if the number is extremely small (ten or twenty, when you have a few thousand images), then the overall system will not perform well. Similarly, if you have too many words (many more than the number of images for example), the system will not perform well. However, in between these two extremes, there is often a very large plateau where you can choose the number of words without a big impact on the result. As a rule of thumb, using a value such as 256, 512, or 1024 if you have very many images, should give you a good result.

We are going to start by computing the features:

```
alldescriptors = []
for im in images:
    im = mh.imread(im, as_grey=True)
    im = im.astype(np.uint8)
    alldescriptors.append(surf.surf(im, descriptors_only))
```

This results in over 100,000 local descriptors. Now, we use **k-means clustering** to obtain the centroids. We could use all the descriptors, but we are going to use a smaller sample for extra speed:

```
concatenated = np.concatenate(alldescriptors) # get all descriptors
into a single array
concatenated = concatenated[::32] # use only every 32nd vector
from sklearn.cluster import Kmeans
k = 256
km = KMeans(k)
km.fit(concatenated)
```

After this is done (which will take a while), we have km containing information about the centroids. We now go back to the descriptors and build feature vectors:

```
features = []
for d in alldescriptors:
    c = km.predict(d)
    features.append(
        np.array([np.sum(c == ci) for ci in range(k)])
    )
features = np.array(features)
```

The end result of this loop is that features[fi] is a histogram corresponding to the image at position fi (the same could have been computed faster with the np.histogram function, but getting the arguments just right is a little tricky, and the rest of the code is, in any case, much slower than this simple step).

The result is that each image is now represented by a single array of features of the same size (the number of clusters; in our case `256`). Therefore, we can use our standard classification methods. Using logistic regression again, we now get 62 percent, a 7 percent improvement. We can combine all of the features together and we obtain 67 percent, more than 12 percent over what was obtained with texture-based methods:

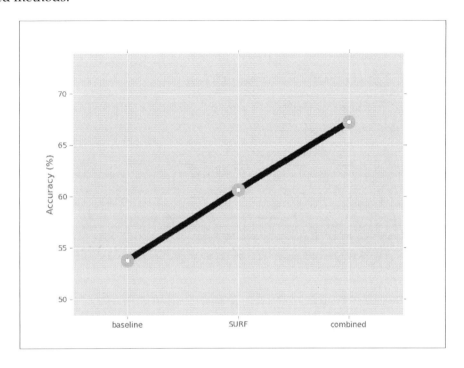

Summary

We learned the classical feature-based approach to handling images in a machine learning context by reducing a million pixels to a few numeric dimensions. All the technologies that we learned in the other chapters suddenly become directly applicable to image problems. This includes classification, which is often referred to as pattern recognition when the inputs are images, clustering, or dimensionality reduction (even topic modeling can be performed on images, often with very interesting results).

We also learned how to use local features in a bag-of-words model for classification. This is a very modern approach to computer vision and achieves good results while being robust to many irrelevant aspects of the image, such as illumination and also uneven illumination in the same image. We also used clustering as a useful intermediate step in classification rather than as an end in itself.

We focused on mahotas, which is one of the major computer vision libraries in Python. There are others that are equally well maintained. Skimage (scikit-image) is similar in spirit, but has a different set of features. OpenCV is a very good C++ library with a Python interface. All of these can work with NumPy arrays and can mix and match functions from different libraries to build complex pipelines.

In the next chapter, you will learn a different form of machine learning: dimensionality reduction. As we saw in several earlier chapters, including when using images in this chapter, it is very easy to computationally generate many features. However, often we want to have a reduced number of features for speed, visualization, or to improve our results. In the next chapter, we will see how to achieve this.

11
Dimensionality Reduction

Garbage in, garbage out, that's what we know from real life. Throughout this book, we have seen that this pattern also holds true when applying machine learning methods to training data. Looking back, we realize that the most interesting machine learning challenges always involved some sort of feature engineering, where we tried to use our insight into the problem to carefully craft additional features that the machine learner hopefully picks up.

In this chapter, we will go in the opposite direction with dimensionality reduction involving cutting away features that are irrelevant or redundant. Removing features might seem counter-intuitive at first thought, as more information is always better than less information. Shouldn't the unnecessary features be ignored after all? For example, by setting their weights to 0 inside the machine learning algorithm. The following are several good reasons that are still in practice for trimming down the dimensions as much as possible:

- Superfluous features can irritate or mislead the learner. This is not the case with all machine learning methods (for example, Support Vector Machines love high-dimensional spaces). But most of the models feel safer with less dimensions.

- Another argument against high-dimensional feature spaces is that more features mean more parameters to tune and a higher risk of overfitting.

- The data we retrieved to solve our task might just have artificial high dimensions, whereas the real dimension might be small.

- Less dimensions mean faster training and more variations to try out, resulting in better end results.

- If we want to visualize the data, we are restricted to two or three dimensions. This is known as visualization.

So, here we will show you how to get rid of the garbage within our data while keeping the valuable part of it.

Sketching our roadmap

Dimensionality reduction can be roughly grouped into feature selection and feature extraction methods. We have already employed some kind of feature selection in almost every chapter when we invented, analyzed, and then probably dropped some features. In this chapter, we will present some ways that use statistical methods, namely correlation and mutual information, to be able to do feature selection in vast feature spaces. Feature extraction tries to transform the original feature space into a lower-dimensional feature space. This is useful especially when we cannot get rid of features using selection methods, but we still have too many features for our learner. We will demonstrate this using **principal component analysis (PCA)**, **linear discriminant analysis (LDA)**, and **multidimensional scaling (MDS)**.

Selecting features

If we want to be nice to our machine learning algorithm, we will provide it with features that are not dependent on each other, yet highly dependent on the value to be predicted. It means that each feature adds some salient information. Removing any of the features will lead to a drop in performance.

If we have only a handful of features, we could draw a matrix of scatter plots – one scatter plot for every feature-pair combination. Relationships between the features could then be easily spotted. For every feature pair showing an obvious dependence, we would then think whether we should remove one of them or better design a newer, cleaner feature out of both.

Most of the time, however, we have more than a handful of features to choose from. Just think of the classification task where we had a bag-of-words to classify the quality of an answer, which would require a 1,000 by 1,000 scatter plot. In this case, we need a more automated way to detect the overlapping features and a way to resolve them. We will present two general ways to do so in the following subsections, namely filters and wrappers.

Detecting redundant features using filters

Filters try to clean up the feature forest independent of any machine learning method used later. They rely on statistical methods to find out which of the features are redundant (in which case, we need to keep only one per redundant feature group) or irrelevant. In general, the filter works as depicted in the workflow shown in the following diagram:

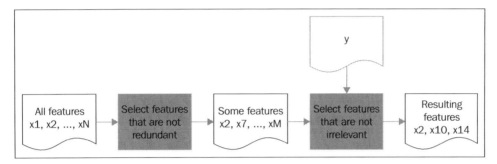

Correlation

Using correlation, we can easily see linear relationships between pairs of features, which are relationships that can be modeled using a straight line. In the graphs shown in the following screenshot, we can see different degrees of correlation together with a potential linear dependency plotted as a red dashed line (a fitted one-dimensional polynomial). The correlation coefficient $Cor(X_1, X_2)$ at the top of the individual graphs is calculated using the common Pearson correlation coefficient (the Pearson r value) by means of the pearsonr() function of scipy.stat.

Given two equal-sized data series, it returns a tuple of the correlation coefficient values and the p-value, which is the probability that these data series are being generated by an uncorrelated system. In other words, the higher the p-value, the less we should trust the correlation coefficient:

```
>> from import scipy.stats import pearsonr
>> pearsonr([1,2,3], [1,2,3.1])
>> (0.99962228516121843, 0.017498096813278487)
>> pearsonr([1,2,3], [1,20,6])
>> (0.25383654128340477, 0.83661493668227405)
```

In the first case, we have a clear indication that both series are correlated. In the second one, we still clearly have a non-zero r value.

However, the p-value basically tells us that whatever the correlation coefficient is, we should not pay attention to it. The following output in the screenshot illustrates the same:

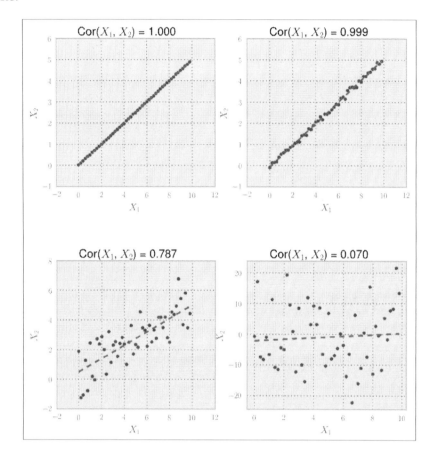

In the first three cases that have high correlation coefficients, we would probably want to throw out either X_1 or X_2 since they seem to convey similar if not the same information.

In the last case, however, we should keep both features. In our application, this decision would of course be driven by that p-value.

Although it worked nicely in the previous example, reality is seldom nice to us. One big disadvantage of correlation-based feature selection is that it only detects linear relationships (a relationship that can be modeled by a straight line). If we use correlation on non-linear data, we see the problem. In the following example, we have a quadratic relationship:

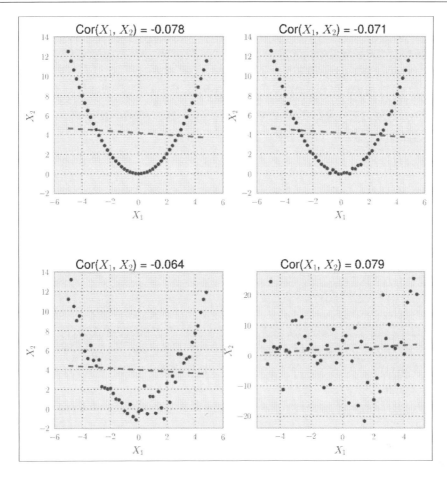

Although the human eye immediately sees the relationship between X1 and X2 in all but the bottom-right graph, the correlation coefficient does not. It is obvious that correlation is useful to detect linear relationships, but fails for everything else.

For non-linear relationships, mutual information comes to the rescue.

Mutual information

When looking at the feature selection, we should not focus on the type of relationship as we did in the previous section (linear relationships). Instead, we should think in terms of how much information one feature provides, given that we already have another.

To understand that, let us pretend we want to use features from the feature set `house_size`, `number_of_levels`, and `avg_rent_price` to train a classifier that outputs whether the house has an elevator or not. In this example, we intuitively see that knowing `house_size` means we don't need `number_of_levels` anymore, since it somehow contains redundant information. With `avg_rent_price`, it is different as we cannot infer the value of rental space simply from the size of the house or the number of levels it has. Thus we would be wise to keep only one of them in addition to the average price of rental space.

Mutual information formalizes the previous reasoning by calculating how much information two features have in common. But unlike correlation, it does not rely on a sequence of data, but on the distribution. To understand how it works, we have to dive a bit into information entropy.

Let's assume we have a fair coin. Before we flip it, we will have maximum uncertainty as to whether it will show heads or tails, as both have an equal probability of 50 percent. This uncertainty can be measured by means of Claude Shannon's information entropy:

$$H(X) = -\sum_{i=1}^{n} p(X_i) \log_2 p(X_i)$$

In our fair coin scenario, we have two cases: let x_0 be the case of heads and x_1 the case of tails, with $p(X_0) = p(X_1) = 0.5$.

Thus, we get the following:

$$H(X) = -p(x_0)\log_2 p(x_0) - p(x_1)\log_2 p(x_1) = -0.5 \cdot \log_2(0.5) - 0.5 \cdot \log_2(0.5) = 1.0$$

 For convenience, we can also use `scipy.stats.entropy([0.5, 0.5], base=2)`. We set the base parameter to 2 to get the same result as the previous one. Otherwise, the function will use the natural logarithm via `np.log()`. In general, the base does not matter as long as you use it consistently.

Now imagine we knew upfront that the coin is actually not that fair, with the heads side having a 60 percent chance of showing up after flipping:

$$H(X) = -0.6 \cdot \log_2(0.6) - 0.4 \log_2(0.4) = 0.97$$

We can see that this situation is less uncertain. The uncertainty will decrease the farther we get from 0.5, reaching the extreme value of 0 for either a 0 percent or 100 percent chance of the head showing up, as we can see in the following graph:

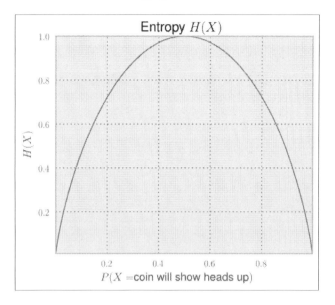

We will now modify the entropy $H(X)$ by applying it to two features instead of one, such that it measures how much uncertainty is removed from X when we learn about Y. Then we can catch how one feature reduces the uncertainty of another.

For example, without having any further information about the weather, we are totally uncertain whether it is raining outside or not. If we now learn that the grass outside is wet, the uncertainty has been reduced (we will still have to check whether the sprinkler had been turned on).

More formally, mutual information is defined as:

$$I(X;Y) = \sum_{i=1}^{m} \sum_{j=1}^{n} P(X_i, Y_j) \log_2 \frac{P(X_i, Y_j)}{P(X_i)P(Y_j)}$$

This looks a bit intimidating, but is really not more than sums and products. For instance, the calculation of $P()$ is done by binning the feature values and then calculating the fraction of values in each bin. In the following plots, we have set the number of bins to 10.

In order to restrict mutual information to the interval [0,1], we have to divide it by their added individual entropy, which gives us the normalized mutual information:

$$NI(X;Y) = \frac{I(X;Y)}{H(X)+H(Y)}$$

The nice thing about mutual information is that unlike correlation, it is not looking only at linear relationships, as we can see in the following graphs:

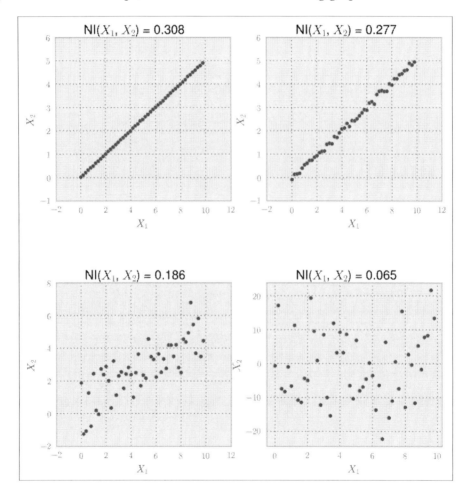

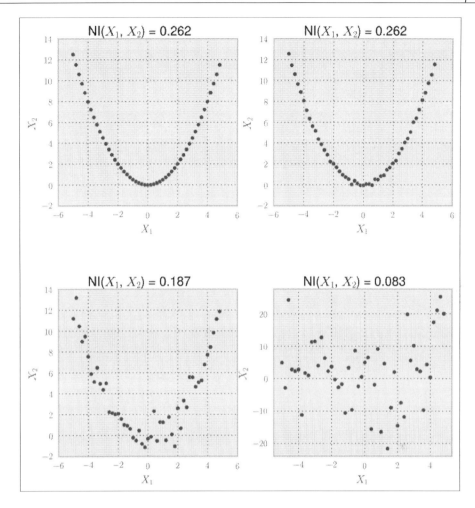

Hence, we have to calculate the normalized mutual information for all feature pairs. For every pair having a very high value (we would have to determine what that means), we would then drop one of them. In case we are doing regression, we could drop the feature that has a very low mutual information with the desired result value.

This might work for a small set of features. At some point, however, this procedure can be really expensive, as the amount of calculation grows quadratically since we are computing the mutual information between feature pairs.

Another huge disadvantage of filters is that they drop features that are not useful in isolation. More often than not, there are a handful of features that seem to be totally independent of the target variable, yet when combined together, they rock. To keep these, we need wrappers.

Asking the model about the features using wrappers

While filters can tremendously help in getting rid of useless features, they can go only so far. After all the filtering, there might still be some features that are independent among themselves and show some degree of dependence with the result variable, but yet they are totally useless from the model's point of view. Just think of the following data, which describes the XOR function. Individually, neither A nor B would show any signs of dependence on Y, whereas together they clearly do:

A	B	Y
0	0	0
0	1	1
1	0	1
1	1	0

So why not ask the model itself to give its vote on the individual features? This is what wrappers do, as we can see in the following process chart diagram:

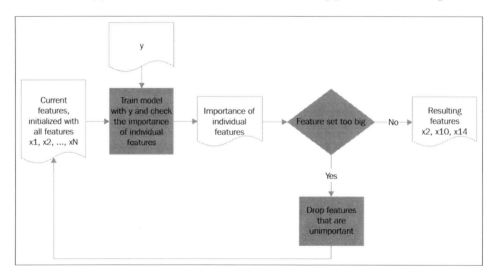

Here we have pushed the calculation of feature importance to the model training process. Unfortunately (but understandably), feature importance is not determined as a binary but as a ranking value. So we still have to specify where to make the cut – what part of the features are we willing to take and what part do we want to drop?

Coming back to Scikit-learn, we find various excellent wrapper classes in the sklearn. feature_selection package. A real workhorse in this field is RFE, which stands for **recursive feature elimination**. It takes an estimator and the desired number of features to keep as parameters and then trains the estimator with various feature sets as long as it has found a subset of the features that are small enough. The RFE instance itself pretends to be like an estimator, thereby, wrapping the provided estimator.

In the following example, we create an artificial classification problem of 100 samples using the convenient make_classification() function of datasets. It lets us specify the creation of 10 features, out of which only three are really valuable to solve the classification problem:

```
>>> from sklearn.feature_selection import RFE
>>> from sklearn.linear_model import LogisticRegression
>>> from sklearn.datasets import make_classification
>>> X,y = make_classification(n_samples=100, n_features=10, n_
informative=3, random_state=0)
>>> clf = LogisticRegression()
>>> clf.fit(X, y)
>>> selector = RFE(clf, n_features_to_select=3)
>>> selector = selector.fit(X, y)
>>> print(selector.support_)
[False  True False  True False False False False  True False]
>>> print(selector.ranking_)
[4 1 3 1 8 5 7 6 1 2]
```

The problem in real-world scenarios is, of course, how can we know the right value for n_features_to_select? Truth is, we can't. But most of the time, we can use a sample of the data and play with it using different settings to quickly get a feeling for the right ballpark.

The good thing is that we don't have to be that exact when using wrappers. Let's try different values for n_features_to_select to see how support_ and ranking_ change:

n_ features_ to_select	support_	ranking_
1	[False False False True False False False False False False]	[6 3 5 1 10 7 9 8 2 4]
2	[False False False True False False False False True False]	[5 2 4 1 9 6 8 7 1 3]
3	[False True False True False False False False True False]	[4 1 3 1 8 5 7 6 1 2]

n_features_to_select	support_	ranking_
4	[False True False True False False False False True True]	[3 1 2 1 7 4 6 5 1 1]
5	[False True True True False False False False True True]	[2 1 1 1 6 3 5 4 1 1]
6	[True True True True False False False False True True]	[1 1 1 1 5 2 4 3 1 1]
7	[True True True True False True False False True True]	[1 1 1 1 4 1 3 2 1 1]
8	[True True True True False True False True True True]	[1 1 1 1 3 1 2 1 1 1]
9	[True True True True False True True True True True]	[1 1 1 1 2 1 1 1 1 1]
10	[True True True True True True True True True True]	[1 1 1 1 1 1 1 1 1 1]

We see that the result is very stable. Features that have been used when requesting smaller feature sets keep on getting selected when letting more features in. Finally we rely on our train/test set splitting to warn us when we go in the wrong direction.

Other feature selection methods

There are several other feature selection methods that you will discover while reading through machine learning literature. Some don't even look like feature selection methods as they are embedded into the learning process (not to be confused with the previously mentioned wrappers). Decision trees, for instance, have a feature selection mechanism implanted deep in their core. Other learning methods employ some kind of regularization that punishes model complexity, thus driving the learning process towards good performing models that are still "simple". They do this by decreasing the less impactful features' importance to zero and then dropping them (L1-regularization).

So watch out! Often, the power of machine learning methods has to be attributed to their implanted feature selection method to a great degree.

Feature extraction

At some point, after we have removed the redundant features and dropped the irrelevant ones, we often still find that we have too many features. No matter what learning method we use, they all perform badly, and given the huge feature space, we understand that they actually cannot do better. We realize that we have to cut living flesh and that we have to get rid of features that all common sense tells us are valuable. Another situation when we need to reduce the dimensions, and when feature selection does not help much, is when we want to visualize data. Then, we need to have at most three dimensions at the end to provide any meaningful graph.

Enter the feature extraction methods. They restructure the feature space to make it more accessible to the model, or simply cut down the dimensions to two or three so that we can show dependencies visually.

Again, we can distinguish between feature extraction methods as being linear or non-linear ones. And as before, in the feature selection section, we will present one method for each type, principal component analysis for linear and multidimensional scaling for the non-linear version. Although they are widely known and used, they are only representatives for many more interesting and powerful feature extraction methods.

About principal component analysis (PCA)

Principal component analysis is often the first thing to try out if you want to cut down the number of features and do not know what feature extraction method to use. PCA is limited as it is a linear method, but chances are that it already goes far enough for your model to learn well enough. Add to that the strong mathematical properties it offers, the speed at which it finds the transformed feature space, and its ability to transform between the original and transformed features later, we can almost guarantee that it will also become one of your frequently used machine learning tools.

Summarizing it, given the original feature space, PCA finds a linear projection of it into a lower dimensional space that has the following properties:

- The conserved variance is maximized
- The final reconstruction error (when trying to go back from transformed features to original ones) is minimized

As PCA simply transforms the input data, it can be applied both to classification and regression problems. In this section, we will use a classification task to discuss the method.

Sketching PCA

PCA involves a lot of linear algebra, which we do not want to go into. Nevertheless, the basic algorithm can be easily described with the help of the following steps:

1. Center the data by subtracting the mean from it.
2. Calculate the covariance matrix.
3. Calculate the eigenvectors of the covariance matrix.

If we start with N features, the algorithm will again return a transformed feature space with N dimensions – we gained nothing so far. The nice thing about this algorithm, however, is that the eigenvalues indicate how much of the variance is described by the corresponding eigenvector.

Let us assume we start with $N = 1000$ features, and we know that our model does not work well with more than 20 features. Then we simply pick the 20 eigenvectors having the highest eigenvalues.

Applying PCA

Let us consider the following artificial dataset, which is visualized in the left plot as follows:

```
>>> x1 = np.arange(0, 10, .2)
>>> x2 = x1+np.random.normal(loc=0, scale=1, size=len(x1))
>>> X = np.c_[(x1, x2)]
>>> good = (x1>5) | (x2>5) # some arbitrary classes
>>> bad = ~good # to make the example look good
```

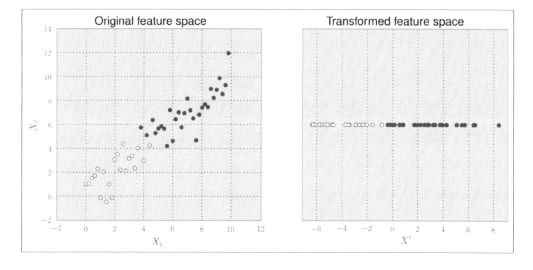

Scikit-learn provides the PCA class in its decomposition package. In this example, we can clearly see that one dimension should be enough to describe the data. We can specify that using the n_components parameter:

```
>>> from sklearn import linear_model, decomposition, datasets
>>> pca = decomposition.PCA(n_components=1)
```

Here we can also use PCA's fit() and transform() methods (or its fit_ transform() combination) to analyze the data and project it into the transformed feature space:

```
>>> Xtrans = pca.fit_transform(X)
```

Xtrans contains only one dimension, as we have specified. You can see the result in the right graph. The outcome is even linearly separable in this case. We would not even need a complex classifier to distinguish between both classes.

To get an understanding of the reconstruction error, we can have a look at the variance of the data that we have retained in the transformation:

```
>>> print(pca.explained_variance_ratio_)
>>> [ 0.96393127]
```

This means that after going from two dimensions to one dimension, we are still left with 96 percent of the variance.

Of course, it is not always that simple. Often, we don't know what number of dimensions is advisable upfront. In that case, we leave the n_components parameter unspecified when initializing PCA to let it calculate the full transformation. After fitting the data, explained_variance_ratio_ contains an array of ratios in decreasing order. The first value is the ratio of the basis vector describing the direction of the highest variance, the second value is the ratio of the direction of the second highest variance, and so on. After plotting this array, we quickly get a feel of how many components we would need: the number of components immediately before the chart has its elbow is often a good guess.

> Plots displaying the explained variance over the number of components is called a Scree plot. A nice example of combining a Scree plot with a grid search to find the best setting for the classification problem can be found at http://scikit-learn.sourceforge.net/stable/auto_examples/plot_digits_pipe.html.

Limitations of PCA and how LDA can help

Being a linear method, PCA has its limitations when we are faced with data that has non-linear relationships. We won't go into details here, but it will suffice to say that there are extensions of PCA, for example Kernel PCA, which introduce a non-linear transformation so that we can still use the PCA approach.

Another interesting weakness of PCA that we will cover here is when it is being applied to special classification problems.

Let us replace the following:

```
>>> good = (x1>5) | (x2>5)
```

with

```
>>> good = x1>x2
```

to simulate such a special case and we quickly see the problem.

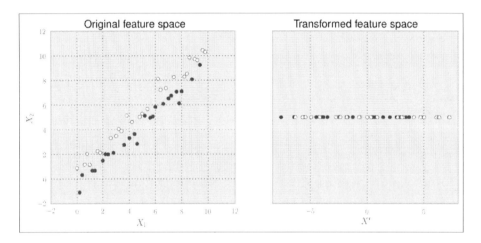

Here, the classes are not distributed according to the axis with the highest variance but the one with the second highest variance. Clearly, PCA falls flat on its face. As we don't provide PCA with any cues regarding the class labels, it cannot do any better.

Linear Discriminant Analysis (LDA) comes to the rescue here. It is a method that tries to maximize the distance of points belonging to different classes while minimizing the distance of points of the same class. We won't give any more details regarding how the underlying theory works in particular, just a quick tutorial on how to use it:

```
>>> from sklearn import lda
>>> lda_inst = lda.LDA(n_components=1)
>>> Xtrans = lda_inst.fit_transform(X, good)
```

That's all. Note that in contrast to the previous PCA example, we provide the class labels to the `fit_transform()` method. Thus, whereas PCA is an unsupervised feature extraction method, LDA is a supervised one. The result looks as expected:

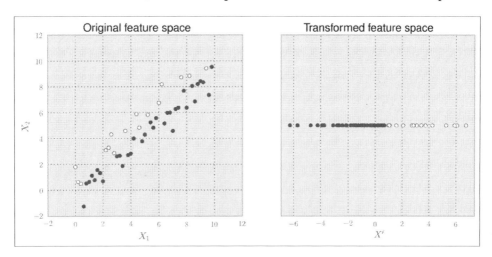

Then why to consider PCA in the first place and not use LDA only? Well, it is not that simple. With the increasing number of classes and less samples per class, LDA does not look that well any more. Also, PCA seems to be not as sensitive to different training sets as LDA. So when we have to advise which method to use, we can only suggest a clear "it depends".

Multidimensional scaling (MDS)

On one hand, PCA tries to use optimization for retained variance, and on the other hand, MDS tries to retain the relative distances as much as possible when reducing the dimensions. This is useful when we have a high-dimensional dataset and want to get a visual impression.

MDS does not care about the data points themselves; instead, it is interested in the dissimilarities between pairs of data points and interprets these as distances. The first thing the MDS algorithm is doing is, therefore, taking all the N data points of dimension k and calculates a distance matrix using a distance function d_0, which measures the (most of the time, Euclidean) distance in the original feature space:

$$\begin{pmatrix} X_{11} \cdots X_{N1} \\ \vdots \quad \ddots \quad \vdots \\ X_{1k} \cdots X_{Nk} \end{pmatrix} \rightarrow \begin{pmatrix} d_0(X_1, X_1) \quad \cdots \quad d_0(X_N, X_1) \\ \vdots \quad\quad \ddots \quad\quad \vdots \\ d_0(X_1, X_N) \quad \cdots \quad d_0(X_N, X_N) \end{pmatrix}$$

Now, MDS tries to position the individual data points in the lower dimensional space such that the new distance there resembles as much as possible the distances in the original space. As MDS is often used for visualization, the choice of the lower dimension is most of the time two or three.

Let us have a look at the following simple data consisting of three data points in a five-dimensional space. Two of the data points are close by and one is very distinct, and we want to visualize that in three and two dimensions as follows:

```
>>> X = np.c_[np.ones(5), 2 * np.ones(5), 10 * np.ones(5)].T
>>> print(X)
[[  1.   1.   1.   1.   1.]
 [  2.   2.   2.   2.   2.]
 [ 10.  10.  10.  10.  10.]]
```

Using the class MDS in Scikit-learn's manifold package, we first specify that we want to transform X into a three-dimensional space as follows:

```
>>> from sklearn import manifold
>>> mds = manifold.MDS(n_components=3)
>>> Xtrans = mds.fit_transform(X)
```

To visualize it in two dimensions, we would have to say so using n_components.

The results can be seen in the following two graphs. The triangle and circle are both close together, whereas the star is far away:

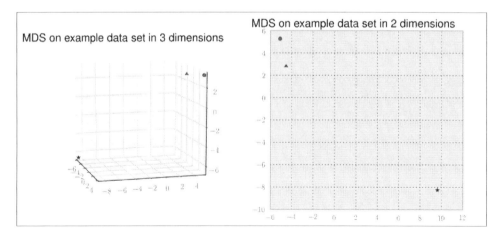

Let us have a look at a slightly more complex Iris dataset. We will use it later to contrast LDA with PCA. The Iris dataset contains four attributes per flower. With the previous code, we would project it into a three-dimensional space while keeping the relative distances between the individual flowers as much as possible. In the previous example, we did not specify any metric, so MDS will default to Euclidean. This means that flowers that were different according to their four attributes should also be far away in the MDS-scaled three-dimensional space, and flowers that were similar should be near together now, as shown in the following screenshot:

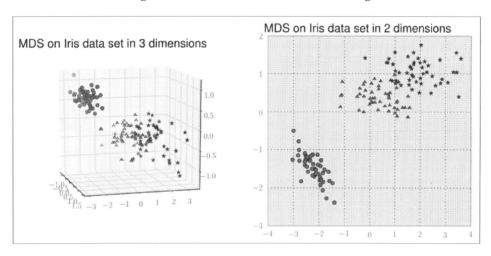

Doing the dimensional reduction to three and two dimensions with PCA instead, we see the expected bigger spread of the flowers belonging to the same class, as shown in the following screenshot:

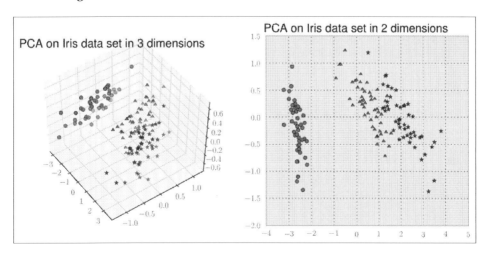

Of course, using MDS requires an understanding of the individual feature's units; maybe we are using features that cannot be compared using the Euclidean metric. For instance, a categorical variable, even when encoded as an integer (0 = red circle, 1 = blue star, 2 = green triangle, and so on), cannot be compared using Euclidean (is red closer to blue than to green?).

But once we are aware of this issue, MDS is a useful tool that reveals similarities in our data that otherwise would be difficult to see in the original feature space.

Looking a bit deeper into MDS, we realize that it is not a single algorithm, but a family of different algorithms, of which we have used just one. The same was true for PCA, and in case you realize that neither PCA nor MDS solves your problem, just look at the other manifold learning algorithms that are available in the Scikit-learn toolkit.

Summary

We learned that sometimes we can get rid of all the features using feature selection methods. We also saw that in some cases this is not enough, and we have to employ feature extraction methods that reveal the real and the lower-dimensional structure in our data, hoping that the model has an easier game with it.

We have only scratched the surface of the huge body of available dimensionality reduction methods. Still, we hope that we have got you interested in this whole field, as there are lots of other methods waiting for you to pick up. At the end, feature selection and extraction is an art, just like choosing the right learning method or training model.

The next chapter covers the use of Jug, a little Python framework to manage computations in a way that takes advantage of multiple cores or multiple machines. We will also learn about AWS – the Amazon cloud.

12
Big(ger) Data

While computers keep getting faster and have more memory, the size of the data has grown as well. In fact, data has grown faster than computational speed, and this means that it has grown faster than our ability to process it.

It is not easy to say what is big data and what is not, so we will adopt an operational definition: when data is so large that it becomes too cumbersome to work with, we refer to it as big data. In some areas, this might mean petabytes of data or trillions of transactions; data that will not fit into a single hard drive. In other cases, it may be one hundred times smaller, but just difficult to work with.

We will first build upon some of the experience of the previous chapters and work with what we can call the medium data setting (not quite big data, but not small either). For this we will use a package called jug, which allows us to do the following:

- Break up your pipeline into tasks
- Cache (memoize) intermediate results
- Make use of multiple cores, including multiple computers on a grid

The next step is to move to true "big data", and we will see how to use the cloud (in particular, the Amazon Web Services infrastructure). We will now use another Python package, starcluster, to manage clusters.

Learning about big data

The expression "big data" does not mean a specific amount of data, neither in the number of examples nor in the number of gigabytes, terabytes, or petabytes taken up by the data. It means the following:

- We have had data growing faster than the processing power
- Some of the methods and techniques that worked well in the past now need to be redone, as they do not scale well

- Your algorithms cannot assume that the entire data is in RAM
- Managing data becomes a major task in itself
- Using computer clusters or multicore machines becomes a necessity and not a luxury

This chapter will focus on this last piece of the puzzle: how to use multiple cores (either on the same machine or on separate machines) to speed up and organize your computations. This will also be useful in other *medium-sized data* tasks.

Using jug to break up your pipeline into tasks

Often, we have a simple pipeline: we preprocess the initial data, compute features, and then we need to call a machine learning algorithm with the resulting features.

Jug is a package developed by *Luis Pedro Coelho*, one of the authors of this book. It is open source (using the liberal MIT License) and can be useful in many areas but was designed specifically around data analysis problems. It simultaneously solves several problems, for example:

- It can memorize results to a disk (or a database), which means that if you ask it to compute something you have computed before, the result is instead read from the disk.
- It can use multiple cores or even multiple computers on a cluster. Jug was also designed to work very well in batch computing environments that use a queuing system such as **Portable Batch System** (**PBS**), the **Load Sharing Facility** (**LSF**), or the **Oracle Grid Engine** (**OGE**, earlier known as Sun Grid Engine). This will be used in the second half of the chapter as we build online clusters and dispatch jobs to them.

About tasks

Tasks are the basic building block of jug. A **task** is just a function and values for its arguments, for example:

```
def double(x):
    return 2*x
```

A task could be "call `double` with argument `3`". Another task would be "call `double` with argument `642.34`". Using jugs, we can build these tasks as follows:

```
from jug import Task
t1 = Task(double, 3)
t2 = Task(double, 642.34)
```

Save this to a file called `jugfile.py` (which is just a regular Python file). Now, we can run `jug execute` to run the tasks. This is something you run on the command line, not at the Python prompt! Instead of Python's `jugfile.py` file (which should do nothing), you run `jug execute`.

You will also get some feedback on the tasks (jug will say that two tasks named "double" were run). Run `jug execute` again and it will tell you that it did nothing! It does not need to. In this case, we gained little, but if the tasks took a long time to compute, it would be very useful.

You may notice that a new directory named `jugfile.jugdata` also appeared on your hard drive, with a few other weirdly named files. This is the memoization cache. If you remove it, `jug execute` will run all your tasks (both of them) again.

> Often it is good to distinguish between pure functions, which simply take their inputs and return a result, from more general functions that can perform actions such as reading from files, writing to files, accessing global variables, modifying their arguments, or anything that the language allows. Some programming languages, such as Haskell, even have syntactic ways in which to distinguish pure from impure functions.
>
> With jug, your tasks do not need to be perfectly pure. It is even recommended that you use tasks to read your data or write your results. However, accessing and modifying global variables will not work well; the tasks may be run in any order in different processors. The exceptions are global constants, but even this may confuse the memoization system (if the value is changed between runs). Similarly, you should not modify the input values. Jug has a debug mode (use `jug execute–debug`), which slows down your computation, but would give you useful error messages if you make this sort of mistake.

The preceding code works but it is a bit cumbersome; you are always repeating the `Task(function, argument)` construct. Using a bit of Python magic, we can make the code even more natural:

```
from jug import TaskGenerator
from time import sleep

@TaskGenerator
def double(x):
```

```
        sleep(4)
        return 2*x


@TaskGenerator
def add(a, b):
    return a + b


@TaskGenerator
def print_final_result(oname, value):
    with open(oname, 'w') as output:
        print >>output, "Final result:", value


y = double(2)
z = double(y)


y2 = double(7)
z2 = double(y2)
print_final_result('output.txt', add(z,z2))
```

Except for the use of TaskGenerator, the preceding code could have been a standard Python file. However, using TaskGenerator, it actually creates a series of tasks, and it is now possible to run it in a way that takes advantage of multiple processors. Behind the scenes, the decorator transforms your functions so that they do not actually execute but create a task. We also take advantage of the fact that we can pass tasks to other tasks and this results in a dependency being generated.

You may have noticed that we added a few sleep(4) calls in the preceding code. This simulates running a long computation. Otherwise, this code is so fast that there is no point in using multiple processors.

We start by running jug status:

Task name	Waiting	Ready	Finished	Running
jugfile.add	1	0	0	0
jugfile.double	2	2	0	0
jugfile.print_final_result	1	0	0	0
Total:	4	2	0	0

Now we start two processes simultaneously (in the background):

```
jug execute &
jug execute &
```

Now we run `jug status` again:

```
Task name                        Waiting    Ready    Finished    Running
..............................................................................
jugfile.add                         1          0          0           0
jugfile.double                      2          0          0           2
jugfile.print_final_result          1          0          0           0
..............................................................................
Total:                              4          0          0           2
```

We can see that the two initial double operators are running at the same time. After about 8 seconds, the whole process will finish and the `output.txt` file will be written.

By the way, if your file was called anything other than `jugfile.py`, you would then have to specify it explicitly on the command line:

```
jug execute MYFILE.py
```

This is the only disadvantage of not using the name `jugfile.py` by the way.

Reusing partial results

For example, let's say you want to add a new feature (or even a set of features). As we saw in *Chapter 10*, *Computer Vision–Pattern Recognition Finding Related Posts*, this can easily be done by changing the computation code feature. However, this would imply recomputing all the features again, which is wasteful, particularly if you want to test new features and techniques quickly:

```python
@TaskGenerator
def new_features(im):
    import mahotas as mh
    im = mh.imread(fname, as_grey=1)
    es = mh.sobel(im, just_filter=1)
    return np.array([np.dot(es.ravel(), es.ravel())])

hfeatures = as_array([hfeature(f) for f in filenames])
efeatures = as_array([new_feature(f) for f in filenames])
features = Task(np.hstack, [hfeatures, efeatures])
  # learning code...
```

Now when you run `jug execute` again, the new features will be computed, but the old features will be loaded from the cache. The logistic regression code will also be run again as those results also depend on the features and those are different now.

This is when jug can be very powerful; it ensures that you always get the results you want without wasteful overcomputation.

Looking under the hood

How does jug work? At the basic level, it is very simple; a task is a function plus its argument. Its arguments may be either values or other tasks. If a task takes other tasks, there is dependency between the two tasks (and the second one cannot be run until the results of the first task are available).

Based on this, jug recursively computes a hash for each task. This hash value encodes the whole computation to get there. When you run `jug execute`, there is a little loop as shown in the following code snippet:

```
for t in alltasks:
    if t.has_not_run() and not backend_has_value(t.hash()):
        value = t.execute()
        save_to_backend(value, key=t.hash())
```

The real loop is much more complex because of locking issues, but the general idea is the one that appears in the preceding code snippet.

The default backend writes the file to the disk (in this funny directory named `jugfile.jugdata/`) but another backend is available which uses a Redis database. With proper locking, which jug takes care of, this also allows for many processors to execute tasks; they will independently look at all the tasks and run the ones which have not run yet and then write them back to the shared backend. This works on either the same machine (using multicore processors) or in multiple machines as long as they all have access to the same backend (for example, using a network disk or the Redis databases). In the next half of this chapter, we will discuss computer clusters, but for now, let us focus on multiple cores.

You can also understand why it is able to memoize intermediate results. If the backend already has the result of a task, it is not run anymore. On the other hand, if you change the task, even in minute ways (by altering one of the parameters), its hash will change. Therefore, it will be recomputed. Furthermore, all tasks that depend on it will also have their hashes changed and they will be recomputed as well.

Using jug for data analysis

Jug is a generic framework, but it is ideally suited for medium-scale data analysis. As you develop your analysis pipeline, it is good to have intermediate results be saved. If you already computed the preprocessing step before and are only changing the features you compute, you do not want to recompute the preprocessing. If you already computed the features but want to try combining a few new ones into the mix, you also do not want to recompute all your other features.

Jug is also specially optimized to work with numpy arrays. So, whenever your tasks return or receive numpy arrays, you are taking advantage of this optimization. Jug is another piece of this ecosystem where everything works together.

We will now look back at *Chapter 10, Computer Vision–Pattern Recognition Finding Related Posts*. We learned how to compute features on images. Remember that we were loading image files, computing features, combining these, normalizing them, and finally learning how to create a classifier. We are going to redo that exercise but this time with the use of jug. The advantage of this version is that it is now possible to add a new feature without having to recompute all of the previous versions.

We start with a few imports as follows:

```
from jug import TaskGenerator
```

Now we define the first task generator, the feature computation:

```
@TaskGenerator
def hfeatures(fname):
    import mahotas as mh
    import numpy as np
    im = mh.imread(fname, as_grey=1)
    im = mh.stretch(im)
    h = mh.features.haralick(im)
    return np.hstack([h.ptp(0), h.mean(0)])
```

Note how we only imported numpy and mahotas inside the function. This is a small optimization; this way, only if the task is run are the modules loaded. Now we set up the image filenames as follows:

```
filenames = glob('dataset/*.jpg')
```

We can use TaskGenerator on any function, even on the ones that we did not write, such as numpy.array:

```
import numpy as np
as_array = TaskGenerator(np.array)

# compute all features:
features = as_array([hfeature(f) for f in filenames])

# get labels as an array as well
labels = map(label_for, f)
res = perform_cross_validation(features, labels)

@TaskGenerator
```

```
def write_result(ofname, value):
    with open(ofname, 'w') as out:
        print >>out, "Result is:", value
write_result('output.txt', res)
```

One small inconvenience of using jug is that we must always write functions to output the results to files as shown in the preceding examples. This is a small price to pay for the extra convenience of using jug.

Not all features of jug could be mentioned in this chapter, but here is a summary of the most potentially interesting ones that we didn't cover in the main text:

- `jug invalidate`: This feature declares that all results from a given function should be considered invalid and in need of recomputation. This will also recompute any downstream computation that depended (even indirectly) on the invalidated results.

- `jug status --cache`: If `jug status` takes too long, you can use the `--cache` flag to cache the status and speed it up. Note that this will not detect any changes to `jugfile.py`, but you can always use `--cache --clear` to remove the cache and start again.

- `jug cleanup`: This feature removes any extra files in the memoization cache. This is a garbage collection operation.

There are other more advanced features, which allow you to look at values that have been computed inside `jugfile.py`. Read up on the use of "barriers" in the jug documentation (online at `http://jug.rtfd.org`).

Using Amazon Web Services (AWS)

When you have a lot of data and a lot of computation, you might start to crave for more computing power. Amazon (`aws.amazon.com/`) allows you to rent computing power by the hour. Thus, you can access a large amount of computing power without having to precommit by purchasing a large number of machines (including the costs of managing the infrastructure). There are other competitors in this market, but Amazon is the largest player, so we briefly cover it here.

Amazon Web Services (AWS) is a large set of services. We will focus only on the **Elastic Compute Cluster** (EC2) service. This service offers you virtual machines and disk space, which can be allocated and deallocated quickly.

There are three modes of use: a reserved mode, whereby you prepay to have cheaper per-hour access; a fixed per-hour rate; and a variable rate which depends on the overall compute market (when there is less demand, the costs are lower; when there is more demand, the prices go up).

For testing, you can use a single machine in the *free tier*. This allows you to play around with the system, get used to the interface, and so on. However, this is a very slow CPU machine. Thus, doing heavy computation using it is not advised.

On top of this general system, there are several types of machines available with varying costs; from a single core to a multicore system with a lot of RAM, or even **graphical processing units (GPUs)**. We will later see that you can also get several of the cheaper machines and build yourself a virtual cluster. You can also choose to get a Linux or Windows server, with Linux being slightly cheaper. In this chapter, we will work our examples on Linux but most of this information would be valid for Windows machines as well.

The resources can be managed through a web interface. However, it is also possible to do so programmatically and by setting up scripts which allocate virtual machines, setting up disks, and all the operations that are possible through the web interface. In fact, while the web interface changes very frequently (and some of the screenshots that we show in the book may be out-of-date by the time it goes to the press), the programmatic interface is more stable and the general architecture has remained stable since the service was introduced.

Access to AWS services is performed through a traditional username/password system, although Amazon calls the username an *access key* and the password a *secret key*. They probably do so to keep it separate from the username/password you use to access the web interface. In fact, you can create as many access/secret key pairs as you wish and give them different permissions. This is helpful for a larger team where a senior user with access to the full web panel can create other keys for developers with less privileges.

Amazon regions

Amazon.com has several regions. These correspond to physical regions of the world: West Coast U.S., East Coast US, several Asian locations, a South American one, and a European one. If you will be transferring data, it is best to keep it close to where you will be transferring to and from. Additionally, if you are handling user information, there may be regulatory issues if you transfer it to another jurisdiction. In that case, do check with an informed counsel on what the implications of transferring data about European customers to the US or vice versa are.

Amazon Web Services is a very large topic, and there are various books exclusively available which cover AWS entirely. The purpose of this chapter is to give you an overall impression of what is available and what is possible with AWS. In the practical spirit of this book, we do this by working through examples, but we will not exhaust all possibilities.

Creating your first machines

The first step is to go to `http://aws.amazon.com/` and create an account. These steps are similar to any other online service. If you want to have more than a single low-powered machine, you will need a credit card. In this example, we will use a few machines, so it may cost you a few dollars if you want to run through it. If you are not ready to take out a credit card just yet, you can certainly read the chapter to learn what AWS provides without going through the examples. Then you can make a more informed decision on whether to sign up.

Once you sign up for AWS and log in, you will be taken to the console. Here you will see the many services that AWS provides:

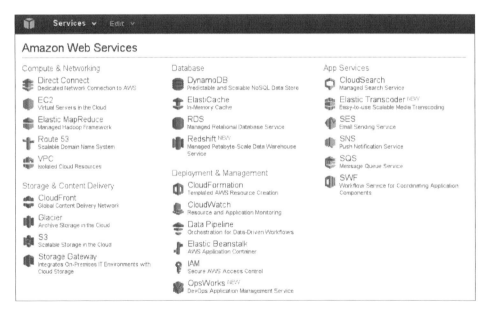

We pick and click on **EC2** (the second element on the leftmost column—this panel is shown as it was when this book was written; Amazon regularly makes minor changes, so you may see something slightly different). We now see the EC2 management console as shown in the following screenshot:

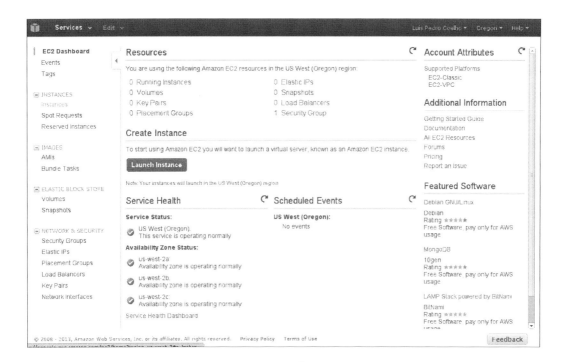

In the top-right corner, you can pick your region (see the *Amazon regions* information box). Note that you will only see information about the region that you have selected at the moment. Thus, if you mistakenly select the wrong region (or have machines running in multiple regions), they may not appear (from casual conversations with other programmers, this seems to be a common pitfall of using the EC2 web management console).

In EC2 parlance, a running server is called an **instance**. So now, we want to select **Launch Instance**. Now, follow the classic wizard. Select the **Amazon Linux** option (if you are familiar with one of the other offered Linux distributions, such as Red Hat, SuSe, or Ubuntu, you can also select one of those, but the configurations will be slightly different). We will start with one instance of the T1.micro type. This is the smallest possible machine, and it is free. Accept all of the defaults until you come to the screen mentioning a key pair:

We will pick the name awskeys for the key pair. Then, click on the **Create & Download your Key Pair** button to download the awskeys.pem file. Save that file somewhere safe! This is the **Secure Shell (SSH)** key that will enable you to log in to your cloud machine. Accept the remaining defaults and your instance will launch.

You will now need to wait for about a minute for your instance to come up. Eventually, the instance will be shown in green with the status "running." Right-clicking on it and selecting the **Connect** option will bring up instructions on how to connect. The following will be a standard SSH command of the form:

```
ssh -i awskeys.pem ec2-user@ec2-54-244-194-143.us-west-2.compute.
amazonaws.com
```

Therefore, we will be calling the ssh command and passing it the key files that we downloaded earlier as the identity (using the -i option). We are logging in as user ec2-user at the machine with the address ec2-54-244-194-143.us-west-2. conompute.amazonaws.com. This address will, of course, be different in your case. If you choose another distribution for your instance, the username may also change. In any case, the web panel will give you the correct information.

Finally, if you are running an Unix-style operating system (including Mac OS), you may have to tweak its permissions by calling the following code:

```
chmod 600 awskeys.pem
```

This sets the read/write permission for the current user only. SSH will otherwise give you an ugly warning.

Now, you should be able to log in to your machine. If everything is OK, you should see the banner as shown in the following screenshot:

```
     __|  __|_  )
     _|  (     /   Amazon Linux AMI
    ___|\___|___|

https://aws.amazon.com/amazon-linux-ami/2013.03-release-notes/
There are 1 security update(s) out of 3 total update(s) available
Run "sudo yum update" to apply all updates.
```

This is a regular Linux box where you have the sudo permission; you can run any command as the super user by prefixing it with sudo. You can run the update command it recommends to get your machine up to speed.

Installing Python packages on Amazon Linux

If you preferred another distribution, you can use your knowledge of that distribution to install Python, NumPy, and others. Here, we will do it on the standard Amazon distribution. We start by installing several basic Python packages as follows:

```
sudo yum -y install python-devel python-dev python-pip numpy scipy
python-matplotlib
```

For compiling mahotas, we will also need a C++ compiler:

```
sudo yum -y install gcc-c++
```

In this system, pip is installed as `python-pip`. For convenience, we will use pip to upgrade itself. We will then use pip to install the necessary packages:

```
sudo pip-python install -U pip
sudo pip install scikit-learn jug mahotas
```

At this point, you can install any other package you like using pip.

Running jug on our cloud machine

We can now download the data and code from *Chapter 10, Computer Vision–Pattern Recognition Finding Related Posts*, as follows:

```
wget FIXME-LET'S-BUILD-A-TAR-GZ-PACKAGE
tar xzf chapter10.tar.gz
cd chapter10
```

Finally, we can do the following:

```
jug execute
```

This would work just fine, but we would have to wait a long time for the results. Our free tier machine (of type `t1.micro`) is not very fast and it only has a single processor. So we will upgrade our machine.

We go back to the EC2 console and right-click on the running instance to get the pop-up menu. We need to first stop the instance. Stopping an instance in a virtual machine is equivalent to powering it off. You can stop your machines at any time. At that point, you stop paying for them (you are still using disk space, which also has a cost that is billed separately).

Once the machine is stopped, the **change instance type** option becomes available. Now we can select a more powerful instance, for example, a `c1.xlarge` instance, which has eight cores. The machine is still off, so you need to start it again (the virtual equivalent to booting up).

> AWS offers several instance types at different price points. Because this information is constantly being revised as more powerful options are introduced and prices are changed (generally getting cheaper), we cannot give you many details in this book; however, you can find the most up-to-date information on Amazon's website.

We need to wait for the instance to appear once again. Once it has, right-click on **Connect** as described earlier to get the connection information as it will almost surely have changed. When you change instance types, your instance will get a new address assigned to it.

You can assign a fixed IP to an instance using Amazon's Elastic IPs functionality, which you will find on the left-hand side of the EC2 console. This is useful if you find yourself creating and modifying instances very often. There is a small cost associated with this feature.

With eight cores, you can run eight jug processes simultaneously, as illustrated in the following code:

```
jug execute &
jug execute &
    (repeat to get 8 jobs going)
```

Use jug status to check whether these eight jobs are in fact running. After your jobs are finished (which should now happen pretty fast), you can stop the machine and downgrade it again to a t1.micro instance to save money; the micro instance is free, while the extra large one costs 0.58 dollars per hour (as of April 2013 — check the AWS website for up-to-date information).

Automating the generation of clusters with starcluster

As we just learned, we can spawn machines using the web interface, but it quickly becomes tedious and error prone. Fortunately, Amazon has an API. This means that we can write scripts which perform all the operations we discussed earlier automatically. Even better, others have already developed tools which can be used for mechanizing and automating many of the processes you want to perform with AWS.

A group at MIT developed exactly such a tool called starcluster. It happens to be a Python package, so you can install it with Python tools:

```
sudo pip install starcluster
```

You can run this from an Amazon machine or from your local machine. Either option will work.

We will need to specify what our cluster will look like. We do so by editing a configuration file. We generate a template configuration file by running the following code:

```
starcluster help
```

Then, pick the option for generating the configuration file in ~/.starcluster/ config. Once this is done, we will manually edit it.

Keys, keys, and more keys

There are three completely different types of keys that are important when dealing with AWS:

- A standard username/password combination, which you use to log in to the website
- The SSH key system, which is a public/private key system implemented with files; with your public key file, you can log in to remote machines
- The AWS access key/secret key system, which is just a form of username/password, which allows you to have multiple users on the same account (including adding different permissions to each one, but we will not cover those advanced features in this book)

To look up our access/secret keys, we go back to the AWS console and click on our name in the top-right corner; then select **Security Credentials**. Now at the bottom of the screen, there should be our access key that may look something like `AAKIIT7HHF6IUSN3OCAA`, which we will use as an example in this chapter.

Now edit the configuration file. This is a standard `.ini` file: a text file where sections start by having their names in brackets and options are specified in the `name=value` format. The first section is the `aws info` section and you should copy and paste your keys there:

```
[aws info]
AWS_ACCESS_KEY_ID =  AAKIIT7HHF6IUSN3OCAA
AWS_SECRET_ACCESS_KEY = <your secret key>
```

Now, we come to the fun part that is defining a cluster. Starcluster allows you to define as many different clusters as you wish. The starting file has one called `smallcluster`. It is defined in the `cluster smallcluster` section. We will edit it to read as follows:

```
[cluster mycluster]
KEYNAME = mykey
CLUSTER_SIZE = 16
```

This changes the number of nodes to `16` instead of the default of two. We can additionally specify which type of instance each node will be and what the initial image is (remember, an image is the initial disk, which defines what operating system you will be running and what software is installed). Starcluster has a few predefined images, but you can also build your own.

We need to create a new `ssh` key with the following:

```
starcluster createkey mykey -o .ssh/mykey.rsa
```

Now that we have configured a 16 node cluster and set up the keys, let's try it out.

```
starcluster start mycluster
```

This may take a few minutes as it allocates 17 new machines. Why 17 when our cluster is only 16 nodes? We always have a master node. All of these nodes have the same filesystem, so anything we create on the master will also be seen by the slaves. This also means that we can use jug on these clusters.

These clusters can be used as you wish, but they come pre-equipped with a job queue engine, which makes them ideal for batch processing. The process of using them is simple:

1. You log in to the master node.
2. You prepare your scripts on the master (or better yet, have them prepared before hand).
3. You submit jobs to the queue. A job can be any Unix command. The scheduler will find free nodes and run your job.
4. You wait for the jobs to finish.
5. You read the results on the master node. You can also now kill all the slave nodes to save money. In any case, do not forget that your system is running over the long term. Otherwise, this will cost you (in the dollars and cents meaning of the word).

We can log in to the master node with a single command:

```
starcluster sshmaster mycluster
```

We could also have looked up the address of the machine that was generated and used an `ssh` command as we did earlier, but when using the preceding command, it does not matter what the address was, as `starcluster` takes care of it behind the scenes for us.

As we said earlier, starcluster provides a batch queuing system for its clusters; you write a script to perform your actions, put it on the queue, and it will run in any available node.

At this point, you will need to repeat the actions to install the needed packages on the cluster. If this was a real project, we would set up a script to perform all the initialization for us, but since it is a tutorial, you should just run the installation steps again.

We can use the same `jugfile.py` system as before, except that now, instead of running it directly on the master, we schedule it on the cluster. First, write a very simple wrapper script:

```
#!/usr/bin/env bash
jug execute jugfile.py
```

Call it using `run-jugfile.sh` and use `chmod +x run-jugfile.sh` to give it an executable permission:

```
For c in 'seq 16'; do qsub run-jugfile.sh; done
```

This will create 16 jobs, each of which will run the `run-jugfile.sh` script, which will simply call jug. You can still use the master as you wish. In particular, you can at any moment run `jug status` and see the status of the computation. In fact, jug was developed in exactly such an environment, so it works very well in it.

Eventually, the computation will be finished and we can kill off all the nodes. Be sure to save the desired results somewhere and run the following:

```
starcluster terminate mycluster
```

Note that terminating will really destroy the filesystem and all your results. Of course, it is possible to change this default. You can have the cluster write to a filesystem which is not allocated and destroyed by starcluster but is available to you on a regular instance; in fact the flexibility of these tools is immense. However, these advanced manipulations could not all fit in this chapter.

Starcluster has excellent documentation online at http://star.mit.edu/cluster/, which you should read for more information about all the possibilities of this tool. We have seen only a small fraction of the functionality and used only the default settings here.

Summary

We saw how to use jug, a little Python framework, to manage computations in a way that takes advantage of multiple cores or multiple machines. Although this framework is generic, it was built specifically to address the data analysis needs of its author (who is also an author of this book). Therefore, it has several aspects that make it fit in with the rest of the Python machine learning environment.

We also learned about AWS, the Amazon cloud. Using cloud computing is often a more effective use of resources than building an in-house computing capacity. This is particularly true if your needs are not constant, but changing. Starcluster even allows for clusters that automatically grow as you launch more jobs and shrink as they terminate.

This is the end of the book. We have come a long way. We learned how to perform classification when we have labeled data and clustering when we do not. We learned about dimensionality reduction and topic modeling to make sense of large datasets. Towards the end, we looked at some specific applications, such as music genre classification and computer vision. For implementations, we relied on Python. This language has an increasingly expanding ecosystem of numeric computing packages built on top of NumPy. Whenever possible, we relied on scikit-learn but also used other packages when necessary. Due to the fact that they all use the same basic data structure (the NumPy multidimensional array), it is possible to mix functionality from different packages seamlessly. All of the packages used in this book are open source and available for use in any project.

Naturally, we did not cover every machine learning topic. In the *Appendix, Where to Learn More About Machine Learning*, we provide pointers to a selection of other resources that will help interested readers learn more about machine learning.

Where to Learn More about Machine Learning

We are at the end of our book and now take a moment to look at what else is out there that could be useful for our readers.

There are many wonderful resources out there to learn more about machine learning (way too much to cover them all here). Our list can therefore represent only a small and very biased sampling of the resources we think are best at the time of writing.

Online courses

Andrew Ng is a Professor at Stanford who runs an online course in machine learning as a **massive open online course** (**MOOC**) at Coursera (`http://www.coursera.org`). It is free of charge, but may represent a significant investment of time and effort (return on investment guaranteed!).

Books

This book focused on the practical side of machine learning. We did not present the thinking behind the algorithms or the theory that justifies them. If you are interested in that aspect of machine learning, then we recommend *Pattern Recognition and Machine Learning, C. Bishop , Springer Apply Italics to this*. This is a classical introductory text in the field. It will teach you the nitty-gritties of most of the algorithms we used in this book.

If you want to move beyond an introduction and learn all the gory mathematical details, then *Machine Learning: A Probabilistic Perspective*, K. Murphy, The *MIT Press,* is an excellent option. It is very recent (published in 2012), and contains the cutting edge of ML research. This 1,100 page book can also serve as a reference, as very little of machine learning has been left out.

Q&A sites

The following are the two Q&A websites of machine learning:

- **MetaOptimize** (`http://metaoptimize.com/qa`) is a machine learning Q&A website where many very knowledgeable researchers and practitioners interact

- **Cross Validated** (`http://stats.stackexchange.com`) is a general statistics Q&A site, which often features machine learning questions as well

As mentioned in the beginning of the book, if you have questions specific to particular parts of the book, feel free to ask them at **TwoToReal** (`http://www.twotoreal.com`). We try to be as quick as possible to jump in and help as best as we can.

Blogs

The following is an obviously non-exhaustive list of blogs that are interesting to someone working on machine learning:

- Machine Learning Theory at `http://hunch.net`
  - This is a blog by *John Langford*, the brain behind *Vowpal Wabbit* (`http://hunch.net/~vw/`), but guest posts also appear.
  - The average pace is approximately one post per month. The posts are more theoretical. They also offer additional value in brain teasers.

- Text and data mining by practical means at `http://textanddatamining. blogspot.de`
  - The average pace is one per month, which is very practical and has always surprising approaches

- A blog by *Edwin Chen* at `http://blog.echen.me`
  - The average pace is one per month, providing more applied topics

- Machined Learnings at `http://www.machinedlearnings.com`
  - ○ The average pace is one per month, providing more applied topics; often revolving around learning big data

- FlowingData at `http://flowingdata.com`
  - ○ The average pace is one per day, with the posts revolving more around statistics

- Normal deviate at `http://normaldeviate.wordpress.com`
  - ○ The average pace is one per month, covering theoretical discussions of practical problems. Although being more of a statistics blog, the posts often intersect with machine learning.

- Simply statistics at `http://simplystatistics.org`
  - ○ There are several posts per month, focusing on statistics and big data

- Statistical Modeling, Causal Inference, and Social Science at `http://andrewgelman.com`
  - ○ There is one post per day with often funny reads when the author points out flaws in popular media using statistics

Data sources

If you want to play around with algorithms, you can obtain many datasets from the **Machine Learning Repository** at **University of California at Irvine (UCI)**. You can find it at `http://archive.ics.uci.edu/ml`.

Getting competitive

An excellent way to learn more about machine learning is by trying out a competition! **Kaggle** (`http://www.kaggle.com`) is a marketplace of ML competitions and has already been mentioned in the introduction. On the website, you will find several different competitions with different structures and often cash prizes.

The supervised learning competitions almost always follow the following format:

- You (and every other competitor) are given access to labeled training data and testing data (without labels).
- Your task is to submit predictions for the testing data.
- When the competition closes, whoever has the best accuracy wins. The prizes range from glory to cash.

Of course, winning something is nice, but you can gain a lot of useful experience just by participating. So, you have to stay tuned, especially after the competition is over and participants start sharing their approaches in the forum. Most of the time, winning is not about developing a new algorithm; it is about cleverly preprocessing, normalizing, and combining the existing methods.

What was left out

We did not cover every machine learning package available for Python. Given the limited space, we chose to focus on Scikit-learn. However, there are other options, and we list a few of them here:

- **Modular toolkit for Data Processing (MDP)** at `http://mdp-toolkit.sourceforge.net`

- **Pybrain** at `http://pybrain.org`

- **Machine Learning Toolkit (MILK)** at `http://luispedro.org/software/milk`

  - ° This package was developed by one of the authors of this book, and covers some algorithms and techniques that are not included in Scikit-learn.

A more general resource is at `http://mloss.org`, which is a repository of open source machine learning software. As is usually the case with repositories such as this one, the quality varies between excellent, well-maintained software and projects that were one-offs and then abandoned. It may be worth checking out if your problem is very specific and none of the more general packages address it.

Summary

We are now truly at the end. We hope you have enjoyed the book and feel well equipped to start your own machine learning adventure.

We also hope you have learned the importance of carefully testing your methods, in particular, of using correct cross-validation and not reporting training test results, which are an over-inflated estimate of how good your method really is.

Index

binary matrix of recommendations,
    using 166, 168
movie neighbors, viewing 168, 169
multiple methods, combining 169-171
MP3 files
converting, into wave format 182
multiclass classification 47, 48
multiclass problems
confusion matrix, used for accuracy
    measurement 188-190
multidimensional regression 151
multidimensional scaling. *See* **MDS**
MultinomialNB 127
music
decomposing, into sine wave
    components 184, 186
music data
fetching 182
Music Information Retrieval (MIR) 193

N

Naive Bayes
used, for classification 121-123
Naive Bayes classifier
about 118-120
accounting, for arithmetic
    underflows 125-127
accounting, for oddities 124
accounting, for unseen words 124
Naive Bayes classifiers
BernoulliNB 127
GaussianNB 127
MultinomialNB 127
Natural Language Toolkit. *See* **NLTK**
ndimage (n-dimensional image) 200
ndimage package 18
nearest neighbor classification 44-46
nearest neighbor search (NNS) 9
Netflix 159
NLTK
installing 58
using 58
NLTK's stemmer
used, for extending vectorizer 59
norm() function 54
np.linalg.lstsq function 150

NumPy
about 200
indexing 15
learning 13-15
non-existing values, handling 15
runtime behaviors, comparing 16, 17
URL, for tutorials 12

O

odr package 18
OpenCV 200
opinion mining 117
optimize package 18
Oracle Grid Engine (OGE) 242
ordinary least squares (OLS) regression 147
Otsu threshold 202, 205
overfitting 25
OwnerUserId attribute 93

P

packages, SciPy
cluster 17
constants 18
fftpack 18
integrate 18
interpolate 18
io 18
linalg 18
maxentropy 18
ndimage 18
odr 18
optimize 18
signal 18
sparse 18
spatial 18
special 18
stats 18
parameters
tweaking 72
partial results
reusing 245
Part Of Speech (POS) 117, 139
pattern recognition 210, 211
PCA
about 222, 233
applying 234, 235

Thank you for buying
Building Machine Learning Systems with Python

About Packt Publishing

Packt, pronounced 'packed', published its first book "*Mastering phpMyAdmin for Effective MySQL Management*" in April 2004 and subsequently continued to specialize in publishing highly focused books on specific technologies and solutions.

Our books and publications share the experiences of your fellow IT professionals in adapting and customizing today's systems, applications, and frameworks. Our solution based books give you the knowledge and power to customize the software and technologies you're using to get the job done. Packt books are more specific and less general than the IT books you have seen in the past. Our unique business model allows us to bring you more focused information, giving you more of what you need to know, and less of what you don't.

Packt is a modern, yet unique publishing company, which focuses on producing quality, cutting-edge books for communities of developers, administrators, and newbies alike. For more information, please visit our website: www.packtpub.com.

About Packt Open Source

In 2010, Packt launched two new brands, Packt Open Source and Packt Enterprise, in order to continue its focus on specialization. This book is part of the Packt Open Source brand, home to books published on software built around Open Source licences, and offering information to anybody from advanced developers to budding web designers. The Open Source brand also runs Packt's Open Source Royalty Scheme, by which Packt gives a royalty to each Open Source project about whose software a book is sold.

Writing for Packt

We welcome all inquiries from people who are interested in authoring. Book proposals should be sent to author@packtpub.com. If your book idea is still at an early stage and you would like to discuss it first before writing a formal book proposal, contact us; one of our commissioning editors will get in touch with you.

We're not just looking for published authors; if you have strong technical skills but no writing experience, our experienced editors can help you develop a writing career, or simply get some additional reward for your expertise.

NumPy Beginner's Guide - Second Edition

ISBN: 978-1-78216-608-5   Paperback: 310 pages

An Action packed guid using real world examples of the easy to use, high performance, free open source NumPy mathematical library

1. Perform high performance calculations with clean and efficient NumPy code.

2. Analyze large data sets with statistical functions

3. Execute complex linear algebra and mathematical computations

OpenCV Computer Vision with Python

ISBN: 978-1-78216-392-3   Paperback: 122 pages

Learn to capture videos, manipulate images, track objects with Python using the OpenCV Library

1. Set up OpenCV, its Python bindings, and optional Kinect drivers on Windows, Mac or Ubuntu

2. Create an application that tracks and manipulates faces

3. Identify face regions using normal color images and depth images

Please check **www.PacktPub.com** for information on our titles

Instant Pygame for Python Game Development How-to

ISBN: 978-1-78216-286-5   Paperback: 76 pages

Create engaging and fun games with Pygame, Python's Game development library

1. Learn something new in an Instant! A short, fast, focused guide delivering immediate results.

2. Quickly develop interactive games by utilizing features that give you a great user experience

3. Create your own games with realistic examples and easy to follow instructions

Programming ArcGIS 10.1 with Python Cookbook

ISBN: 978-1-84969-444-5   Paperback: 304 pages

Building rigorously tested and bug-free Django applications

1. Develop Django applications quickly with fewer bugs through effective use of automated testing and debugging tools.

2. Ensure your code is accurate and stable throughout development and production by using Django's test framework.

4. Understand the working of code and its generated output with the help of debugging tools.

Please check **www.PacktPub.com** for information on our titles

Printed in Great Britain
by Amazon.co.uk, Ltd.,
Marston Gate.